Anna-Maria Perissutti, Sor
Ursula Doleschal (Eds.)

WRILAB2

TransLIT

Sprach-, Literatur- und Kulturkontraste

herausgegeben von

Dr. Halyna Leontiy
(Universität Münster)

Prof. Dr. Elena Polledri
(Università degli Studi Udine)

Prof. Dr. Sonja Kuri
(Università degli Studi Udine)

Band 3

LIT

WRILAB2

A Didactical Approach to Develop Text Competences in L2

edited by

Anna-Maria Perissutti, Sonja Kuri,
Ursula Doleschal

LIT

This publication has been funded with support from the European Commission. It reflects the views only of the authors, and the Commission cannot be held responsible for any use which may be made of the information contained therein.

Lifelong Learning Programme

Gedruckt auf alterungsbeständigem Werkdruckpapier entsprechend ANSI Z3948 DIN ISO 9706

Bibliographic information published by the Deutsche Nationalbibliothek
The Deutsche Nationalbibliothek lists this publication in the Deutsche Nationalbibliografie; detailed bibliographic data are available in the Internet at http://dnb.d-nb.de.

ISBN 978-3-643-90859-9

A catalogue record for this book is available from the British Library

Klosbachstr. 107
CH-8032 Zürich
Tel. +41 (0) 44-251 75 05
E-Mail: zuerich@lit-verlag.ch http://www.lit-verlag.ch

Distribution:

In the UK: Global Book Marketing, e-mail: mo@centralbooks.com
In North America: International Specialized Book Services, e-mail: orders@isbs.com
In Germany: LIT Verlag Fresnostr. 2, D-48159 Münster
Tel. +49 (0) 2 51-620 32 22, Fax +49 (0) 2 51-922 60 99, e-mail: vertrieb@lit-verlag.de
In Austria: Medienlogistik Pichler-ÖBZ, e-mail: mlo@medien-logistik.at
e-books are available at www.litwebshop.de

Contents

Preface 7

PART I: THEORETICAL INSIGHTS

Gerd Bräuer
The Didactic Framework for WRILAB2 13

Ursula Doleschal, Sonja Kuri
WRILAB2: On-line Reading and Writing Laboratory for Czech, German, Italian and Slovenian L2. Insights from Theory and Application 23

Anna-Maria Perissutti
The Use of Thematic Progression to Improve Students' Essay Structure 37

Ineke Vedder
Assessing Functional Adequacy in L2 and L1 Writing. Proposal of a Rating Scale 55

PART II: DIDACTIC APPLICATIONS

Ana Adamovičová, Zuzana Hajíčková
Česká verze projektu Wrilab2 75

Sonja Kuri, Ursula Doleschal
Zwölf Module für die Entwicklung von Textkompetenz in DaF/DaZ. Didaktische Anmerkungen für Unterrichtende 101

Gianluca Baldo
Guida alla sezione italiana di Wrilab2 127

Mihaela Knez, Damjana Kern
Razvijanje pisne zmožnosti v slovenščini kot drugem jeziku s pomočjo spletnega laboratorija za branje in pisanje (WRILAB2) 149

Contributors 163

Preface

The current volume has grown out of the research and the discussions related to the implementation of Wrilab2, an "On-line Reading and Writing Laboratory for Czech, German, Italian and Slovenian as L2", which is part of a European project co-financed by the EU Lifelong Learning Programme, Transversal actions, KA2-Languages, for the years 2014-2016.

Wrilab2 intends to cover a gap in the training provisions devoted to functional writing in the four European languages mentioned, thus responding to a higher demand in this field caused by the recent increase of foreign students in schools and universities in the respective European countries.

During the three years of the project implementation, the project partners – universities and secondary schools in five European countries (Austria, Czech Republic, Germany, Italy and Slovenia) – developed a methodology for the teaching of functional reading and writing skills in Czech, German, Italian and Slovenian as L2 (for the levels B1-C1), as well as criteria to assess L2 functional writing.

The output of the project consists in a free, on-line virtual laboratory based on Moodle, which offers interactive materials for the teaching of Czech, German, Italian and Slovenian L2 writing to foreign and second language students in high schools and colleges as well as to professionals in any writing-intensive field.

The current volume addresses the needs of university and secondary school teachers and aims at offering them both the state of the art of current research related to important issues in the field of teaching L2 writing, as well as a practical guideline to the four language sections of the Wrilab2 portal.

The full spectrum of the project topics is covered here: analysis and assessment of L2 writing, text linguistics, theory of writing didactics, and best practices in the teaching of L2 writing. Moreover, this volume presents one contribution by a researcher (Ineke Vedder) who did not take part in the project implementation but was invited to join due to the relevance of the topics she deals with.

The volume includes two parts. Part I, entitled "Theoretical Insights", is written in English and focuses on the theoretical background of Wrilab2. It begins with a chapter by Gerd Bräuer "The Didactic Framework for WRILAB2", which outlines the course design framework shared by all the courses in the four languages of the portal. The chapter by Ursula Doleschal and Sonja Kuri "WRILAB2: On-line Reading and Writing Laboratory for Czech, German, Italian and Slovenian L2. Insights from Theory and Application" provides a comprehensive account of the current state of the art of writing research as it is reflected in WRILAB2 and explains how principles of modern writing didactics are incorporated into the different parts of the courses.The third contribution by Anna-Maria Perissutti entitled "The Use of Thematic Progression to Improve Students' Essay Structure" is dedicated to one micro-competence which represents a real challenge for the L2 writer, especially at lower levels: the competence to appropriately introduce new referents into the discourse and create referential chains, linking new information to the old one presented in the preceding clauses. The author presents the linguistic tool of Thematic Progression and proposes to apply it to L2 writing teaching. Finally, Ineke Vedder's essay "Assessing Functional Adequacy in L2 and L1 Writing. Proposal of a Rating Scale" deals with L2 writing proficiency assessment. The author argues that both the linguistic and finctional ('how to get the message through') dimensions are crucial when assessing learners' written performance in a second language (L2). With this purpose in mind, a rating scale for assessing L2 writing is developed.

The second part of the volume, entitled "Didactic Applications", presents the manuals to the four language sections of the portal, namely, for Czech, German, Italian and Slovenian. In fact, despite the shared didactic framework outlined by Gerd Bräuer's chapter, some differences can be noticed on the micro-level of instruction and material design in the four language sections. These differences are due to the cultural peculiarities in learning and instruction, to the different literacy cultures and to the specific needs of the targeted learners.

The contributions of this part are written in the respective language. This is in line with the general aim of the project, which intends to highlight the peculiarity of the different European literacy cultures, as well as the importance for the L2 student to learn them.

The chapter by Ana Adamovičová and Zuzana Hajíčková „Česká verze projektu Wrilab2" reports the results of the survey on Czech L2 writing processes and strategies as well as the results of the preliminary Wrilab2 studies aimed at identifying the main tendencies and oddities in L2 Czech writing as compared to L1 Czech writing. It further presents the twelve textual genres analysed in the Czech didactic units of the portal as well as the structure of each unit.

The chapter by Sonja Kuri and Ursula Doleschal "Zwölf Module für die Entwicklung von Textkompetenz in DaF/DaZ – didaktische Anmerkungen für Unterrichtende" deals with the German language section of the portal. Starting from the theoretical bases of WRILAB2 the authors explain how these have been put into practice in the German modules. A special focus is set on the significance of the genres on the one hand, and feedback and collaborative writing on the other.

Gianluca Baldo's chapter "Guida alla sezione italiana di Wrilab2" presents the Italian language section of the Wrilab2 portal. It explains the structure of the twelve Italian didactic units as well as the genres analysed. It also suggests possible strategies for teachers to design writing courses for L2 Italian based on Wrilab2.

Finally, Mihaela Knez's and Damjana Kern's chapter "Razvijanje pisne zmožnosti v slovenščini kot drugem jeziku s pomočjo spletnega laboratorija za branje in pisanje (WRILAB2)" is dedicated to the Slovenian language section of the portal. The authors relate the tasks to the Common European Framework of Reference for Languages and explain the structure of the single units relating it to the results of the preliminary survey. They also stress the necessity of feedback and make recommendations on how to give feedback.

We want to thank everybody who contributed to this volume, particular thanks go to Deborah Saidero from the University of Udine for editing the contributions in English, and Michaela Gindl for the technical support.

Anna-Maria Perissutti

Sonja Kuri

Ursula Doleschal

PART I
THEORETICAL INSIGHTS

Gerd Bräuer

The Didactic Framework for WRILAB2

1 Introduction

This chapter will outline the didactic framework for the project that aimed to develop a system of digital courses in Czech, German, Italian and Slovenian for foreign and (second language) L2 students in high schools and colleges as well as for professionals in any writing-intensive field. These courses will either be used by individual L2 writers autonomously on an Internet-based e-learning platform (Moodle) or by L2 writers joining a blended learning course based on Moodle and combined with a local classroom face-to-face setting.

For both learning arrangements the overall course structure and the accompanying course materials will be self-explaining, although the material for the blended learning courses can be sometimes more complex due to the opportunity of face-to-face interaction in class and personal online facilitation.

The design of all the courses in all the languages of this project follows the same principles that will be outlined below. As a result of a shared course design framework, users of the course portal will be encouraged to switch between courses and languages and profit from contextual learning effects, which can occur when learners start to compare linguistic practices. Due to the fact that the languages of this project have much in common at a linguistic, cultural, geographic and historical level, it is also hoped that noticing the other courses may also motivate some students to learn a new language. The similarity in course and task design will hopefully also encourage instructors to learn from other courses and languages and get inspired methodologically by individual tasks and supplementary materials provided in each course. Last but not least, the aim of the project to provide a shared didactic framework for all courses and languages has also stimulated discussion among the project partners about L2 didactics and triggered learning from and with each other.

Despite the shared didactic framework, which will be outlined below in more detail, cultural differences in learning and instruction, peculiarities of the partner institutions, including different literacy cultures, and specific needs of the targeted learners resulted in some differences at the micro-level of instruction and material design.

Here are the principles for both task and course design, which all project partners agreed upon at the beginning of the course and material development (cf. Bräuer 2016).

Each task by itself should be:

a) **authentic and situated** with regard to solving a concrete rhetorical problem which leads to additional practical value for both writers and readers (e.g. summarizing a reading material in order to use the summary for other tasks within a specific group of learners);
b) **linked to other tasks** and as such represent a flexible building block for task arrangements (see also below "task arrangements");
c) **process-oriented** (including drafting, multiple feedback/partners, revision);
d) **supportive of the individual differences of the learners**, e.g. different types of learners (writers/readers), configuration of the personal learning environment (e.g. use of mobile devices, Internet availability);
e) **inclusive toward different levels of comprehension**, especially through ways of scaffolding (e.g. breaking down complex tasks into several steps that will be taken according to the learner's individual ability).

Each task arrangement should be:

a) **authentic and situated** with an exponential practical value for both individual learners and a community of learners at large;
b) **supportive toward the different needs of the learners** (e.g. types of learners and levels of comprehension);
c) **focused on the transfer of competences** with regard to future tasks and levels of practice (e.g. moving from B2 to C1, or from secondary to higher education);
d) **linked to reflective practice on emotional experience**, self-assessment of process/product qualities, procedural and factual knowledge (e.g. in learning logs and/or portfolios).

In addition, the description of individual tasks and of task arrangements should include:

- pedagogical and organizational suggestions for task implementation in individual teaching practices;
- additional suggestions for sustainable inclusion in both the curriculum and institution;
- strategies for task adaptation with regard to local / individual needs;
- recommendations for specific instructional competences and possible teacher training;
- guidelines for assessment of the effectiveness of the task / task arrangement.

The key aspects of this didactic framework will be further explained below and contextualized in learning and literacy theory, always illustrated with examples from the practice of L2 writing.

2 Authentic tasks and task arrangements

Very often students learn how to write a certain genre because the curriculum says so and the instructor feels obligated to follow the curriculum. In this rather common scenario the main motivation for learning is to receive a good grade for the final product, the finished text, which will often be written during a staged achievement test. Unfortunately, this kind of learning is not very sustainable which means the knowledge a student gained about the writing of a certain genre does not last very long and the instruction about that genre has to be repeated in the next curricular cycle.

The students' learning motivation can be quite different and result in more sustainable competence when the writing of a certain genre happens in response to an authentic communicative need, e.g. high school students in their final year before graduation learn how to write an application letter due to the upcoming college application process. If in such a moment students receive information (either through self-learning material or face-to-face instruction) about the specific communicative situation they face when applying for college entry, they will not only be more receptive but also better understand why they will have to write an application letter in a certain way, e.g. in order to persuade the audience of the application about their qualification for college. They may not be successful with their first application, but with each rejection letter, they will learn to understand better the making of the genre and the expectations of the audience they are aiming at.

The writing task described above is called *authentic* and *situated*, because the writer experiences a concrete practical value of his/her action (e.g. applying for college and getting accepted) in a specific moment of time (transition between high school and college). The "authenticity" and "situatedness" of the task does not happen by coincidence but is the result of a conscious didactic decision – a staging within a given institutional framework – and not just the result of executing a canon of genres required for a successful high school graduation.

While in a traditional face-to-face classroom situation, the moments of instruction and practice are often forgotten quickly, in a so-called *blended learning scenario* or in an *online self-learning scenario*, both the information about the subject and the traces of the learning activities (e.g. in a forum or blog) remain accessible on the e-learning platform and can be revisited whenever needed by the student or be reminded of by peers and/or the instructor.

Speaking of the latter: An exponential *practical value* of any learning activity carried out in the past can be experienced by the students when they notice that the effort they invested in a certain writing task matters beyond the moment of immediate action and can – or even needs to – be used further in future activities and tasks. In other words, a writing task can be even more authentic in the perception of the learner whenever this task in its design is linked to other tasks both before and after the task-related action, e.g. the writing of a college application will be prepared with the help of a task to write an application for a high school scholarship or something similar. In addition, the task description for the college application includes the information that this application can later be used as a model text for future applications of any kind.

3 Scaffolding and transfer of competence

Writing in a genre with complex rhetorical functions, e.g. a college application with aspects of describing, informing and persuading, can be quite challenging for less experienced writers. Whenever a writing task is rhetorically complex, the flow of writing is in severe danger due to the complex nature of writing by itself. If the writer is composing in a language different than his/her native tongue, the mental overload is even heavier.

In this case, *scaffolding* (Vygotsky 1987) as a means to break down complex actions into smaller, less complex steps within reach for the student needs to be applied to the task design. In this way, a complex task gives rise to a *task arrangement*, a didactic orchestration of several smaller tasks that consists of so-called *help tasks*, sometimes combined with so-called *transfer tasks*. "Help tasks" are tasks that will be carried out only for the direct benefit of the writer and not with an additional audience in mind, e.g. in preparation of a college application, a list of the most important biographical dates of the applicant and/or a list of competences the applicant can prove to have acquired.

In contrast to the *writer-based* prose of the help texts, "transfer texts" are *reader-based* and written with an audience in mind. After the testing of its effectiveness a transfer text will be included in, and sometimes adapted for, a more complex text, e.g. a biographical sketch for a high school's *Who is who?* becomes embedded in a college application.

The concept of *scaffolding* should not be applied to task design in a generalized manner, but should take into consideration the specific needs of the targeted group of learners, such as the specific linguistic needs of a B1 language learner versus the needs of a C1 language learner. In addition, material complementing the tasks, such as model texts, linguistic building blocks, and grammar structures and exercises, could further individualize instruction based on the anticipated *zone of proximal development* (ibid.) of the targeted learners.

In addition to the aspect of scaffolding, difficulties in the transfer of prior knowledge should be taken into account when designing singe tasks as well as whole task arrangements. Applying existing competences to a new task should not be seen as an automatism but rather as something that needs to be didacticly initiated and linguistically triggered by so-called *Anschlusskommunikation* (Bräuer 2016), that is, information integrated in the task description that reminds the student of what he/she should know or may have experienced with regard to a certain task, such as certain help texts or transfer texts that where worked on prior to the current task (see 1, above).

4 Facilitating the different needs of individual learners

The design of tasks and related materials should support the different needs of individual learner types. Based on Kolb's typology (1984), there are four main types of learners: the converging (1: abstract, active), diverging (2: concrete, reflective), assimilating (3: abstract, reflective), and accommodating (4: concrete, active) style. The design of instruction, tasks, supplemental materials and overall learning environment should, therefore, include aspects of expert input (specifically for type 1), guided practice and feedback (specifically for type 2), coaching and meta-reflection (specifically for type 3), and problem-based learning (specifically for type 4).

For the specific competence of writing, research (Bräuer 2009, Galbraith 2009) identified different types that indicate a certain tendency in carrying out text production: a*) structure followers* (Galbraith 2009 says "high self-monitors"), writers who early in the writing process come up with a structure and in the main part of text production follow these patterns of thinking in a highly focused manner; b) *structure creators* (Galbraith 2009 says "low self-monitors", writers who start drafting right away and, in the process of text production, carve out the structure of their intended message through extensive higher-order revision.

While the action patterns of the structure follower (a) seem to be a combination of Kolb's converging style (1) and assimilating style (3), the action patterns of the structure creator (b) seem to show parallels to Kolb's diverging style (2) and accommodating style (4). There are still no research results on the impact foreign and/or second language practice can have on the carrying out of these two types of writers. It is, therefore, still speculative whether writer types in L1 are transferred into L2 text production, but it is, however, strongly anticipated since the types identified for L1 writing so far are based on how people monitor a highly complex cognitive task such as writing (Galbraith 2009, Baaijen et al. 2012).

In addition to the aspects already mentioned with regard to the different needs of individual learners, research on the conditioning of L2 learners (Aguado/Riemer 2010) has found differences between learners' *language aptitude*, a combination of different competences such as phonetic encoding (ability to identify phonemes in writing), grammatical sensitivity (ability to identify grammatical functions in a sentence), inductive language learning ability (ability to identify linguistic patterns), and rote learning ability (ability to memorize linguistic information).

Based on the learner's language aptitude, research assumes the existence of individual profiles of language learners in the context of mental capacities on the one hand and analytical skills on the other. Personality factors also seem to contribute to whatever someone is able to accomplish as a L2 writer, e.g. handling of tasks, tolerance of ambiguity, introverted vs. extroverted behavior, readiness to assume a risk, preference of perception channels (auditory, visual, and kinesthetic). All in all, learning and instruction should always provide students with a chance to identify personal strengths and urge chances for further learning and, with it, the ability to acknowledge ones' own "comfort zone" and to enable oneself to go beyond this comfort zone in a responsible manner (Aguado/Riemer 2010).

5 Process-oriented learning and (peer) interaction

The courses of all the languages in this portal for L2 writing are designed around text models for genres that are important for the targeted groups of learners. The importance of text models, especially for inexperienced writers, has been highlighted many times since Hyland/Milton (1997) identified their positive impact on the development of genre knowledge, writing fluency, evolving active vocabulary, and effective writing strategies (Chenoweth/Hayes 2001, Fidalgo et al. 2015). A successful instructional strategy for less experienced writers seems to require the following steps (ibid.):

1. Examination of commented text models and working on tasks that lead to a better understanding of what works/does not work with the text model;
2. Input on genre features (e.g. through self-learning materials or face-to-face instruction;
3. Planning/drafting and peer feedback;
4. Revision and further individual practice.

In the design of the courses for the different languages, there have been steps added whenever the targeted genre seemed rather complex with regard to its rhetorical features, required style and grammatical particularities. These tasks will help to create beginning routine in applying specific features of the targeted genre.

Feedback, both by peers and instructors, seems to relieve the tension that usually builds up in moments of transition from one phase to the next of text production, e.g. between planning and drafting or drafting and revising. Even though feedback would certainly be helpful for all writers, the two writer types mentioned in chapter (3) show different motivation with regard to feedback (Bräuer 2014). While structure followers tend to avoid feedback until the very end of text production and then urge feedback on formal aspects of text accuracy, structure creators seek feedback early on and focus on feedback that inspires them to reconsider and further develop their overall text structure (ibid.). These differences in the writers' motivation for feedback need to be taken into consideration when designing writing tasks as part of a learning environment that is highly individualized.

6 Reflective practice

Since the shaping of writing skills is a lifelong endeavor, writers should reflect upon their development in order to monitor and steer both effort and progress. For this long-term reflection, electronic portfolios (e.g. Mahara), ideally realized as plugin of the e-learning platform Moodle, work best. Based on the four levels of reflection – documenting, analyzing, evaluating, planning (Bräuer 2016, 2009) – both learning and insights can be shared with peers and the instructor and finally turned in as part of the assessment including grading. Especially in a learning scenario where the writer would act autonomously, the portfolio could provide important information about how to proceed with the shaping of one's writing skills.

Personal blogs as part of the learning environment on Moodle can be used as a learning log for short-term reflection during the unfolding of a specific writing project. Information about expectations from both the writer and the instructor, emotional sensitivities during the work process, questions, doubts, moments of strength and contentedness and intermediary results (milestones) should be collected, as well as impressions with regard to overall satisfaction at the end of work. The essence of such entries in the personal blog would trigger the abovementioned electronic portfolio, usually during transition from one writing project to the next.

Since not all people are naturally interested in reflection and reflective practice can sometimes be experienced as a tedious effort, it needs initiation through regular reflective tasks, encouragement and recognition for working with the personal blog as well as the e-portfolio. Both formats should be considered part of feedback, assessment and grading. In other words, the regular communication with instructors and peers should make students realize that blogs and portfolios are necessary elements of successful writing and learning.

7 Consequences for the use and adaptation of the courses and materials

Genres, understood as means of communication within ever-changing communities of practice – in the academe also communities of knowledge – have changed in the past and will continue to change in the future. Academic genres are, therefore, also an expression of specific scientific cultures, which can also change whenever institutions of education and its members change their practices. The consequence of all this for the courses of WRILAB2 is that they should not be seen as static but rather as a starting point to keep thinking about efficient ways to help writers cope best with the challenges of text production in general, with the special challenges of writing in other languages beyond their native tongue and with their personal needs as individual writers which also keep changing. It is, therefore, essential to adapt the proposed courses, methods and materials within WRILAB2 to whatever is needed of a certain target group within a local learning environment. If the insight gained from local adaptation becomes part of the shared wisdom of the network being created by WRILAB2 users, the potential for sustainable change in the way people write texts in other languages will be given.

Literature

Aguado, Karin & Riemer, Claudia (2010): Lernstile und Lernertypen. In: Krumm, Hans-Jürgen, Fandrych, Christian, Hufeisen, Britta & Riemer, Claudia (Eds.): Deutsch als Fremd- und Zweitsprache. Ein internationales Handbuch (Handbücher zur Sprach- und Kommunikationswissenschaft/HSK). Berlin, New York: de Gruyter, Bd. 1, 850-858.

Baaijen, Veerle M., Galbraith, David & Glopper, Kees de (2012): Effects of writing beliefs and planning in writing performance. In: Learning and Instruction, 33, 81-91. Available online at: http://authors.elsevier.com/sd/article/S0959475214000358 [last accessed: dec. 14th 2016].

Bräuer, Gerd (Hrsg.) (2009): Scriptorium – Ways of Interacting With Writers and Readers. Freiburg i. Br.: Fillibach.

Bräuer, Gerd (2014): Grundprinzipien der Schreibberatung. Eine pragmatische Sicht auf die Schreibprozesstheorie. In: Dreyfürst, Stephanie & Sennewald, Nadja (Eds.): Schreiben. Grundlagentexte zur Theorie, Didaktik und Beratung. Opladen & Toronto: Barbara Budrich, 257-282.

Bräuer, Gerd (2016): Vertieftes Lernen im Fach in einem Online-Kurs zur akademischen Literalität. In: *Zeitschrift für Hochschulentwicklung*, 11, 231-245.

Bräuer, Gerd (2016a): Das Portfolio als Reflexionsmedium für Lehrende und Studierende. (2. Auflage). Opladen, Toronto: Barbara Budrich.

Chenoweth, Ann N. & Hayes, John R. (2001): Fluency in Writing. Generating Text in L1 and L2. In: *Written Communication*, 1, 80-98.

Galbraith, David (2009): Writing about what we know: Generating ideas in writing. In: Beard, Roger, Myhill, Debra, Riley, Jeni & Nystrand, Martin (Eds.): The SAGE Handbook of Writing Development. Los Angeles: SAGE, 48-64.

Hyland, Ken & Milton, John (1997): Qualification and certainty in L1 and L2 students' writing. In: *Journal of Second Language Writing*, 6, 183-205.

Fidalgo, Raquel, Torrance, Mark, Rijlaarsdam, Gert, Bergh, Huub van den & Alvarez, Ma Lourdes (2015): Strategy-focused writing instruction: Just observing and reflecting on a model benefits 6th grade students. In: *Contemporary Educational Psychology*, 41, 37-50.

Kolb, David A. (1984): Experiential learning: experience as the source of learning and development. Englewood Cliffs, NJ: Prentice Hall.

Vygotsky, Lev (1987): Thinking and speech. In: Rieber, Robert W. & Carton Aaron S. (Eds.): The collected works of L. S. Vygotsky, Volume 1: Problems of general psychology. New York: Plenum Press, 39–285. (Original work published 1934).

Ursula Doleschal, Sonja Kuri

WRILAB2: On-line Reading and Writing Laboratory for Czech, German, Italian and Slovenian L2
Insights from Theory and Application

1 Introduction

In this chapter we will show how modern writing theory and text linguistics contribute to our learning platform on writing in L2. The aim of WRILAB2 is to enable L2 learners and practitioners to improve their writing in Czech, German, Italian and Slovenian as a second or foreign language. This involves the following two aspects: **improvement of the writing process** – in other words, writing more easily, and **improvement of the writing products** – better texts.

Writing texts encompasses different kinds of knowledge and different skills. According to Beaufort & Iñesta (2014: 146) a skilled writer masters the following kinds of knowledge: **1. subject matter knowledge, 2. genre knowledge, 3. rhetorical knowledge, 4. writing process knowledge, 5. discourse community knowledge**.

1. In order to be able to write a text, we need to know what we are writing about, i.e., we have to be acquainted with the topic or the problem, we need to have extra-linguistic, declarative knowledge about a certain **subject matter**. E.g., if I want to write a synthesis about a research project in order to obtain a scholarship I have to know quite thoroughly what I want to do research on, what I want to find out and how I will achieve the result.

2. All texts belong to a certain **genre**. Genres are patterns of language use, patterns of texts, cultural products and may differ from language community to language community. In order to write effectively, one has to be acquainted with the genre to which the text belongs. If I want to write a motivational letter, I have to know the formal characteristics of this genre, such as structure and layout as well as obligatory formal parts. I also have to know how to formulate the text, which stylistic devices are expected, and, last but not least, what may and what has to be the content of such a letter, in order to achieve the communicative purpose and ultimately reach the addressee.

3. **Rhetorical knowledge** is the ability to adapt our knowledge of genre to the concrete writing situation and the concrete writing task. E.g., I have to proceed differently if I have to write a summary of three newspaper articles on a certain topic for my boss or for a press review addressed at the whole organization I work in.

4. Knowledge of the **writing process** means knowing the steps it takes to write a text in general and of a certain genre in particular. It means knowing that writing is more than to write down a text in one go; that writing involves a planning stage, a drafting stage and a revising stage and how to organize these stages in-

dividually. It means having experience with and awareness of one's own writing habits.

5. Knowledge of the **discourse community** comprises the four kinds of knowledge mentioned above and the values and communication norms of the community in question. E.g., is it appropriate in my disciplinary field to write a personal reflection in a seminar paper or should I take an impersonal stance? In order to be a competent writer one has to be able to put this knowledge "into action when solving specific writing tasks" (Beaufort & Iñesta 2014: 149).

WRILAB2 provides information, materials and exercises in order to enhance this kind of knowledge. The modules or units[1] are organized according to the stages of the **writing process**. In the planning phase there are exercises for developing the **subject matter** and for collecting relevant information. The **genres** are explained and illustrated. The explanations also refer to the **discourse community**. Examples of **rhetorical devices** are incorporated into the genre descriptions on the one hand and into concrete exercises on the other.

There are also tasks and exercises for collecting vocabulary which aim at developing both the **subject matter** and the **rhetorical devices**, since in L2 writing the development of a topic is inseparably intertwined with vocabulary knowledge, and lack of the latter often hampers the former (cf. Krings 1989, Börner 1989, Cumming 1990, 1994, Silva 1993, Grieshammer 2011).

The teaching of writing has mostly focussed on two different aspects of the model described above: either on the **genre as the product** that has to be achieved or **on the process as the way** in which one reaches the goal of writing (cf. Machowicz 2011: 101). Wrilab2 combines the genre-based and the process-based approaches.

2 The writing process and consequences for L2-writing

Writing is a complex problem-solving process. This is what the seminal model put forward by Linda Flower and John Hayes comes down to. The writing process is usually subdivided into phases or stages called **prewriting** or **planning, transcribing** or **drafting**, and **revising.** Traditional writing didactics views these phases as a sequence of steps from idea generation to final product, the written text. Flower and Hayes (1981), however, argue against such a linear modelling of writing. They point out that planning, drafting and revising are distinct activities which occur recursively. So, for example, plans that were made before the drafting stage are often modified after writing down a piece of text, because a sentence may make a certain continuation more plausible and

---

1 For each language twelve Moodle courses for twelve genres have been prepared. They are referred to either as "units" or "modules".

logical than the one envisaged before. Such a change in planning also implies the revision of the written piece.

Flower and Hayes' model has been influential in L2 writing research, and has been adapted by various authors to explain L2 writing (e.g., Börner 1987, Krings 1989, Grießhaber 2009). However, the use of phase models has also proven to be useful in teaching writing, especially in the case of longer texts. Kruse (2010: 62), for instance, suggests four macrophases in academic writing. In the first phase, "planning", one gets acquainted with the subject matter, defines the topic and the genre, finds out who the addressees are and should also make a time schedule for the whole writing process. The next phase, "collecting material or data", is about reading, making notes, collecting the data one wishes to write about and structuring the material. In the third phase "working on the text, revising", the first draft is written and consequently revised regarding contents and language. Feedback is a crucial element in this phase. In the fourth phase, "finalizing and signing in", the text receives its final layout and is signed in. Eventual feedback may either be incorporated or used for further writing projects.

In a similar vein, Bräuer (2010 and http://schreibzentrum.ph-freiburg.de/zisch/Mein%20Schreibprozess.pdf) proposes eight methodical steps, four of which he calls "production phases": "finding the topic, collecting material and structuring the material", "first draft", "revision of the first draft" and "revision of the second draft and final version". The first three steps contain a feedback phase, which is carried out collaboratively. At the end of the process there is a reflection phase reserved for individual reflection.

As Ruhmann and Kruse (2014: 25) write, these phase models are justified insofar as planning, drafting and revising are crucial to writing and the models help writers understand the writing process as a whole, but they are not descriptions of the real course of writing. Drawing attention to process models is useful for writing in L2, too, for L2-writers (similar to L1-writers, cf. Brinkschulte 2012: 74-75) seldom have a realistic idea of how long it will take them to produce an acceptable text, and how this is done. Therefore WRILAB2 is organized along these lines and has sections for planning, drafting and revising.

In our mind this is especially important as in L2 writing both planning and revising are often rather restricted. It has been observed that L2 writers tend to plan their texts locally, sentence by sentence, depending on their vocabulary proficiency (Krings 1989, Börner 1989, Cumming 1989, Ortner 2002: 242). Revision, on the other hand, is confined to surface phenomena, especially grammar and vocabulary (cf. Silva 1993). Machowicz (2011: 108-109) discovered that secondary school teachers ensured that pupils were acquainted with the topics of writing assignments, but neither the selection of contents nor the elaboration of vocabulary for a concrete writing task were usually carried out together in class. The same is true for revision and feedback. She concludes that important phases of the writing process and their characteristics were thus not made transparent to the learners. This is a typical situation in L2 writing in the four languages in question: writing assignments are usually delegated to homework and learners are left alone to figure out writing strategies on their own. This leads to the aforementioned approaches. We have observed the same phenomenon when testing the materials on the WRILAB2-platform with students: they started drafting without paying attention to the exercises and materials available on the platform. Revision by teachers, on the other hand, concerned only mistakes in vocabulary and grammar and did not lead to revised versions of the texts.

WRILAB 2 is based on a didactic model of writing phases. It encourages both revision tasks, taking into account that ideas come up during drafting, and feedback by teachers and peers. It shows that the writing process comprises different stages by dedicating single sections to **planning**, **writing**, **revising** and **reflecting** and making their interaction visible where this is possible. At the same time it leaves it up to the users to move through these sections according to their needs.

3 Writing strategies and types of writers

In writing research different strategies of coping with the writing process have been identified. Bräuer (2009: 21) speaks of "mental programs for directing text production". Usually two different strategies are singled out: top-down vs. bottom-up (Molitor 1985: 342, cited according to Sennewald 2014: 170), knowledge telling vs. knowledge transforming (Bereiter & Scardamalia 1987), radical brain-stormer vs. radical outliner (Reid 1984, cited according to Plag 1996: 241), structure creator vs. structure follower (Bräuer 2009), emergent planner vs. advance planner (Cumming 1989) etc. Although these dichotomies do not refer to exactly the same phenomena, they nevertheless cover the basic observation that writers may begin to solve a writing task either by immediately drafting or by starting with an elaborate outline of their future text.

Writing strategies can be used intentionally for different tasks and different genres, e.g., writing a short private e-mail can be carried out in a bottom-up manner, while top-down planning is more appropriate when writing an essay or a scientific monography.

Writing strategies are also domain-specific (cf. Jakobs & Spinuzzi 2014) – journalists need different strategies than academic writers – and may be culture-specific (cf. Lieber & Posset 1988, Riehl 2001, Hufeisen 2002, Ortner 2002). Moreover, they are also influenced by the writing medium: drafting in an exercise book provides other possibilities than drafting on a personal computer (cf. Eßer 1997: 115).

It has also been observed that people adopt strategies as their habitual ways of dealing with the writing process without regarding the task in question. We can, therefore, also speak of types of writers. Hanspeter Ortner (2000) has identified 10 different types of writers (see Sennewald 2014 for a concise account), among which there are, for example, "flow writers" who mainly follow their stream of consciousness, "planners" who make an outline before starting to draft, and "puzzle writers" who write text fragments. Sennewald (2014) discusses the advantages and drawbacks of each of Ortner's types and points out that there may be even more combinations of strategies forming more types of writers. In the context of writing didactics it is important to understand that there is not the one and only, perfect way for carrying out the writing process, but that several successful approaches exist and writers have to try which one suits them best.

Writing strategies can be successfully transferred from L1 to L2 (Cumming 1989, Gračner 2011), but there are also clear differences between writing in L1 and L2 (cf. Silva 1993, Grieshammer 2011). L2 writers are slower and they make more and longer pauses. Moreover, as has been observed above, L2 writers are often overwhelmed by the linguistic difficulties of their writing task and therefore turn to local planning strategies. In other words, they write sentence by sentence and tend to adapt the content of their writing to their vocabulary proficiency (Krings 1989, Börner 1989, Silva 1993, Cumming 1989, 1990, Plag 1996, Eßer 1997: 183). Cumming (1989) points out that some of them do not want to even read through the produced text, let alone revise it. He noticed, too, that both writing strategies and text quality in L2 depends on the writing experience in L1 and that writing strategies are automatically transferred from L1 to L2: experienced writers produce better texts in L2, independently of L2-proficiency, while the opposite is not the case: a higher language proficiency does not influence text quality. It is, therefore, of the utmost importance to help L2 writers acquire adequate writing strategies. This comes down to making them aware of the necessity of planning in terms of **content and vocabulary** as well as **genre knowledge**, regardless of the stage where this planning comes into play. It also means understanding that revising does not just entail correcting inadequacies of lexis and grammar, but also of content and structure.

One of the central aims of WRILAB2 is to raise the awareness of L2 writers and L2 instructors for different approaches to writing which should ideally lead to their trying out new strategies and adapting their strategies to individual writing tasks. L2 instructors should act as facilitators in this learning process, guiding learners by giving them formative feedback which takes the textual level (communicative function, contents, structure) into account. The writing platform, therefore, provides room and suggestions for feedback both by peers and teachers, as well as criteria for revision and the possibility to upload revised versions of texts.

4 Genre

Genre is a central notion of text linguistics and writing research. All writing ideally aims at adhering to a certain genre.

Genres can be defined as **conventionalized patterns of language use**. The expression "patterns of language use" has a twofold meaning. On the one hand, it considers texts as patterns of language use – products of writing which show certain characteristics. On the other hand, it means the use of language itself in a conventionalized, patterned way and, as such, comprises not only the product of writing but also the situation in which certain textual patterns are produced.

Therefore we also speak of "genres as typified recurrent situations" (Devitt & Reiff 2014: 265), including both the processual aspect of writing and the product aspect of the text-to-be. Genres are deeply entrenched in communities of practice – discourse communities in Swales' (1990) sense, and hence follow community norms.

In order to communicate effectively with this community (in our case – the language community of the L2 in question) it is necessary to learn certain genre conventions. However, as is pointed out in the literature (cf. Devitt & Reiff 2014), it is not sufficient to master structural patterns and stylistic characteristics and be able to reproduce them in a mechanic way. One also has to understand the conventionalized role of the writer and the addressee, the situation in which the text is written, the domain and discourse community where it is usually used and the function it has for this discourse community. These extralinguistic factors shape the textual patterns on the one hand, and are also responsible for the expected and expectable contents of the genre on the other (Fandrych & Thurmair 2011: 16-22). Ideally, this leads to pattern-related writing following community norms.

Every text exemplar is an individual instantiation of the genre. As such it contains individual elements which are seen as the necessary and expected outcome for the solving of a concrete rhetorical problem. Since genres relate to typified situations, their characteristics cannot be instantiated fully and exactly, but have to be modified in each concrete situation, in order to meet the necessities of the concrete writing task. With regard to these aspects the teaching of genre in L2 writing instruction has also been criticized for being too normative and mechanic, since it runs the risk of presenting genre in terms of a set of patterns that can be followed like rules of thumb (see Devitt & Reiff 2014: 273-274 for an overview).

As mentioned above, communicative aspects of writing are often neglected in L2 writing and formal characteristics are put in the fore. One of Plag's (1996: 249-250) informants, for instance, said that she had written an introduction and a conclusion because she felt that this was expected in an educational context, even if personally she did not find these parts of the text necessary or meaningful. Moreover, because of the obvious problems of language proficiency both teachers and learners focus mostly on grammatical correctness and lexical problems (Eßer 1997: 183, Machowicz 2011).

Yet, if L2 writers want to acquire writing competence, they have to master the textual characteristics of genre, i.e., communicative aspects and structure.

Therefore we contend that the acquaintance with and awareness of the characteristics of genres are an essential prerequisite for writing texts, both in L1 and L2, and have to be communicated. Inexperienced writers usually do not take the conventionalized and concrete role of the writer and the addressee into account and thus write texts which poorly fit the communicative norms of the genre. This is one of the reasons why the tasks in WRILAB2 are situated and should be meaningful for pupils and students (who are the main target group of the platform). In such a way users should experience the writing task as valuable and it will eventually lead to deep learning (cf. Bräuer, this volume).

Awareness of genres as patterns of language use is crucial for experienced writers, too, because the conventions are hardly ever the same as in L1 (cf. Eßer 1997, Krause 2002, Brinkschulte 2012). The discourse communities may be different and they may have different norms and expectations. This has been demonstrated by Ruth Eßer (1997) who analyzed German and Mexican seminar papers in literary science with regard to their cultural backgrounds. She found that the differences in history and tradition of the two countries led to different communicative situations and shaped the expectations of the academic discourse communities as to the contents of seminar papers. While in the German tradition universities are primarily a place of research with a corresponding socialization of students as "beginning researchers", Mexican universities are more a place of education with an emphasis on tradition and fine arts. Correspondingly, German seminar papers focussed on the abstract presentation of theory, while their Mexican counterparts were practically oriented (cf. Eßer 1997: 94-96 and studies cited in Brinkschulte & Mudoh 2009: 304-306 as well as the research by Brinkschulte 2012).

The characteristics of genres are also taken into account in the evaluation of text exemplars by untrained raters, as Zimmermann (1996) shows. This pertains among other things to such communicative prerequisites as contents and the depth of their elaboration, as well as the reflection of text function and role of writer and addressee in an adequate style.

Therefore the genre descriptions of WRILAB2 include details of the communicative situation and domain, the roles of writer and reader, the function of the genre, text structure and typical linguistic means. Genres are illustrated by sample texts which are the basis for exercises on various genre features. In such a way users of the platform can get acquainted with the genre from different angles.

5 Planning, Feedback, Revising

Both planning and even more so revising are usually not taken into account by unexperienced writers and especially so when writing in a foreign or second language (cf. Plag 1996) or they are not so efficient as in L1 (see Silva 1993: 661-662).

This is also due to teaching practices which usually delegate writing to individual homework (cf. Machowicz 2011, similarly Grießhaber 2009). Research on the writing process in L2 has shown that planning mostly involves the immediate co-text, sentence by sentence (cf. Silva 1993, Krings 1989, Börner 1989). Therefore Eßer (1997: 182-184) and Machowicz (2011) suggest giving room to prewriting in class, where diverse planning tasks can be performed in collaboration and feedback can be given on the validity of this planning for the drafting phase.

According to Beaufort and Iñesta (2014: 145) early cognitive studies have shown that the planning stage (where, among other things, idea generation is situated) is crucial for a good text. Eigler et al. (1990: 153-182) show that a deepened knowledge of the subject matter (acquired by reading specialized texts) leads to a greater depth of the produced text, in terms of the hierarchical organization of propositions.

Therefore the modules of WRILAB2 provide special sections for the planning stage with materials for idea generation, structuring and collecting the necessary vocabulary in L2. The pretexts of this phase do not necessarily need to be in L2. It is, however, important to use this phase for the elaboration of the linguistic devices in L2 as an interaction of subject matter and expression, in order to avoid a mechanic translation of a draft from L1 to L2. And again, it is important that these efforts are documented and receive formative feedback. We also encourage the use of forums on the platform for collaborative planning.

Feedback is of great importance in the writing process both for motivation and for the quality of the texts (see, e.g., Hyland & Hyland 2016, Schnetzer 2006, Nelson & Schunn 2007, Lammertz & Heinke 2016, Guasch & Esposa 2015, Finnegan, Kauppinen & Wärnsby 2015). In order to improve writing, feedback, too, must conform to certain rules. In the first place, feedback has to appreciate the writer's effort. It also has to be explicit (formative), not just a mark (summative). It has to be relevant and argumentative; this means that it must express not only an evaluation, but give reasons for it. It should ideally be in the form of meutic questions, in order to help the authors revise the text on their own (Ruhmann & Kruse 2014). It should not come as a correction. It should refer to criteria that were clear from the beginning.

In L1 writing didactics it is common to give text feedback first on "higher order concerns", which are structure and contents, and only when this feedback has led to revision "later order concerns" are taken into consideration, i.e., vocabulary, style, grammar and orthography. We recommend to proceed in a similar way in L2 writing, although some adaptations will be in place. One of them is the necessity of feedback before drafting. Thus Börner (1989: 371) points out that feedback is necessary already in prewriting. Planning activities need to receive feedback in L2 writing, in order to help writers choose the materials that are in line with their topic or writing task. As Silva (1993: 661) notes, L2 writers tend to collect a huge amount of material during planning without using it in their written texts. The same is found by Machowicz (2011) and Börner (1989). They note that teachers encourage the collection of material during class, often in a collaborative process, but do not help learners to judge the relevance of this material. Therefore, revision based on feedback by teacher and peers should be included in teaching practices.

This is why the units in WRILAB2 foresee feedback in all phases. There are also elaborate instructions for giving feedback. Teachers who want to work with WRILAB2 should be aware that they have to give feedback not only on vocabulary and grammar, but on the adequacy and completeness of content, on structure and on the communicative function.

It has also to be taken into account that feedback makes sense only if it leads to revision. Therefore the necessity of revision must be stressed and another round of feedback must be envisaged. These recursive phases of feedback and revision are not cherished either by learners or by teachers. The sense of feedback becomes clearer if it is included in collaborative work, if it is made transparent, and if it is done not only by teachers but also by peers.

6 The cultural specificity of writing

One of the *desiderata* for a future development of WRILAB2 is to incorporate the intercultural aspect of writing into the learning platform. Genres, as patterns of language use, are bound to certain discourse communities that may also be language communities or cultures. The study of contrastive rhetoric has shown that genres within the same domain, such as academia, may differ substantially in their communicative function and hence also content, structure and linguistic means. The roles of writer and addressee, too, may be different – more or less hierarchical, for example. This entails a certain style and tone which may consequently differ from community to community, culture to culture and ultimately language to language (cf. Clyne 1987, Eßer 1997, Adamzik 2001, Fix, Habscheid & Klein 2001, Hufeisen 2002, Kuri 2005, Čmejrková & Daneš, Załęska 2007, Doleschal 2005, 2007, Riehl 2014: 165-171 and many others).

Usually L2 writers unconsciously transfer genre characteristics from L1 to L2 (Eßer 1997: 122, Hufeisen 2002: 68-70). This leads to strange-sounding (cf. Krause 2002) or even unreadable texts. In order to overcome such difficulties, it is necessary to raise the awareness of genre characteristics in L1 and L2. We have tried to facilitate this by creating forums for discussing experiences with certain genres and comparing them among languages in the German WRILAB2 course. We would appreciate extensive use of these forums, in order to find out more about personal experiences with writing in L2.

7 Summary

In this chapter we have shown different directions in writing research related to L2 writing and how the results of this research have been incorporated into the learning platform "WRILAB2". Moreover, we have pointed out some didactic consequences for using the platform in teaching writing to L2 learners. Last but not least, we have tried to instigate the use of WRILAB2 and its further development by users who, in such a way, might build a community of practice across languages and cultures and facilitate the teaching and learning of L2 writing.

Literature

Adamzik, Kirsten (Ed.) (2001): Kontrastive Textologie. Tübingen: Stauffenburg Verlag.

Adamzik, Kirsten & Krause, Wolf-Dieter (2005): Text-Arbeiten. Textsorten im fremd- und muttersprachlichen Unterricht an Schule und Hochschule. Tübingen: Narr (Europäische Studien zur Textlinguistik, Bd. 1).

Beaufort, Anne & Iñesta, Anna (2014): Author profiles: Awareness, competence, and skills. In: Jakobs, Eva-Maria, Perrin, Daniel & Knapp, Karlfried (Hg): Handbook of Writing and Text Production. Berlin: De Gruyter Mouton, 141-158.

Bereiter, Carl & Scardamalia, Marlene (1987): The Psychology or Written Composition. Hillsdale, New York: Erlbaum.

Börner, Wolfgang (1987): Schreiben in der Fremdsprache: Überlegungen zu einem Modell. In: Löscher, Wolfgang & Schulze, Rainer (Eds.): Perspectives on Language in Performance. To Honour Werner Hüllen on the Occasion of His Sixtieth Birthday. Tübingen: Narr, Bd. 2, 1336-1349.

Börner, Wolfgang (1989): Didaktik schriftlicher Textproduktion in der Fremdsprache. In: Gerd Antos, Hans P. Krings (Eds.): Textproduktion. Ein interdisziplinärer Forschungsüberblick. Tübingen: Niemeyer (Konzepte der Sprach- und Literaturwissenschaft, 48).

Börner, Wolfgang & Vogel, Klaus (Eds.) (1996): Texte im Fremdsprachenerwerb. Verstehen und produzieren. Tübingen: Narr (Tübinger Beiträge zur Linguistik, 418).

Bräuer, Gerd (2009): Schreiben. In: Bräuer, Gerd (Ed.): Scriptorium. Ways of Interacting with Writers and Readers. Freiburg i. Br.: Fillibach, 15-26.

Bräuer, Gerd (2010): Schreibprozesse begleiten. In: *Deutschunterricht* 3, 4-9.

Brinkschulte, Melanie (2012): Akademisches Schreiben in der Fremd- und Zweitsprache Deutsch. In: Draheim, Kristin, Liebetanz, Franziska & Vogler-Lipp, Stefanie (Eds.): Schreiben(d) lernen im Team. Ein Seminarkonzept für innovative Hochschullehre. Wiesbaden: VS Verlag für Sozialwissenschaften (Key Competences for Higher Education and Employability), 59–81.

Brinkschulte, Melanie & Mudoh, Annett (2009): Ressourcenaktivierung durch akademische Schreibberatungin der Fremdsprache Deutsch. In: Lévy-Tödter, Magdalène & Meer, Dorothee (Hg.): Hochschulkommunikation in der Diskussion. Frankfurt (Main): Peter Lang, 301–322.

Cumming, Alister (1990): Metalinguistic and Ideational Thinking in Second Language Composing. In: *Written Communication* 7 (4), 482–511.

Cumming, Alister (1989 [1994]): Writing Expertise and Second-Language Proficiency. In: *Language Learning* 39 (1), 81–135. DOI: 10.1111/j.1467-1770.1989.tb00592.x. [reprinted in Cumming 1994: 173-221]

Cumming, Alister (Eds.) (1994): Bilingual performance in reading and writing. Ann Arbor [u.a.]: Ann Arbor [u.a.]: Benjamins (The best of language learning series).

Devitt, Amy & Reiff, Mary Jo (2014): Reproducing genres: Pattern-related writing. In: Jakobs, Eva-Maria, Perrin, Daniel & Knapp, Karlfried (Eds.): Handbook of Writing and Text Production. Berlin: De Gruyter Mouton, 263-284.

Clyne, Michael (1987): Cultural differences in the organization of academic texts. English and German. In: *Journal of Pragmatics* 11, 211-247.

Čmejrková, Světla & Daneš, František (1996): Academic Writing in Czech and English. In: Ventola, Eja & Mauranen, Anna (Eds.): Academic Writing. Intercultural and Textual Issues. Amsterdam: Benjamins, 137-152.

Doleschal, Ursula (2005): Nationalsprachliche Besonderheiten von wissenschaftlichen Texten – Überlegungen zu einem Forschungsprojekt. In: Wingender, Monika (Ed.): Linguistische Beiträge zur Slavistik XII. München: Sagner, 9-22.

Doleschal, Ursula (2007): Implicitness in Academic Texts. A Case Study of Slovene and Russian Texts. In: Doleschal, Ursula & Gruber, Helmut (Eds.): Wissenschaftliches Schreiben abseits des englischen Mainstreams. Academic Writing in Languages Other than English. Bern, Frankfurt, Wien: Lang, 58-81.

Dreyfürst, Stephanie & Sennewald, Nadja (Eds.) (2014): Schreiben. Grundlagentexte zur Theorie, Didaktik und Beratung. Leverkusen: Barbara Budrich (UTB, 8604: Schlüsselkompetenzen).

Eigler, Gunther et al. (1990): Wissen und Textproduzieren. Tübingen: Narr (ScriptOralia, 29).

Fandrych, Christian & Thurmair, Maria (2011): Textsorten im Deutschen. Linguistische Analysen aus sprachdidaktischer Sicht. Tübingen, Narr.

Eßer, Ruth (1997): Etwas ist mir geheim geblieben am deutschen Referat. Kulturelle Geprägtheit wissenschaftlicher Textproduktion und ihre Konsequenzen für den universitären Unterricht von Deutsch als Fremdsprache. München: iudicium.

Finnegan, Damian, Kauppinen, Asko & Wärnsby, Anna (2015): Automated Feedback in a Blended Learning Environment: Student Experience and Development. In: Deane, Mary & Guasch, Teresa (Eds.) (2015): Learning and teaching writing online. Strategies for success, 31-45.

Fix, Ulla, Habscheid, Stephan & Klein, Josef (2001): Zur Kulturspezifik von Textsorten. Tübingen: Stauffenberg (Textsorten, Bd. 3).

Flower, Linda & Hayes, John (1981): A Cognitive Process Theory of Writing. In: *College Composition and Communication* 32, 365-387.

Gračner, Doris Mlakar (2011): Schreibstrategien beim gemeinsamen Verfassen mutter- und fremdsprachlicher Texte (Slowenisch/Deutsch): Eine Fallstudie. In: *Jezikoslovlje* XII (2), 229–248. Available online at https://www.ceeol.com/content-files/document-119620.pdf.

Grießhaber, Wilhelm (2009): Schreiben mit ausländischen Kindern. In: Berning, Johannes, Keßler, Nicola & Koch, Helmut K. (Ed.): Schreiben im Kontext von Schule, Universität, Beruf und Lebensalltag. Berlin: LIT.

Grieshammer, Ella. (2011): Der Schreibprozess beim wissenschaftlichen Schreiben in der Fremdsprache Deutsch und Möglichkeiten seiner Unterstützung. Schreiben im Zentrum: Schreibdidaktische Schriftenreihe der Europa-Universität Viadrina, OPUS, Open Access-Reihe. Magisterarbeit. Technische Universität Berlin, Fakultät I, Institut für Sprache und Kommunikation, Fachbereich Deutsch als Fremdsprache, Berlin. Fachbereich Deutsch als Fremdsprache, checked on feb, 10th 2016.

Guasch, Teresa & Esposa, Anna (2015): Collaborative Writing Online: Unravelling the Feedback Process. In: Deane, Mary & Guasch, Teresa (Eds.): Learning and teaching writing online. Strategies for success. Leiden: Brill, 13-30.

Hyland, Ken & Hyland, Fiona (2016): Feedback on second language students' writing. In: Language Teaching, 39 (2), 83-101.

Hufeisen, Britta (2002): Ein deutsches *Referat* ist kein englischsprachiges *Essay*. Theoretische und praktische Überlegungen zu einem verbesserten textsortenbezogenen Schreibunterricht in der Fremdsprache Deutsch an der Universität. Innsbruck: Studienverlag.

Jakobs, Eva-Maria & Spinuzzi, Clay (2014): Professional Domains: Writing as creation of economic value. In: Eva-Maria, Perrin, Daniel & Knapp, Karlfried (Eds.): Handbook of Writing and Text Production. Berlin: De Gruyter Mouton.

Krause, Wolf-Dieter (2002): Text und Textsorte in der fremdsprachigen Kommunikation. In: Adamzik, Kirsten (Ed.): Texte. Diskurse. Interaktionsrollen: Analysen zur Kommunikation im öffentlichen Raum.Tübingen: Stauffenburg, 191-210.

Krings, Hans P. (1989): Schreiben in der Fremdsprache – Prozeßanalysen zum 'vierten skill'. In Gerd Antos, Hans P. Krings (Eds.): Textproduktion. Ein interdisziplinärer Forschungsüberblick. Tübingen: Niemeyer, 377-436.

Kruse, Otto (2010): Lesen und Schreiben. Der richtige Umgang mit Texten im Studium. Wien: Huter und Roth.

Kuri, Sonja (2005): Im Spannungsfeld der Mehrsprachigkeit. Deutsch an italienischen Universitäten. In: Glaboniat, Manuela, Rastner, Eva Maria & Wintersteiner, Werner (Eds.): Sprachbegegnungen (Heft 2 – 2005 *ide*), 74-84.

Lammertz, Ines & Heinke, Heidrun (2016): Wissenschaftliches Schreiben und Peer-Feedback: Lerngelegenheiten im Physikpraktikum. In: *Zeitschrift für Hochschulentwicklung* 11 (2), 147-162.

Lieber, Maria & Posset, Jürgen (Eds.) (1988): Texte schreiben im Germanistik-Studium. München: iudicium.

Machowicz, Iwona (2011): Schreiberfahrungen aus dem schulischen DaF-Unterricht – Ergebnisse einer empirischen Untersuchung. In: *Lublin Studies in Modern Languages and Literature* (35), 101-118.

Molitor, Sylvie (1985): Personen- und aufgabenspezifische Schreibstrategien. Fünf Fallstudien. In: *Unterrichtswissenschaft* 4/1985, 334-345.

Nelson, Melissa M. & Schunn, Christian D. (2007): The nature of feedback: how different types of peer feedback affect writing performance. In: *Instructional Science* 37, 375-401.

Ortner, Hanspeter (2000): Schreiben und Denken. Tübingen: Niemeyer.

Ortner, Hanspeter (2002): Schreiben für Fortgeschrittene – vom kreativen zum wissenschaftlichen Schreiben. In: Portmann-Tselikas, Paul R. & Schmölzer-Eibinger, Sabine (Eds.): Textkompetenz. Neue Perspektiven für das Lernen und Lehren. Innsbruck: Studienverlag, 233-246.

Plag, Ingo (1996): Individuelle Schreibstrategien beim Verfassen mutter- und fremdsprachlicher Texte (Deutsch/Englisch). In: Wolfgang Börner & Klaus Vogel (Eds.): Texte im Fremdsprachenerwerb. Verstehen und produzieren. Tübingen: Narr (Tübinger Beiträge zur Linguistik, 418), 237–252.

Reid, Joy (1984): The Radical Outliner and the Radical Brainstormer: a Perspective on the Composing Process. In: *Tesol Quarterly* 18, 529-534.

Riehl, Claudia Maria (2001): Schreiben, Text und Mehrsprachigkeit. Zur Textproduktion in mehrsprachigen Gesellschaften am Beispiel der deutschsprachigen Minderheiten in Südtirol und Ostbelgien. Tübingen: Stauffenburg.

Riehl, Claudia Maria (2014): Sprachkontaktforschung. Eine Einführung. 3. Auflage. Tübingen: Narr.

Ruhmann, Gabriela & Kruse, Otto (2014): Prozessorientierte Schreibdidaktik: Grundlagen, Arbeitsformen, Perspektiven. In: Dreyfürst, Stephanie & Sennewald, Nadja (Eds.): Schreiben. Grundlagentexte zur Theorie, Didaktik und Beratung. Leverkusen: Barbara Budrich, 15-34.

Schnetzer, Adrian (2006): Peer-Feedback an Mittel- und Hochschule. In: Kruse, Otto, Berger, Katja & Ulmi, Marianne (Eds.): Prozessorientierte Schreibdidaktik. Schreibtraining für Schule, Studium und Beruf. Bern: Haupt, 195-214.

Sennewald, Nadja (2014): Schreibstrategien. Ein Überblick. In: Dreyfürst, Stephanie & Sennewald, Nadja (Eds.): Schreiben. Grundlagentexte zur Theorie, Didaktik und Beratung. Leverkusen: Barbara Budrich, 169–192.

Silva, Tony (1993): Toward an Understanding of the Distinct Nature of L2 Writing. The ESL Research and Its Implications. In: *TESOL Quarterly* 27 (4), 657. DOI:10.2307/3587400.

Swales, John (2000): Genre analysis. Oxford: Oxford University Press.

Załęska, Maria (2007): Argumentation within different traditions. The case of Polish and Italian academic discourse. In: Doleschal, Ursula & Gruber, Helmut (Eds.): Wissenschaftliches Schreiben abseits des englischen Mainstreams. Academic Writing in Languages Other than English. Bern, Frankfurt, Wien: Lang, 142-175.

Zimmermann, Rüdiger (1996): Asking for belated admission: Produktion und (Selbst-) Evaluation beim Schreiben in der Fremdsprache Englisch. In: Wolfgang Börner & Klaus Vogel (Eds.): Texte im Fremdsprachenerwerb. Verstehen und produzieren. Tübingen: Narr (Tübinger Beiträge zur Linguistik, 418), 211–235.

Anna-Maria Perissutti

The Use of Thematic Progression to Improve Students' Essay Structure

1 Introduction

As we have seen in Bräuer's introduction (this volume), one of the key aspects of the Wrilab2 task design is "scaffolding" (Vygotsky 1987) as a means to break down complex actions into smaller, less complex steps for the student.

In this sense, this chapter is dedicated to a micro-competence which represents a real challenge for the L2 writer, especially at lower levels: the competence to appropriately introduce new referents into the discourse and create referential chains, linking the new information to the old one presented in the preceding clauses. The linguistic term for the structuring of given and new information is "*thematization*". While native speakers may subconsciously acquire such competence through extensive reading without needing instruction, L2 students are less likely to have had sufficient exposure to texts in the target language and, even with lengthy exposure, may find it difficult to discern any patterns in information structuring in a foreign language. The reason for this could be that there are too many different elements of the unfamiliar language to concentrate on simultaneously. Moreover, as pointed out in numerous studies on L2 writing (see among others Olson et al. 2013, Chini et al. 2003, Bräuer this volume), due to their limited grammatical resources or their lack of confidence in a new L2, low level learners tend to concentrate on the sentence level, failing to see the organization of the text as a whole.

Since thematization is a key factor in text writing because it acts as a bridge between sentence level and discourse level, in this chapter it is proposed to apply the linguistic tool of Thematic Progression to L2 writing didactics, in the hope that it may help L2 teachers provide their students with the basic knowledge necessary to discern and produce L2 patterns in information structuring[2].

This chapter is based on the results of the preliminary studies conducted in the framework of Wrilab2, aimed at identifying the main tendencies and oddities in Thematic Progression in L2 Czech writing, compared to L1 Czech writing (see Perissutti 2016 A, 2016 B, Adamovičová & Hajíčková this volume). The chapter is structured as follows: after a brief section in which the concepts of Theme and Rheme are introduced, the Thematic Progression patterns proposed by F. Daneš (1974) are outlined; next, the most frequent "oddities" in Thematic Pro-

---

2 Despite being aware of the difficulties of applying linguistic theories to teaching, we are convinced that the two disciplines should go hand in hand, trying to enrich each other, instead of proceeding separately.

gression found in a small corpus of 40 argumentative compositions written by L2 Czech students (level B1, B2, C1)[3] will be identified.

The chapter ends with a series of didactic suggestions to improve L2 students' textual organization.

2 Theme and Rheme

Introduced by Vilém Mathesius in the framework of the Prague Linguistic School in the 1930s, the concepts of Theme and Rheme were later developed and spread all over the world in the 1970s mainly by two other famous representatives of the Prague School, František Daneš and Jan Firbas. Nowadays these notions are among the most debated in linguistics[4]. In this chapter I adopt the definition proposed by K. Lambrecht (1994), the author of a comprehensive and recognised study that explores the relationship between the structure of sentences and the linguistic and extra-linguistic contexts in which they are used. Theme refers to "what the text is about". Within the proposition, one (or more) **textual referent** has the function of Theme as, in Lambrecht's words (1994):

> "In a given situation the proposition is construed as being about this referent, i.e. as expressing information which is relevant to and which increases the addressee's knowledge of this referent (Lambrecht 1994: 131)".

As pointed out by Halliday and Kirkwood (1985: 38), the Theme comes to function naturally as the "point of departure of the message". In addition, it is particularly evident in the communicative context and is, therefore, usually expressed by a bound personal pronoun or by a pre-verbal nominal or prepositional phrase. In a sentence with normal word order, the Theme tends to coincide with the syntactic subject (even when it is not phonetically realized).

The semantic element functionally related to the Theme is the Rheme. The Rheme follows the linguistic expression of the Theme and coincides with the

---

3 These argumentative compositions were taken from the learner corpus CzeSL (Czech as a Second Language), which is the first Czech learner corpus and is part of the Czech National Corpus. It contains a total of about 2.3 million tokens, i.e. transcripts of essays written by non-native speakers of 54 different mother tongues, in language teaching classes of various types and levels. The texts were collected in 2009-2012 mostly in schools, i.e. in a formal environment, and included in the corpus with the consent of the relevant institutions and individuals. The original forms and automatic corrections are tagged, lemmatized and assigned error labels.

4 Some linguists interpret this concept as a pragmatic universal (Lambrecht, 1994), others in the frame of cognitive semantics (Maslova & Bernini 2006), while linguists working in the generative framework interpret it as a functional head at the left periphery of the sentence (Rizzi 1997). Different and not always equivalent are also the terms used in the literature to express the concept: some use the term "psychological subject", others use the term "topic". For a summary see Berretta (1995).

predicate of a proposition (it can also include circumstantial information). Consider the following example (the Theme is in bold, while the Rheme is in italics):

(1) **Leica Macroscopes** *are among the most precise on the market.* (http://www.leica-microsystems.com/)

Usually the Theme is chosen among Given information (old information), while the Rheme coincides with the New information, the true enrichment of the proposition. To explain this tendency, the Czech linguist J. Firbas (1974) introduced the concept of Communicative Dynamism, stating that the Theme of the utterance is the semantic element associated with the lowest degree of Communicative Dynamism, while the Rheme is the element with the highest degree of Communicative Dynamism.

3 Thematic progression

From an informational perspective, the Themes in a text are linked together; they form a sequence that ensures semantic continuity and creates the skeleton of the texts, while the Rhemes develop the textual content. Consider the following example:

(2) A. **Stereo microscopes and macroscopes from Leica Microsystems** enable you to view, analyze and document your specimens in two and three dimensions. B. **These imaging systems** provide powerful solutions for precise analysis and documentation. (http://www.leica-microsystems.com)

While sentence A introduces the textual referents fulfilling the role of Theme (i.e. **Stereo microscopes** and **macroscopes from Leica Microsystems**), sentence B resumes them through the Nominal Phrase **These imaging systems.**

This sequence of thematic elements participating in creating text cohesion is called "thematic progression". Defined by the Czech linguist František Daneš in the 1970s[5], this concept has to do with **textual organization**, and in particular with the selection of the successive Themes in the text[6]. In Daneš's words (1974: 114):

---

5 The concept of Thematic Progression was created to define an important textual (macro-syntactic) effect of the sentence-related phenomenon known as "Functional Sentence Perspective".

6 As soon as it was defined, the concept of thematic progression was immediately used in Text Linguistics, where it came to denote an important condition of text

> By this term [thematic progression] we mean the choice and ordering of utterances themes, their mutual concatenation and hierarchy, as well as their relationship to the hyperthemes of the superior text units (such as the paragraph, chapter, etc.), to the whole text, and to the situation. Thematic progression might be viewed as the skeleton of the plot.

Basically, according to the nature of the preceding informational unit being thematized (i.e. whether it is a thematic and/or a rhematic element), Daneš posited three types of thematic progression: constant, simple linear, and derived progression.

1. In "Constant Theme Progression", successive clauses retain the same **Theme.** This may be represented as **Th1-Th2, Th2-Th3, Th3-Th4,** etc. (where Th denotes Theme, i.e. the theme of clause 1 links up with the Theme of clause 2, the Theme of clause 2 with the Theme of clause 3, and so on. See the abovementioned example 2;

2. In "Simple Linear Theme Progression", the Theme repeats or transforms the Rheme of the preceding clause and this may be depicted as **Rh1-Th2, Rh2-Th3, Rh3-Th4,** etc. (Rh denoting Rheme); see example (3):

(3) A. **Communication** is a process of transmitting a message.

B. **The message** can be delivered through oral or written expression.

3. In "Derived Theme Progression", the Themes connect to an implicit overall 'hypertheme' of the whole text (which could be shown as **Th(D1), Th(D2), Th(D3),** etc., where an implied link to the hypertheme is represented by the 'D' in brackets). Confront example (4):

(4) A. **Ecuador** is situated on the equator in the northwest of South America.

B. **The economy** is based on oil and agricultural products.

C. **More oil** is produced **in Ecuador** than in any other South American country except Venezuela.

D. **Bananas, coffee, and cocoa** are grown there.

Ecuador is the Theme of the entire paragraph (the hyper-theme) and the the themes of sentences A, B, C, and D are all related to this hyper-theme.

---

coherence: utterances forming a coherent text are typically characterized by the presence of thematic contents with a low degree of Communicative Dynamism, and these thematic elements are responsible for linking more dynamic information to the immediate and less immediate contexts (the phenomenon involves the preceding as well as the succeeding context, cf. Givón 1983).

Besides the three TP proposed by Daneš, one more TP was considered[7], which was introduced by the Italian linguist Mortara Garavelli (1979) i.e.:

4. "thematization of a Theme+Rheme sequence", or "thematization of more than one Theme+Rheme sequences". The following example shows the thematization of a Theme+Rheme sequence: the pronoun *ciò* in Italian, *this* in English, encapsulates the content of the entire preceding context:

(5) A. **The sunrays that reach the mountains** are hotter than those that reach the plains. B. **This** is known to all who were in the mountains and have burned their skin despite the very low temperatures.

The different types of thematic progression typically alternate, cross each other and overlap in a text. In order to illustrate the four thematic progressions presented above, consider the following example, proposed in Ferrari & Zampese (2000: 354)[8]:

(6) A. **Il microscopio** permette di osservare oggetti molto piccoli, tanto piccoli da non essere visibili ad occhio nudo. B. **(zero subject)** È uno strumento che funziona così: C. **un primo gruppo di lenti, l'obbiettivo,** ingrandisce l'oggetto da vedere; D. **un secondo gruppo di lenti, l'oculare,** ingrandisce l'immagine creata dall'obbiettivo.

E. **Il segreto del microscopio** è dunque l'ingrandimento dell'ingrandimento.
F. **Con il microscopio, (zero subject)** possiamo osservare le parti delle piante. G. **(zero subject)** Iniziamo con una pelle di cipolla: H. **essa** infatti è sottile e si osserva con facilità (Ferrari & Zampese 2000: 354).

A. **The microscope** makes it possible to observe very small objects, so small that **they** are not visible to the naked eye. B. **It** is a tool that works like this: C. **a first group of lenses, the objective,** enlarges the object to be seen; D. **a second group of lenses, the eyepiece**, enlarges the image created by the lens.

E. **The microscope's secret** is, thus, the enlargement of the enlargement.

F. **With the microscope, we** can observe the parts of the plants. G. Let's start with an onion skin: H. In fact, **it** is thin and is observed with ease. (Ferrari & Zampese 2000: 354).

---

7 The typology proposed by Daneš (1974) has been slightly changed under the influence of the numerous later studies that added other Thematic Progressions (TP).

8 The English translation is mine.

In the text reproduced in (6), Constant Theme Progression can be observed between utterances A and B: through the omitted subject in Italian and the pronoun *it* in English, the Theme of Utterance B resumes the nominal phrase *il microscopio/ the micorscope*, which is the Theme of the preceding utterance. Utterances G and H show an instance of Linear Theme Progression: the Theme of Utterance 8, *essa* in Italian, *it* in English, resumes the nominal phrase *una pelle di cipolla (an onion skin)*, which is part of the Rheme of utterance G. In turn, sentences C and D illustrate Derived Theme Progression: the two Themes, "a first group of lenses, the objective", and "a second group of lenses" connect, the eyepiece" connect to an implicit overall hypertheme, "the functioning of the microscope".

4 Applying theThematic Progression tool to L2 writing analysis

Having briefly reviewed Daneš's progression types, this linguistic tool will now be applied to the study of Czech L2 argumentative compositions[9], compared to L1 Czech essays. In this section the most frequent "oddities" in L2 Czech Thematic Progression will be pointed out, as well as the Thematic Progression patterns present in Czech L1 but absent in L2 Czech writings. Considering the aim of this publication, instead of presenting quantitative data the attention will be drawn to the ways in which teachers can enrich their students' knowledge of thematic progression and solve the problems they encounter in organizing information.

4.1 Overuse of Constant Progression

L2 students, especially at a lower level, tend to overuse Constant Progression, resulting at worst in a series of unrelated statements about the Theme. Consider the following examples (note that the Czech L2 and L1 texts are divided in

[9] As far as the L2 Czech data are concerned, we selected a small corpus of 40 argumentative compositions (level B1-B2-C1) from the corpus CzeSL - Czech as a Second Language with Spelling, Grammar and Tags, which is part of the Czech National Corpus. The L1 Czech compositions instead are taken from the portal Český jazyk Literatura aneb studentský underground, <www.cesky-jazyk.cz>, which provides assignments of different genres written by L1 Czech secondary students, as well as many other useful materials concerning the Czech language and literature. The analytical procedure was to first divide the compositions in clauses, locate and mark each independent clause with a letter (A, B, C...) in the L2 Czech learners' writing as well as in that of Czech mother tongue students. Next the theme of each clause was identified and marked in boldface. Finally, the category of Thematic Progression (and any others discernible) at work across each inter-clause boundary in Czech L1 and L2 writings was identified and the results from the two groups were compared, in order to single out oddities, deviations, L2 tendencies and missing Thematic Progression patterns in L2 Czech writings. All reported examples are authentic, uncorrected.

clauses, marked with a letter (A, B, C....). The Themes of the clauses are marked in boldface):

(7)

A.	**Jídlo**	v lidském životě	hraje	velkou roli.
	Food $^{\text{NOM.SG}}$	in human life ^{LOC}	play $^{\text{PRS.IPF.3SG}}$	big role^{ACC}

B.	**Pro mne**	**jídlo**	je	jako	prostředek k životu $^{\text{DAT.SG}}$
	For me ^{ACC}	**food** $^{\text{NOM.SG}}$	be $^{\text{PRS.3.SG}}$	as	mean$^{\text{NOM.SG}}$for living$^{\text{DAT.SG}}$

C.	a	take	je	**pro me**	velmi důležité,
	and	also	be $^{\text{PRS.3.SG}}$	**for me** ^{ACC}	very important

D.	aby **to jídlo**	bylo	zdravé.
	that **that food** $^{\text{NOM.SG}}$	be $^{\text{PST.3.SG}}$	healthy $^{\text{NOM.SG}}$

"Food plays an important role in human life. For me food is a means for living. And it is also important for me that that food is healthy".

Despite the fact that every Theme in example (7) includes the word '**jídlo - food**', there is no clear development pattern for the reader to hold on to as s/he navigates the text[10]. In the effort to be clear and to produce grammatically correct sentences, L2 students repeat the same information, creating a clumsiness that unnecessarily labours the obvious.

The analysis of the *TP with Constant Theme* can give teachers the opportunity to explain the linguistic expression of anaphora, i.e. the resumption of a referent already introduced in the preceding text, a linguistic phenomenon which may seem trivial to the L1 writer, but hides many pitfalls for the L2 writer.

The linguistic coding of anaphora in L2

As shown by numerous linguistic studies since the 1980s, (Givón 1983, Fox 1987, Tomlin 1987, Berretta 1990 among other), there is an interaction between the structuring of the texts and the linguistic coding of anaphora. What is crucial

---

10 The relationship of Themes to their Rhemes (i.e. progression proper) is vital. Co-operative writers select something in theme as the starting point for a clause which will make it easier for their readers to immediately see how the information that will come in the remainder of the clause is likely to fit in with what has already been written.

in determining the choice of anaphoric devices is the distance in the discourse from the most recent occurrence of the referent. When the referent is distant or discontinuous (because it is interrupted by another referent), the more marked forms (full Nominal Phrases and stressed pronouns) are used for its anaphoric resumption. In contrast, when the referent to be resumed is near, accessible and continuous, anaphora will be marked by reduced forms (unstressed pronouns, zero anaphora and agreement). Besides this cross-linguistic principle, which can be learned quite easily by L2 learners due to its universal nature, the linguistic coding of anaphora is also language specific, thus depending on the structural and typological features of each language. This can be observed considering example (6), which we repeat in (8):

(8) A. **Il microscopio** permette di osservare oggetti molto piccoli, tanto piccoli da non essere visibili ad occhio nudo. B. **(zero subject)** È uno strumento che funziona così:

A. **The microscope** makes it possible to observe very small objects, so small that **they** are not visible to the naked eye. B. **It** is a tool that works like this:

If you compare the original Italian text with its English translation, you can see that the devices used to mark anaphoric reference in the two languages are different: while Italian is a pro-drop language and enables the use of null subjects to resume the preceding referent *(il microscopio)*, English requires the expression of the pronominal subject *it.* As Berretta (1990) has shown, besides depending on the structural properties of each language, the linguistic coding of anaphora also depends on the register and the text typology, thus challenging not only the writer's morphological and lexical mastery, but also his/her stylistic and pragmatic competences. Due to its complexity, the linguistic expression of anaphora is thus likely to represent a problematic area for the L2 writer, one which deserves more attention.

As a sample of the difficulties that L2 writers may encounter, we present the tendencies that emerged from the study of our L2 Czech written text corpus, compared to argumentative texts written by L1 Czech students[11].

To introduce a distant or discontinuous referent (i.e., a referent interrupted by another referent), the Czech L2 student tends to repeat the same Nominal Phrase used in the antecedent, without using adjectives and determiners such as *vyše zmíňený* / *nahoře uvedený* 'above mentioned', *onen* 'that', to signal that the referent was already introduced, thus losing textual coherence.

[11] For the study concerning the Italian L2 linguistic coding of anaphora see Chini, Marina, Ferraris, Stefania, Valentini, Ada & Businaro, Barbara (2003).

The repetition of the same NP used in the antecedent seems to be the strategy preferred by L2 writers even when they have to resume a near, accessible referent, mentioned in the preceding clause: this is a context where the repetition of the same NP in Czech is forbidden; Czech L1 writers use synonyms, hyperonyms and hyponyms instead and accompany the NP with a rich variety of determiners (*ten, tento, tenhle... the, this, that…*).

To understand this phenomenon better, let us look at the following examples: (9) is taken from a Czech L1 essay (*Sdělovácí prostředky 2*), while (10) is taken from a Czech L2 essay:

(9)

A.	**Sdělovací prostředky**	vznikly	už před miliony let (...),
	Mass media $^{\text{NOM.PL}}$	arise $^{\text{PST.PFV.3PL}}$	ago million ^{INS} year $^{\text{GEN.PL}}$

B.	kde	se začala	rozvíjet	řeč.
	where	initiate $^{\text{PST.PFV.REFL.3SG}}$	develop $^{\text{INF.IPFV}}$	language^{NOM}

C.	**Tento způsob sdělování informací**	se vyvinul
	This system transmission ^{GEN} information $^{\text{GEN.PL}}$	evolve $^{\text{PST.PFV.3SG REFL}}$

D.	z potřeby	pravěkého člověka	se dorozumět […].
	from need ^{GEN}	prehistorical man ^{GEN}	communicate $^{\text{INF.IPFV}}$

"The mass media arose millions of years ago in the ancient world where language was initiated. This information transmission system evolved from the prehistorical man's need to communicate [...]".

In (9) the referent expressed by NP **sdělovací prostředky** 'mass media' in A. is resumed in B. by the synonym – **tento způsob sdělování informací** 'this information communication system'. In the following, observe a typical textual sequence from the Czech L2 corpus:

(10)

A.	**Média**	pro nás	jsou	absolutně nezbytné.
	Mass media $^{\text{NOM.PL}}$	for us ^{ACC}	be $^{\text{PRS.3PL}}$	absolutely essential.

B.	**To**	je	hlavní	důvod,
	This NOM.3SG	be PRS.3SG	main	reason NOM

C.	proč	můžou	**média**	řídit	náš	život.
	why	can PRS.3PL	**media** NOM.PL	control INF.IPFV	our ACC	life ACC

"The mass media are absolutely essential for us. This is why the media can influence our lives".

In (10) the referent expressed by NP **média** 'mass media' in clause A is anaphorically resumed in clause C by the same NP.

This redundancy, which is particularly frequent in Constant Theme TP, may be explained by recalling the L2 tendency to over-explicitness, often noticed in the writings of L2 learners and aimed at avoiding misunderstanding. We believe that it could also depend on the different textual planning from L1 and L2: due to their limited competence, L2 learners tend to divide the text into smaller syntactical units which are autonomous and thus easier to control at the morphological and lexical level. However, being autonomous, these single smaller units need lexical (heavier) linguistic means to be resumed.

4.2 Simple Linear Progression - Thematic jumps

As far as simple linear progression is concerned, where the Rheme of the preceding clause becomes the Theme of the following one, a sort of "mechanical" use of it can be noticed in Czech L2 writers, resulting in Themes linked to the Rhemes of the preceding sentences without really developing the text and thus rendering it incoherent. See example (11):

(11)

A.	**Kulturní člověk**	miluje	přirodu
	Cultivated person NOM	love PRS.IPF.3SG	nature ACC

B.	**Ø** Velmý	mnoha	zná
	very	much	know PRS.IPF.3SG

C.	a	**Ø** myslí	velmý	oblišně
	and	think PRS.IPF.3SG	very	originally

D.	**Ø** Hodně	čte	knih
	many	read [PRS.IPF.3.SG]	book [GEN.PL]

E.	a	**Ø** divá se	**na**	**filmy**
	and	watch [PRS.IPF.3SG REFL]	at	film [ACC.PL]

F.	**Můj oblíbený**	**film**	je	Hatiko
	My favourite	**film** [NOM.SG]	be [PRS.3SG]	Hatiko

> "An educated person loves nature. He/she knows many things and he/she thinks in an original way. He/she reads many books and watches films. My favourite film is Hatiko".

As you can see in the preceding example, while clauses A, B, C, D and E present a TP with constant Theme (the omitted subjects of utterances B, C, D, and E ensure semantic continuity with utterance A through the anaphoric resumption of the NP *Kulturni clovek* in A), sentence F presents a Linear Theme Progression, transforming the Rheme of the preceding sentence E (*film*) into the Theme of sentence F. The problem here lies in the abrupt introduction of the NP *my (favourite film)* in F, which introduces the writer's person in the text, without logically justifying his presence and thus rendering the text incoherent. Since similarly random Theme changes are frequent in the writings of Czech L2 students, it can be concluded that students have little knowledge of progression theory and fail to consider their audience, placing material which is completely new, or at least insufficiently known to the reader, in the Theme.

4.3 Derived Progression

In the context of derived progression, one problem that can be observed is the difficulty to clearly state the hyper-theme from which two following subthemes split: often it is difficult to understand how the two split Themes are connected to the hyper-theme, as in the following example:

(12)

A.	Když to	bude	musulmanska	zemí
	If it	be [PRS.3SG]	muslim	country [NOM]

B.	určite	nikdy	vy	nemůžete	vidět
	of course	never	you	can [NEG.PRS.1PL]	see [INF.IPF]

C.	abych lídí	kouřilí	ven	a samozrejme	v restauracich.
	that people	smoke$^{PST.IPF.1.PL}$	out	and of course	in restaurant $^{LOC.PL}$

D.	**Prvny typ**	bude	dovolat	kouření	v restauracích
	First type	^{AUX}	admit $^{INF.IPF}$	smoke ^{ACC}	in restaurant $^{LOC.PL}$

E.	a	**jiný**	nikdy	nemůže
	and	other	never	can $^{NEG.PRS.3SG}$

F.	Pro	mě	je	---	**to**	duležita	vec
	For	me ^{ACC}	be $^{PRS.3SG}$		it	important	thing ^{NOM}

G.	při	vybery	**restauraci**
	in	choice $^{STR.}$	restaurant $^{GEN.PL}$

> "In a Muslim country you can't see people smoking neither in nor outside the restaurants. The first type will admit smoking inside, the other never. For me it is an important factor in the choice of the restaurant".

Poor thematization in at least three cases makes this passage difficult to process. The denotation of the two split thematic expressions in clauses D **"prvny typ"** – *the first type*, and E **"jiny"** *the other* is not clear. One can guess that the denotation of *the first* type in D represents countries where people can smoke in restaurants and *the other* in E represents countries where people cannot smoke in restaurants. Even the denotation of the pronoun "**to**"- *it* in sentence F (which creates a complex pattern, resuming a Theme – Rheme structure) is hard to discern, unless the reader is interested enough to simply continue to the subsequent clause.

This problematic thematization is probably due to the writer's low linguistic competence. To create Derived Theme Progression one needs to master complex syntactical structures, such as secondary sentences and nominalizations, in order to "compress" the content of the preceding sentences in one single thematic element.

The writers' limited linguistic competence leads to another problem in thematization that can be noticed in Czech L2 written compositions, namely the absence of a Theme-Rheme structure.

4.4 Absence of a discernable Theme-Rheme structure

This is the most basic difficulty with students' progression. It is most likely to occur if the writer attempts an unusually long sentence and loses her/his way. To understand the problem, let us observe the following example, taken from a Czech L2 composition (a film review):

(13)

A.	V tomto případě	je	to	riskantnější	než	obvykle:
	in this case ^{LOC}	be $^{\text{PRS.3SG}}$	it	more risky	then	usually

B.	mluví se	o	horách,	o nebezpečnosti (...)
	talk $^{\text{PRS.IPF.3SG REFL}}$	about	mountain $^{\text{LOC.PL}}$,	about danger $^{\text{LOC.SG}}$ (...)

C.	Existuje	však	negativní	aspekt:
	exist $^{\text{PRS.3SG}}$	however	negative	aspect ^{NOM}:

D.	**horolezectví**	je	to	riskantní	činnost
	climbing $^{\textbf{NOM}}$	be $^{\text{PRS.3SG}}$	it	risky	aktivity ^{NOM}

E.	a	**Ø** záleží	nejenom na	schopnost	člověka,
	and	depend $^{\text{PRS.3SG}}$	not only on	ability	person, $^{\text{GEN.SG}}$

F.	ale	i	na	horu	a	na	přírodu.
	but	also	on	mountain ^{ACC}	and	on	nature ^{ACC}

> "In this case it is riskier: we talk about mountains and danger. There is however one negative aspect: climbing is a risky activity and it depends not only on one's ability but also on the mountains and nature".

In C the writer, using the connector "však" – *however,* announces to the reader that the next sentence is going to present the Rheme proper, i.e., the true textual enrichment. But the following sentence D repeats instead the same information (*climbing is a risky activity*) already presented in sentences A and B, thus violating the informational role which states that new, dynamic information should be placed in the Rheme. This textual structuring confuses the reader, who does not understand neither the textual development pattern nor the writer's communicative intention.

This writer's difficulty is probably due to low linguistic competence. The student should have put all the information THE RISKS IMPLICIT IN CLIMBING in the Theme, thus highlighting the Rheme CANNOT BE CONTROLLED BY THE CLIMBER BECAUSE IT DEPENDS LARGELY ON NATURE. Even here, in order to compress a big amount of information in the Theme, the writer has to master complex syntactical structures, such as nominalizations (which transform sentences into a noun clause) and secondary sentences.

4.5 Absence of more complex TPs such as the thematization of a "Theme+Rheme sequence"

In the Czech L2 corpus, the absence of complex thematic progression patterns can be remarked. One of these complex TP patterns is the thematization of a "Theme+Rheme sequence through NPs" having a generic meaning (such as, for example *otázka* 'question', *věc* 'thing', *směr* 'tendency', *skutečnost* 'reality'), which refer not only to the previous NP but also to entire portions of the preceding text, as in the example (14):

(14)

A.	**Křivka znázorňující**	**počet vražd**	**ve Spojených státech [...]**
	Curve^{NOM} indicating	number homicides$^{GEN.PL}$	in United States^{LOC} [...]

B.	sleduje	křivku	rustu	počtu televizorů,
	follow $^{PRS.IPFV.3SG}$	curve ^{ACC}	growth ^{GEN}	number television ^{GEN}

C.	**což**	by mělo být	jako	velice alarmující	zjištění
	thing	should be considered	as	very alarming	fact ^{NOM}

"The curve indicating the number of homicides in the United States follows the curve of the increase in the number of televisions, a thing that should be considered as an alarming fact [...]".

2. another complex TP, which is absent in L2 Czech compositions and which is sometimes present in Czech L1 writings in the context of the Simple Linear Progression is the phenomenon of diatheme: the NP that performs the anaphoric function, transforming the Rheme of the preceding sentence into the Theme of the new sentence, also provides new information about the Theme. Consider the following example:

(15)

A.	Autor	zde	publikuje	svou	novou báseň
	Author^{NOM}	here	publish $^{PRS.IPFV.3SG}$	his ^{ACC}	new poetry ^{ACC}

B.	**V lyrickém obraze**	**podzimní přírody**	nechává promlouvat	
	In lyrical image ^{LOC}	autumn nature	let $^{CAUS.PRS.IPFV.3SG}$	speak $^{INF.IPFV}$

"Here the author publishes his new poetry. **In the lyrical image of nature in autumn** he lets speak [...]".

5 Concluding remarks and suggestions for teachers

Considering the main difficulties identified in Czech L2 thematic progression patterns I suggest the following activities to improve L2 writers' textual information structure.

- In order to limit the repetition of Constant Theme Progression, the students should be coached in alternative Thematic Progression patterns (simple linear, derived), helping them realize the effect that the repetition of this TP has on the reader;
- in the context of Constant Theme Progression, it is of the utmost importance to enrich the students' lexical vocabulary and their scale of morphological devices (pronouns, determiners) in order to enlarge their pool of anaphoric means useful for the resumption of near and distant referents;
- in the context of Simple Linear Progression, teachers should draw the students' attention to the need to constantly figure out the state of the reader's knowledge in order to avoid the abrupt introduction of new Themes in the discourse;
- the importance to define a clear Theme – Rheme structure in the sentences should be explained to the students;
- to enable students to compress a large amount of information into the Theme while highlighting the proper new information in the Rheme, teachers should train them in complex syntactical structures, such as nominalizations, secondary sentences, abstract names that refer to an entire preceding context (such as *question, phenomenon…*).

Literature

Adamovičová, Ana & Hajíčková, Zuzana (2016): Česká verze projektu Wrilab2, this volume.

Berretta, Monica (1995): Ordini marcati dei costituenti maggiori di frase: una rassegna. In: *Linguistica e Filologia* (1), 125-170.

Berretta, Monica (1990): Catene anaforiche in prospettiva funzionale: antecedenti difficili. In: *Rivista di Linguistica*, II, 1, 91-120.

Bräuer, Gerd (2016): The Didactic Framework for WRILAB2, this volume.

Chini, Marina, Ferraris, Stefania, Valentini, Ada & Businaro, Barbara (2003): Aspetti della testualità. In: Giacalone Ramat, Anna (Ed.): Verso l'italiano. Percorsi e strategie di acquisizione. Roma: Carocci, 179-219.

Conte, Maria Elisabeth (1988): Determinazione del tema. In: Conte, Maria Elisabeth (Ed.): Condizioni di coerenza. Ricerche di linguistica testuale. Firenze: La Nuova Italia, 49-56.

Daneš, František (1974): Functional sentence perspective and the organization of the text. In: Daneš, František (Ed.): Papers on Functional Sentence Perspective. Prague and Paris: Academia-Mouton, 106-28.

Ferrari, Angela & Zampese, Luciano (2000): Dalla frase al testo. Una grammatica per l'italiano. Bologna: Zanichelli.

Ferrari, Angela & De Cesare Anna-Maria (2009): La progressione tematica rivisitata. In: *Vox Romanica*, LXVIII, 98-128.

Firbas, Jan (1974): Some aspects of the Czechoslovak approach to problems of function sentence perspective. In: Daneš, František (Ed.): Papers on Functional Sentence Perspective. Prague, Paris: Academia, 11-37.

Fox, Barbara (1987): Anaphora in Popular Written English Narratives. In: Tomlin, Russell S. (Eds.): Coherence and Grounding in Discourse, Amsterdam and Philadelphia, 157-174.

Givón, Talmy (1983): Topic continuity in discourse: a quantitative cross-language study, Amsterdam and Philadelphia: J. Benjamins.

Halliday, Michael & Kirkwood, Alexander (1985): An introduction to functional grammar. London: Arnold.

Lambrecht, Knud (1994): Information structure and sentence form. Topic, focus and the mental representations of discourse referents. Cambridge: Cambridge University Press.

Maslova, Elena & Bernini, Giuliano (2006): Sentence Topics in the Languages of Europe and Beyond. In: Bernini, Giuliano & Schwarz Marcia L. (Eds.): Pragmatic Organization of Discourse in the Languages of Europe. Berlin, New York: de Gruyter, 67-120.

Mortara Garavelli, Bice (1979): Il filo del discorso, Torino: Giappichelli.

Olson, Booth Carol, Scarcella, Robin & Matuchniak, Tina (2013): Best Practices in Teaching Writing to English Learners. Reducing Constraints to Facilitate Writing Development. In: Graham, Steve (Ed.): Writing Instruction. New York, London: The Guilford Press, 381-402.

Perissutti, Anna-Maria (2016A): Scelta del topic e codificazione anaforica nelle composizioni argomentative in ceco L2. In: Benigni, Valentina, Gebert, Lucyna & Nikolaeva, Julija: Le lingue slave tra struttura e uso. Biblioteca di studi Slavistici. Firenze: University Press, 243-260.

Perissutti, Anna-Maria (2016B): Progressioni tematiche nell'interlingua: studio longitudinale sull'acquisizione della abilità di scrittura in ceco L2. In: Inkova, Olga & Trovesi, Andrea: Lingue slave a confronto. Bergamo: University Press, 343-363.

Rizzi, Luigi (1997): The Fine Structure of the Left Periphery. In: Haegeman, Liliane (Ed.): Elements of Grammar. Dordrecht: Kluwer Academia Publishers, 281-337.

Tomlin, Russell (1987): Linguistic Reflections of Cognitive Events. In: Tomlin, Russell (Eds.): Coherence and grounding in Discourse. Amsterdam, Philadelphia: J. Benjamins, 455-479.

Vygotsky, Lev (1987): Thinking and speech. In: Rieber, Robert W. & Carton Aaron S. (Eds.): The collected works of L. S. Vygotsky, Volume 1: Problems of general psychology. New York: Plenum Press, 39–285. (Original work published 1934).

Zimová, Ludmila (1994): Způsoby vyjadřování větných členů v textu. Konkurence pojmenování, pronominalizace a elize. Ústí nad Labem: Univerzita Jana Evangelisty Purkyně.

Ineke Vedder

Assessing Functional Adequacy in L2 and L1 Writing. Proposal of a Rating Scale

1 Introduction

In second language research (SLA) general measures for assessing linguistic performance, operationalized in terms of complexity, accuracy and fluency (CAF) are often employed (Housen, Kuiken & Vedder 2012). In this essay it is argued that not only the linguistic dimension but also the functional dimension ('how to get the message through') is crucial when assessing learners' oral and written performance in a second language (L2). With this purpose in mind a rating scale for assessing L2 speaking and writing was developed.

The main goal of the study presented herein is to investigate the role of functional adequacy in assessing L2 proficiency within a task-related framework (TBLT: Task Based Learning and Teaching). The overarching research question is: How can we measure a multifaceted construct such as functional adequacy?

In order to answer this question three experiments were set up. In the first study (study 1) we investigated how functional adequacy in L2 and L1 writing in three languages (Dutch, Italian and Spanish) could be defined and measured by means of a global rating scale inspired by the scale descriptors of the CEFR (Council of Europe 2001; Kuiken, Vedder & Gilabert 2010; Kuiken & Vedder 2014).

Based on the outcomes of this first study the original global rating scale was adjusted and a new one developed. In the new rating scale four distinct components of functional adequacy were distinguished inspired by Grice's conversational maxims (1975: 1) content, 2) task requirements, 3) comprehensibility, 4) coherence and cohesion. In the second and third study the applicability of the rating scale for functional adequacy was put to the test. In study 2 the rating scale was tried out for L2 and L1 writing, for Dutch and Italian (Kuiken & Vedder 2016). In study 3 we tested the applicability of the scale for the assessment of oral performance, for Dutch L2 and Italian L2 (Kuiken & Vedder forthcoming).

The present contribution focuses on the written data for Italian L2 and L1 of study 2, without considering the data for Dutch L2 and L1. It is structured as follows. In order to illustrate the concept of functional adequacy, section 2 presents some examples for L2 writing and L1 speaking, respectively, functionally adequate and inadequate written and oral text samples. In section 3 the problem of how to define and assess functional adequacy is discussed. In section 4 the theoretical underpinnings, levels and descriptors of the rating scale for functional adequacy are presented. Section 5 describes the participants of the study, the collection of the data, the raters and the writing tasks that were assigned to the L2 and L1 writers. In section 6 the main findings of the study are reported. Section 7 and 8 focus on the pedagogical implications of the study for classroom practice, particularly with respect to the assessment of L2 writing.

2 Functional (in)adequacy: examples

Before moving to the definition of the construct of functional adequacy, let us first consider a few examples of functionally adequate (or inadequate) messages, in relation to a particular context or with respect to the specific requirements of the task. Example 1 and 2 ('Caro Orlando'; 'Cara Valentina') are taken from a corpus of written L2 data produced by first-year university students of Italian, with Dutch as their native language. Examples 3 and 4 are taken from a corpus of natural data from a study on the use of pragmatic markers and modifiers in requests and apologies, in phone messages in Italian L1 and Dutch L1. The messages were left on the answering machine of an Italian dentist, with a dental practice in both Naples and Amsterdam.

In example 1 (a letter to a friend) the participants were asked to recommend a B&B in Italy, on the basis of a number of criteria to be taken into account (e.g. vicinity to the city centre and public transport). Despite some syntactic and lexical errors or a few odd formulations, such as 'locomozioni fino a tardi' ('things to do'? 'public transport'?), the first letter ('Caro Orlando') is largely comprehensible and functionally adequate regarding the specific requirements of the writing task.

Example 1: Caro Orlando (Italian L2)

Caro Orlando,[12]

Secondo gli tuoi condizione creo che il nummer 3, B&B Hotel Migani Spiaggia è il più appropriata. Non è vicino al centro, ma è vicino al boulevard, che anche è interessante. E di notte ha abbastanza movimento e locomozioni fino a tardi. Va per te, lo so sicuro!

Things are somewhat different in the second letter ('Cara Valentina'). Although the letter is lexically and syntactically more varied and contains fewer errors compared to 'Caro Orlando', the text is functionally inadequate, with respect to the task requirements, register and genre. Instead of suggesting a B&B

---

[12] Dear Orlando, taking into account your requirements I think that number 3, B&B Hotel Migani Spiaggia is the best one. It is not close to the city centre, but close to the waterfront, which is also interesting. And at night there is a lot of movement [?] and public transport [?] until late at night. I am sure you will like it.

accomodation and providing reasons for this choice, the author has written a love letter to his girlfriend Valentina. This is shown by the presence of numerous 'inadequate' expressions, such as 'tu ci sei per me, non c'è importante per me dove siamo'('You are here for me, and it doesn't matter where we are'); 'ti amo, ti vorrei abbracciare e non lasciare mai ('I love you', 'I want to hold you in my arms and never leave you'); 'goderci la vita e l'un l'altro' ('to enjoy life and each other'); 'ti desidero' ('I want you'); 'un baciozzo' ('bacione'?; 'big kiss').

Example 2: Cara Valentina (Italian L2)

Cara Valentina,[13]

Sono molto felice che hai scelto cinque diverse opzione per andare in vacanza. Non te ho visto lungo. C'è una scelta difficile. Però tu ci sei per me, non c'è importante per me dove siamo. Ti amo. Ti vorrei abbracciare e non lasciare mai. Quindì penso che la prima scelta è ottima, perché il B&B assomiglia molto tranquillo. Inoltre c'è un giardino e fanno una prima colazione fantastica. Per di píu abbiamo la tutto di tempo per goderci La vita e l'un l'altro. Ti desidero.

Un baciozzo.

The voice mail messsages in Italian L1 and Dutch L1 (examples 3 and 4), were taken from a corpus of voice mail messages left by the patients of a dental practice in Naples and Amsterdam, in order to reschedule their appointment.

Cancelling an appointment, viewed within the theoretical framework of Politeness Theory (Brown & Levinson 1987), is considered a face-threatening speech act (FTA), which requires the employment of a number of modifiers and pragmatic and linguistic devices, in order to avoid losing face.

Example 3 is taken from the data collected in Naples. The patient on the phone – a native speaker of Italian – wishes to change her appointment with the dentist, as she is unable to come. In relation to the particular situation, setting and task, the voice mail message is functionally adequate. In order to reduce the risk of face-threat, the caller apologies by using a large number of internal and external modifiers and pragmatic devices (Trosborg 1995). The message contains two external modifiers, 'perché non ho modo di arrivare da voi' ('because I do not have any means to get there'), and 'perché sono al lavoro'

---

13 Dear Valentina, I am very happy that you have chosen five different options for our holiday. I haven't seen you for a long time. It is a difficult choice. But you are here for me, and it doesn't matter where we are. I love you, I want to hold you in my arms and never leave you. So I think the first option is perfect, because the B&B seems very quiet. There is also a garden and breakfast is delicious. And we will have plenty of time to enjoy life and each other. I want you. A big kiss.

('because I am at work'), Next to these two justifiers, the phone message comprises various syntactic and lexical mitigators and pragmatic markers, such as 'dovrei' ('I should'), 'mi dispiace ('I am sorry'), 'sono mortificata' ('I am mortified'), 'purtroppo' ('unfortunately'), 'scusatemi'('excuse me'), 'gentilmente' ('kindly').

Example 3. Ehm, mi dispiace (Italian L1)[14]

Ehm, mi dispiace, sono mortificata, ma purtroppo devo annullare l'appuntamento di oggi, perché non ho modo di arrivare da voi, non ho la macchina, e purtroppo, scusatemi, dovrei fissare un altro appuntamento. Se gentilmente mi può richiamare sul cellulare, perché sono al lavoro, grazie.

Example 4 comes from the corpus of voice mail messages collected in Amsterdam. The patient, a native speaker of Dutch, wishes to change his appointment. Compared to the Italian phone call, the Dutch message is very different, as the caller does not apologize or provide any reasons for having to cancel the appointment. His request to be called back is phrased as an imperative rather than as a request. Furthermore, unlike the Italian example, the phone message does not contain any pragmatic markers or modifiers. Notwithstanding possible socio-pragmatic and rhetorical differences between Italian and Dutch regarding politeness strategies and the employment of courtesy markers, the message is functionally inadequate and would be considered as impolite also in the Dutch context.

Example 4. Goedemiddag (Dutch L1)[15]

Goedemiddag, u spreekt met [+ name]*, ik wil een andere afspraak maken, ik had een afspraak op 4 december, telefoonnummer is [+cell phone number] en anders* [+ phone number], *bedankt.*

3 Functional Adequacy: Defining the construct

The importance of functional adequacy as an essential component of L2 proficiency has been observed by authors such as Pallotti (2009), Kuiken, Vedder

14 Ehm, I am so sorry, I am mortified, but unfortunately I have to cancel my appointment for today, because I have no means to reach you. I don't have a car, and so, unfortunately, I'm sorry, I need to reschedule the appointment. Would you be so kind to call me back on my mobile phone, because I am at work. Thank you.

15 Good afternoon, this is [+ name] speaking, I want to make another appointment, I had an appointment on December 4, my phone number is [+ cell phone number], or otherwise {+ phone number].

& Gilabert (2010) and De Jong et al. (2012a, b). However, whereas in language teaching and testing practice both the linguistic and the communicative dimension are often independently assessed by teachers, in SLA research functional adequacy is generally overlooked.

A possible reason for the paucity of studies in which the relationship between functional adequacy and the linguistic complexity, accuracy and fluency of L2 production is investigated may be the absence of a clear-cut definition of the construct. Until now, there has been no unanimity in the literature as to how functional adequacy should be defined or assessed and by which features it is determined (Iwashita, Brown, McNamara & O'Hagan 2008). In recent studies in which functional adequacy is taken into account, the definition varies greatly and different terms, such as 'communicative adequacy' (Pallotti 2009), 'communicative competence' (McNamara & Roever 2007), 'communicative effectiveness' (Bridgeman, Powers, Stone & Mollaun 2011; Sato 2012), 'intercultural competence' (Hismanoglu 2011), or 'communicative functionality' (Fragai 2001, 2003), have been employed to designate the construct.

Even McNamara and Roever (2007) considering functional adequacy within a socio-pragmatic perspective emphasize the importance of the assessment of functional adequacy in L2 teaching. In other studies functional adequacy is defined on the basis of successful task performance (Pallotti 2009; Kuiken et al. 2010; Alanen, Huhta, & Tarnanen 2010), success of transfer of information (Upshur & Turner 1995), or presented in an intercultural perspective (Hismanoglu 2011). Relating linguistic and socio-pragmatic factors, Fragai (2001, 2003) distinguishes a number of features that determine functional adequacy, such as adequate use of syntax and lexicon and the ability to select appropriate linguistic forms for different communicative contexts. In the study by Knoch (2009, 2011) functional adequacy is considered within a discourse-analytic perspective and defined in terms of coherence and cohesion of the text (for a discussion of definitions of functional adequacy viewed from different theoretical angles, see also Leung 2005 and Leung & Lewkowicz 2012).

There is no unanimity in the literature either as to how functional adequacy could best be assessed. Contrary to the indices often used for measuring overall complexity, accuracy and fluency (CAF), general and quantitative measures to rate functional adequacy are lacking. Moreover, it is unclear by which textual and linguistic features functional adequacy, in the eyes of raters, is mainly determined (see however the study by Iwashita, Brown, McNamara & O'Hagan 2008, for an investigation of the relationship between certain features of the oral L2 production of test-takers and the holistic scores awarded by raters).

For the assessment of functional adequacy, it is thus necessary to resort to proficiency scales, like the ones of the CEFR, which contain a set of descriptors to evaluate the features of L2 performance relevant for a particular level of proficiency. However, as has been pointed out in a number of studies, one of the problems of the use of proficiency scales is that they are generally not calibrated or empirically validated and do not refer to any theoretical paradigm (Alanen, Huhta, & Tarnanen 2010; Hulstijn, Alderson & Schoonen 2010).

The definition of functional adequacy underlying the present study is that of functional adequacy viewed as a task-related, interpersonal construct, involving two participants (the writer A and the reader B). Functional adequacy is thus considered in terms of successful task fulfilment (Alanen, Huhta, & Tarnanen 2010; De Jong et al. 2012a, b; Kuiken, Vedder & Gilabert 2010; Kuiken & Vedder 2014; Kuiken & Vedder 2016; Kuiken & Vedder forthcoming). The focus in this definition is on the specific task to be carried out by A, and on the reception of the message by B. What is considered 'adequate' by the receiver B will depend on the particular language task to be performed by A (e.g. a letter to the student office, a short note to a housemate, an email to the teacher). In terms of Grice's conversational maxims (1975), the adequacy of the message transmitted by the writer A is understood and interpreted by the reader B with respect to the quantity, relation, manner and quality of the message by A.

4 Rating scale of functional adequacy: description and scale levels

The rating scale of functional adequacy was developed on the basis of two main sources: the general descriptors provided by the CEFR (Council of Europe 2001) and the scale descriptors of the rating scale of De Jong et al. (2012a, b). The scale that was used in the study at hand is an adaptation of the overall rating scale employed in study 1 (Kuiken, Vedder & Gilabert 2010; Kuiken & Vedder 2014). On the basis of the outcomes of study 1 it was decided to adapt the rating scale, by separating it more clearly from the linguistic CAF descriptors and by splitting up the overall scale into four subscales.

The requirements of the rating scale are the following: (i) deconstruction of the relevant components of functional adequacy; (ii) independency of descriptors of functional adequacy from linguistic descriptors in terms of CAF; (iii) 'objective' and 'countable' scale descriptors; (iv) applicability both for expert and non-expert raters; (v) the possibility to use the scale in both L2 and L1.

The new rating scale of functional adequacy, a six-point Likert scale, is inspired by Grice's conversational maxims (1975), focusing on the quantity, relevance, manner and quality of the message of the speaker/writer A to be transmitted to the interlocutor B. The rating scale, defined in terms of successful task completion of A in conveying a message to B, in relation to Grice's conversational maxims, thus comprises the following four scale dimensions (see Appendix 1).

1. Content: Is the number of information units (in terms of ideas, concepts, thematic elaboration) provided in the text adequate and relevant?

This dimension takes into account the adequacy of the number and type of information units in the text and their consistency and relevance, independently from the specific requirements of the language task to be carried out.

2. Task requirements: Have the requirements of the task been fulfilled successfully, with respect to e.g. text genre, register and speech act?

This dimension focuses on the specific instructions and requirements of the task to be completed and the adequacy of the message transmitted by the speaker/writer A to the listener/reader B.

3. Comprehensibility: How much effort is required of the interlocutor B in order to understand text purpose and ideas expressed by A?

This dimension takes into account the extent to which the message of A turns out to be adequate and comprehensible for the interlocutor B (Bridgeman et al., 2012; De Jong, et al., 2012a, b).

4. Coherence and cohesion: Is the text produced by A coherent and cohesive?

This dimension focuses on the adequacy of the message of A for the interlocutor B in terms of the occurrence of cohesive ties (the presence or absence of deictic elements, anaphoric devices and strategies), use of conjunctions, coherence breaks, and number of repetitions (Knoch 2007, 2009, 2011).

5 Testing out the rating scale for functional adequacy

5.1 Research questions

The main goal of the current study was to test out the applicability of the rating scale of functional adequacy. The overarching research question was formulated as follows: How do (non-expert) raters investigate the functional adequacy of argumentative texts of L2 and L1 writers? More particularly, we were interested in (i) the reliability of the judgments of the raters; (ii) correlations between the four scale dimensions, (iii) correlations between the ratings for Italian L2 and Italian L1 and (iv) correlations between task 1 and task 2. The following questions were thus formulated:

1. What are the interrater reliability scores on the four dimensions of FA?
2. How are raters' judgments on the 4 dimensions of FA correlated?
3. How are raters' judgments in L2 and L1 correlated?
4. How are the raters' judgments in the two tasks correlated?

5.2 Participant, tasks and raters

The data for Italian L2 and L1 discussed in this chapter were derived from a corpus of argumentative texts written by three groups of intermediate L2 writers of Dutch, Italian and Spanish. All writers had been subjected to two writing tasks, prompting the participants to write two short argumentative texts. In the first task, learners were required to make a decision about which of three non-governmental organizations to propose as a candidate for receiving a grant (see Appendix 2). In the second writing task they had to decide which topic they would like to see published as the main article on the front page of the monthly magazine of their favorite newspaper. As a benchmark the same writing tasks were administered to a group of native speakers of the three languages. The data of the two writing tasks of the 39 Italian L2 writers and the 18 L1 writers of Italian who participated in the study (Kuiken, Vedder, & Gilabert 2010) are here reported. An example of a text written by an L2 writer of Italian is provided below (Example 5)

Example 5 (Italian L2; task 2)[16]

Secondo me l'articolo sull'esercizio fisico deve essere scelto per il prossimo numero. E' vero che la gente diventa sempre più grassa e fa meno esercizio fisico. Spesso questo è il risultato di una vita comoda. Cioè una vita senza molto bisogno di muoversi.

Nell'articolo bisogna non solo dare consigli su come dimagrire ma anche su come vivere in modo sano/mantenere un modo di vivere sano/. Così non sarà interessante solo per le persone grasse ma anche per tutti che vogliono sapere più su questo tema.

L'articolo deve appararire in prima pagina perché il problema è molto d'attualità. Interesserà a tante persone di sicuro. Poi sarebbe qualcosa di nuova perché di solito si vedono solo degli articoli tristi o noiosi su questa pagina.

A C-test was used to establish the general proficiency level of the Italian L2 participants. In the C-test the second half of each second word was omitted.

---

16 In my view the article on physical excercise should be chosen for the next issue of the monthly magazine. It is true that people always grow fatter and do little physical exercise. Often this is the result of a comfortable life. In other words, a life without much need to move.The article must not only give advice on how to lose weight but also on how to live healthily/maintain a healthy way of life. So it will be interesting not only for fat people but also for anyone who wants to know more about this topic. The article should appear on the front page because the problem nowadays is very common. It certainly affects very many people. It would also be something new because what you usually see on the front page are only sad or boring articles.

There were five short texts and 100 cancellations. The same version of the C-test was also administered to the native writers of Italian. Example 6 shows an example of one of the five texts.

Example 6: C-test (Italian L2 and L1)[17]

Terra di poeti, viaggiatori e innamorati. Il B - - Paese ris - - - - il cu- - - dei gio- - - -? Pare pro- - - di s-. I gio- - - - italiani so - - i p- - innamorati d- tutti. N- - credono a- - amore ete- - - , ma a- colpo d- fulmine s-. Nove ital- - - - su di- - - hanno de- - - di ess- - - già st- - - innamorati. Ma solo un giovane su due crede all'amore eterno

In order to try out the applicability and reliability of the rating scale, the written data for Italian L2 that was collected in study 1 (Kuiken, Vedder & Gilabert 2010; Kuiken & Vedder, 2014) were presented to a group of four raters. The raters were asked to assess the functional adequacy of the written data of study 1 for Italian L2 and L1, by means of the new rating scale. Whereas in study 1 all texts had been rated by four *expert* raters (native speakers of Italian and language teachers), in study 2 the texts were assessed by four *non-expert* raters (native speakers of Italian and university students). Since expert raters (language teachers) may be biased in their judgments being sometimes either too lenient or too severe in their judgments, in this second experiment we decided to work with non-expert raters instead.

6 Results

In this section the statistical analysis of the data and the main outcomes of the study are presented and summarized. For a more detailed report of data analysis and results the reader is referred to Kuiken and Vedder (2016) and Kuiken and Vedder (forthcoming).

6.1 Data analysis

In order to assess the interrater reliability of the scores assigned by the four raters (RQ1), intra-class correlations were calculated (for L2 and L1 combined). Interrater reliability was high across all raters, ranging between .725 (for task

17 Land of poets, travelers and lovers. Does the Bel Paese warm the hearts of young people? Apparently it does. Young Italians are the ones who have most often been in love. Although they don't believe in eternal love, they do believe in love at first sight. Nine out of ten Italians say they have already been in love. But only one out of two believes in eternal love.

requirements in Italian) and .901 (for comprehensibility). These correlations were all statistically significant ($p < .01$ for all correlation pairs), implying that raters indeed agree in their judgments of the L2 and the L1 texts.

To find out the extent to which the judgments of the raters on the four separate dimensions of functional adequacy correlate (RQ2), Pearson's product–moment correlations were calculated. All correlations were significant ($p < .01$ for all correlation pairs), particularly with respect to the relation between comprehensibility and coherence/cohesion (.938).

Regarding the correlations between the raters' judgments of the L2 texts compared to the L1 texts (RQ3), not surprisingly, it was found that raters assigned higher scores on all dimensions of functional adequacy to the texts written by the native writers. Scores for the L2 texts range from 3.54 for coherence/cohesion to 4.32 for task requirements, whereas the L1 scores range from 4.94 (coherence/cohesion) to 5.39 (comprehensibility). A paired sample *t*-test (and a Bonferroni correction) demonstrated that the observed differences between writers in L2 and L1 are on the whole significant (content, comprehensibility, coherence/cohesion), except for task requirements.

Research question 4 investigates whether raters differed in their judgments of the two texts written by the same participant (task 1 and task 2). On the basis of the calculation of Pearson's correlation coefficients one can conclude that the correlations between the two writing tasks (combined for L2 and L1) are in all cases high for the four dimensions of functional adequacy, indicating that raters judge both texts in more or less the same way. The lowest correlation is obtained on task requirements (.455), the highest on coherence/cohesion (.802). All correlations are significant ($p < .001$).

6.2 Summary of results

The results of the study show that functional adequacy can reliably be measured by a rating scale containing four different subscales. Content was assessed by considering the number and relevance of information units. It is, thus, distinct from task requirements, which focus on the specific task to be carried out in terms of genre, register, and speech act. For raters it appeared to be fairly easy to distinguish the two constructs.

Comprehensibility, operationalized in terms of the amount of effort and 're-reading' required of the reader in order to understand the text could be assessed in a countable way. This was also true for coherence and cohesion, which could also be assessed in a quantifiable way by considering the presence or absence of cohesive and anaphoric devices, strategies, coherence breaks, and repetitions.

The intra-class correlations among the four raters varied from acceptable to excellent. The correlations between the four subscales were generally high. Lower correlations were found, not surprisingly, between task requirements and the other scale dimensions. It is, indeed, perfectly possible to write a comprehensible and coherent text that is, however, unsuccessful in terms of specific task requirements. The study also demonstrated that the scales could be employed by raters for assessing the texts of both L2 and L1 writers, although raters found it easier to differentiate between L2 learners compared to L1 writers who, compared to L2 writers, all performed at the upper end of the scale. Correlation coefficients of the ratings on both writing tasks produced by the same participants were good and in all cases significant, implying that raters were generally stable in their judgments of the two texts.

7 Implications for teaching practice

The outcomes of the study presented in this chapter demonstrate that functional adequacy, as a fundamental component of L2 proficiency, can be reliably assessed (Kuiken & Vedder 2014). The findings of study 3, in which the rating scale for functional adequacy was put to the test also for oral L2 production, point in the same direction: the functional adequacy of oral speech, measured in two monologue tasks, can also reliably be assessed by means of the new rating scale for functional adequacy (Kuiken & Vedder, forthcoming).

Regarding the implications for L2 writing practice we may conclude that functional adequacy of oral and written learner production should preferably be assessed by means of a rating scale comprising four distinct subscales. As these dimensions are conceptually different, it is important to keep them apart, despite significant correlations between them. The results of the study at hand (see also Kuiken & Vedder 2016) and of those of study 3 (Kuiken & Vedder, forthcoming) show that the rating scale is applicable to non-expert raters as well, since they were able to become familiar with the scales in just two training sessions. The scale also allows teachers to provide L2 writers with specific feedback and focused comments on their writing skills on the four different dimensions of functional adequacy. The rating scale of functional adequacy thus appears to be a reliable and efficient tool for L2 teachers for the assessment of the functional adequacy of written (and oral) learner production.

8 Conclusion

Assessing student writing is, according to Weigle (2007), one of the most fundamental duties of a writing teacher. Writing both in L2 and L1, as claimed by Murray (1980), is first of all *rewriting*. Writers rarely move through a piece of writing in any linear fashion. Generally they shuffle back and forth through the various phases of planning, revision, reflection, researching and drafting. This is where assessment comes in. Through assessment and feedback writers learn to be careful evaluators of their own writing (Crusan 2010: 15). This is why writing assessment is so important.

White (1996: 14) describes a number of features of writing assessment that writing teachers consider essential, such as assessment that recognizes the complexity of writing and of the teaching of writing, assessment that respects teachers as professionals and their students as individuals, and assessment that will not be misused to provide simple, damaging and misleading information. Next to these general characteristics that White defines as being important for good writing assessment, it is crucial, as argued in this chapter, to assess not only the complexity, accuracy and fluency (CAF) of L2 performance, but to evaluate also the functional adequacy of learner language. Hopefully the rating scale presented in this chapter will be a step forward in that direction and will prove be a useful instrument for the assessment of L2 writing.

References

Alanen, R., Huhta, A., & Tarnanen, M. (2010): Designing and assessing L2 writing tasks across proficiency levels. In: Bartning, I., Martin, M. & Vedder, I. (Eds.): Communicative proficiency and linguistic development. Intersections between SLA and language testing research. Eurosla Monograph Series 1, 21-56.

Bridgeman, B., Powers, D., Stone, E., & Mollaun, P. (2012): TOEFL iBT speaking test scores as indicators of oral communicative language proficiency. In: *Language Testing*, 29(1), 91-108.

Brown, P. & Levinson. S.D. (1987): Politeness: Some universals in language usage. Cambridge: Cambridge University Press.

Council of Europe (2001): Common European Framework of Reference for Languages: Learning, teaching, assessment. Cambridge: Cambridge University Press.

Crusan, D. (2010): Assessment in the second language writing classroom. Ann Arbor: The University of Michigan Press.

De Jong, N.H., Steinel, M.P., Florijn, A.F., Schoonen, R., & Hulstijn, J.H. (2012a): The effect of task complexity on functional adequacy, fluency and lexical diversity in speaking performances of native and non-native speakers. In: Housen, A., Kuiken, F. & Vedder, I. (Eds.), Dimensions of L2 performance and proficiency. Complexity, accuracy and fluency in SLA. Amsterdam: J. Benjamins, 121-142.

De Jong, N.H., Steinel, M.P., Florijn, A.F., Schoonen, R., & Hulstijn, J.H. (2012b): Facets of speaking proficiency. In: *Studies in Second Language Acquisition*, 34(1), 5-34.

Fragai, E. (2001): La programmazione didattica: Il Glotto-Kit come strumento per valutare i livelli in entrata. In: Barni, M. & Villarini, A. (Eds.): La questione della lingua per gli immigrati stranieri. Insegnare, valutare e certificare l'Italiano L2. Milano: Franco Angeli, 191-208.

Fragai, E. (2003): Valutare la competenza linguistico-comunicativa in italiano L2: Il Glotto-Kit per bambini e adolescenti stranieri. In: *Didattica & Classe Plurilingue*, 7, 1-5.

Grice, H.P. (1975): Logic and conversation. In: Cole, P. & Morgan, J.L. (Eds.): *Speech acts.* New York: Academic Press, 41-58.

Hismanoglu, M. (2011): An investigation of ELT students' intercultural communicative competence in relation to linguistic proficiency, overseas experience and formal instruction. In: *International Journal of Intercultural Relations,* 35(6), 805-817.

Housen, A., Kuiken, F. & Vedder, I. (Eds.) (2012): Dimensions of L2 performance and proficiency. Complexity, accuracy and fluency in SLA. Amsterdam: J. Benjamins.

Hulstijn, J. H., Alderson, J.C., & Schoonen, R. (2010): Developmental stages in second-language acquisition and levels of second-language proficiency: Are there links between them? In: Bartning, I., Martin, M. & Vedder, I. (Eds.): Communicative proficiency and linguistic devel- opment: Intersections between SLA and language testing research. Eurosla Monographs Series 1, 11-20.

Iwashita, N., Brown, A., McNamara, T., & O'Hagan, S. (2008): Assessed levels of second language speaking proficiency: How distinct? In: *Applied Linguistics,* 29(1), 24-49.

Knoch, U. (2007): 'Little coherence, considerable strain for reader': A comparison between two rating scales for the assessment of coherence. In: *Assessing Writing,* 12(2), 108–128.

Knoch, U. (2009): Diagnostic assessment of writing: A comparison of two rating scales. In: *Language Testing*, 26(2), 275.

Knoch, U. (2011): Rating scales for diagnostic assessment of writing: What should they look like and where should the criteria come from? In: *Assessing Writing*, 16(2), 81-96.

Kuiken, F., & Vedder, I. (2014): Rating written performance: What do raters do and why? In: *Language Testing*, 31(3), 329-348.

Kuiken, F. & Vedder, I. (2016): Functional adequacy in L2 writing. Towards a new rating scale. In: *Language Testing*. DOI: 10.1177/0265532216663991.

Kuiken, F, & Vedder, I. (forthcoming): Assessing functional adequacy of L2 performance in a task-based approach. Amsterdam/Philadelphia: J. Benjamins.

Kuiken, F., Vedder, I., & Gilabert, R. (2010): Communicative adequacy and linguistic complexity in L2 writing. In: Bartning, I., Martin, M. & Vedder, I. (Eds.): Communicative proficiency and linguistic development: Intersections between SLA and language testing research. Eurosla Monographs Series 1, 81-100.

Leung, C. (2005): Convivial communication: Recontextualizing communicative competence. In: *International Journal of Applied Linguistics*, 15(2), 119-144.

Leung, C. & Lewkowicz, J. (2012): Language communication and communicative competence: A view from contemporary classrooms. *Language and Education*, 26(6), 1-17.

McNamara, T., & Roever, C. (2007): Testing: The social dimension. Malden, Oxford: Blackwell.

Murray, D. M. (1980): Writing as process: How writing finds its own meaning. In: Donovan, T.R. & McClelland, B.W. (Eds.): Eight approaches to teaching composition. Urbana, IL: National Council of Teachers of English, 3-20.

Pallotti, G. (2009): CAF: Defining, refining and differentiating constructs. Special Issue, Complexity, Accuracy and Fluency (CAF) in Second Language Acquisition. In: *Applied Linguistics*, 30(4), 590-601.

Sato, T. (2012): The contribution of test-takers' speech content to scores on an English oral proficiency test. In: *Language Testing*, 29(2), 223-241.

Trosborg, A. (1995): Interlanguage Pragmatics: Requests, Complaints and Apologies. Berlin, New York: Mouton de Gruyter.

Upshur, J. A., & Turner, C. E. (1995): Constructing rating scales for second language tests. In: *ELT Journal*, 49(1), 3-12.

Weigle, S.C. (2007): S.C. Teaching writing teachers about assessment. In: *Journal of Second Language Writing*, 16, 194-209.

White, E.M. (1996): Writing assessment beyond the classroom. Will writing teachers play a role? In: Bloom, L. Z., Daiker, D.A. & White, E.M. (Eds.): Composition in the twenty-first century. Crisis and change. Carbondale: Southern Illinois University Press, 101-111.

Appendix 1: Rating scale for functional adequacy

Content: Is the number of information units provided in the text adequate and relevant?

1	2	3	4	5	6
The number of ideas is *not at all adequate* and insufficient and the ideas are unrelated to each other.	The number of ideas is *scarcely adequate*, the ideas lack consistency.	The number of ideas is *somewhat adequate*, even though they are not very consistent.	The number of ideas is *adequate* and they are sufficiently consistent.	The number of ideas is *very adequate*, they are very consistent to each other.	The number of ideas is *extremely adequate* and they appear very consistent to each other.

Task Requirements: Have the task requirements been fulfilled successfully (e.g. genre, speech acts, register)?

1	2	3	4	5	6
None of the questions and the requirements of the task have been answered.	*Some (less than half)* of the questions and the requirements of the task have been answered.	*Approximately half* of the questions and requirements of the task have been answered.	*Most (more than half)* of the questions and the requirements of the task have been answered.	*Almost all* the questions and the requirements of the task have been answered.	*All* the questions and the requirements of the task have been answered.

Comprehensibility: How much effort is required to understand text purpose and ideas?

1	2	3	4	5	6
The text is *not at all comprehensible*. Ideas and purposes are unclearly stated and the efforts of the reader to understand the text are ineffective.	The text is *scarcely comprehensible*, its purposes are not clearly stated and the reader struggles to understand the ideas of the writer. The reader has to guess most of the ideas and purposes.	The text is *somewhat comprehensible*, some sentences are hard to understand at a first reading. A second reading helps to clarify the purposes of the text and the ideas conveyed, but some doubts persist.	The text is *comprehensible*, only a few sentences are unclear but are understood, without too much effort, after a second reading.	The text is *easily comprehensible* and reads smoothly, comprehensibility is not an issue.	The text is *very easily comprehensible* and highly readable, the ideas and the purpose are clearly stated.

Coherence and cohesion: Is the text coherent and cohesive (e.g. cohesive devices, strategies)?

1	2	3	4	5	6
The text is *not at all coherent.* Unrelated progressions and coherence breaks are very common. The writer does not use any anaphoric device. The text is *not at all cohesive.* Connectives are hardly ever used and ideas are unrelated.	The text is *scarcely coherent.* The writer often uses unrelated progressions; when coherence is achieved, it is often done through repetitions. Only a few anaphoric devices are used. There are some coherence breaks. The text is *not very cohesive.* Ideas are not well linked by connectives, which are rarely used.	The text is *somewhat coherent.* Unrelated progressions and/or repetitions are frequent. More than two sentences in a row can have the same subject (even when the subject is understood). Some anaphoric devices are used. There can be a few coherence breaks. The text is *somewhat cohesive.* Some connectives are used, but they are mostly conjunctions.	The text is *coherent.* Unrelated progressions are somewhat rare, but the writer sometimes relies on repetitions to achieve coherence. A sufficient number of anaphoric devices is used. There may be some coherence breaks. The text is *cohesive.* The writer makes good use of connectives, sometimes not limiting this to conjunctions.	The text is *very coherent*: when the writer introduces a new topic, it is usually done by using connectives or connective phrases. Repetitions are very infrequent. Anaphoric devices are numerous. No coherence breaks. The text is *very cohesive* and ideas are well linked by adverbial and/or verbal connectives.	The writer ensures *extreme coherence* by integrating new ideas in the text with connectives or connective phrases. Anaphoric devices are used regularly. There are few incidences of unrelated progressions and no coherence breaks. The structure of the text is *extremely cohesive*, thanks to a skillful use of connectives (especially linking chunks, verbal constructions and adverbials), often used to describe relationships between ideas.

Appendix 2

Task 1 (Translated from Italian)

Every year your university supports a charitable organization with an amount of € 50.000. The University Board has nominated three organizations:

Back to Nature,
SPMC (Sports for the Physically and Mentally Challenged),
Animals First.

Out of these three organizations one has to be selected. The selection is made by a Committee consisting of students. Every member of the committee has to write a report in which s/he states who the winner should be and why. On the basis of the arguments given in the reports the University Board will then decide who the winner will be.

This year you are on the Selection Committee. Read the brief descriptions of the organizations below. Determine which organization should receive the money this year. Write a text in which you give at least three arguments for your choice. Try to be as clear as possible and include the following points in your report:

to which organization the money should go;

what the aim of the organization is;

who will be helped by the organization;

why the university needs to support this organization (give three arguments)

You have 35 minutes to write your report and you need to write at least 150 words (about 15 lines). The use of a dictionary is not allowed.

PART II
DIDACTIC APPLICATIONS

Ana Adamovičová, Zuzana Hajíčková

Česká verze projektu Wrilab2

1 Úvod

Mezinárodní projekt Wrilab2 – což je ve skutečnosti anglický akronym slov Writing Laboratory, si klade za cíl rozvíjení kompetencí čtení a psaní v druhém/cizím jazyce. Do projektu On-line Reading and Writing Laboratory jsou zapojeny čtyři středo/jihoevropské jazyky – němčina, čeština, italština a slovinština a řada evropských univerzit a středních škol. Přestože jde o typologicky odlišné jazyky, je mezi nimi jistá spojitost: jednak podobný zeměpisný prostor, jednak spletité vzájemné vztahy, ať už historické, či sahající do současnosti. Projekt vznikl z iniciativy vynikající zahraniční bohemistky Anny Marii Perissutti působící na Univerzitě v Udine, která již delší dobu pociťovala potřebu věnovat se svým studentům více po stránce psaného projevu. Z dalších univerzit jsou do projektu zapojeny Univerzita Karlova – Ústav bohemistických studií, Univerzita v Lublani, Univerzita v Klagenfurtu a Pedagogická fakulta ve Freiburku. Na projektu se též podílí několik slovinských, italských a českých středních škol – např. pražské Gymnázium Na Pražačce, dvojjazyčná italsko-slovinská škola v San Pietro al Natisone či střední škola Ingeborg Bachmann v Tarvisiu (s intenzivní výukou němčiny). Z přidružených partnerů na projektu participují pouze české instituce, což zajisté významným způsobem vyzdvihuje roli češtiny v celém projektu: Asociace učitelů češtiny jako cizího jazyka, Ústav jazykové a odborné přípravy Univerzity Karlovy v Praze anebo česko-italský spolek Camera di Commercio e dell'Industria Italo-Ceca, Praha, Česká republika.

Hlavním cílem projektu bylo vytvoření interaktivních učebních materiálů jako podkladu pro on-line kurzy psaní ve zmíněných čtyřech jazycích. Projekt zároveň podporuje virtuální komunity umožňující studentům kontakt s rodilými mluvčími a učiteli za účelem výměny materiálů a osvědčených lingvodidaktických postupů.

Kurzů češtiny se mohou zúčastnit středoškolští a vysokoškolští studenti, pro něž je čeština druhým/cizím jazykem, nerodilí mluvčí (včetně dospělých z řad migrantů, nebo například pracovníků v oblasti cestovního ruchu, žurnalistiky, obchodu, veřejné správy či diplomacie), kteří se potřebují zdokonalit v písemném projevu.

1.1 První fáze projektu

Projekt byl zahájen v roce 2014, kdy proběhla implementace portálu pro Wrilab2 v Moodlu a též dotazníkové šetření o procesech a strategiích při psaní v druhém a cizím jazyce, jež se teoreticky opíralo o dosavadní poznatky v této oblasti (viz Albertini 2008; Hyland, 2007, 2009, 2013; Kobayashi & Rinnert 2013; Kormos 2012).

1.1.1 Dotazníkové šetření

Dotazník týkající se názorů a potřeb studentů ohledně procesů a strategií psaní obsahoval několik okruhů otázek (zkušenosti se psaním, jistota v psaní, postoje ke psaní, strategie psaní, žánry v psaní, preferovaná témata apod.) a paralelně zkoumal názory respondentů na tyto otázky jak v jejich mateřštině, tak v cizím/druhém jazyce.

Na dotazníkovém šetření se celkově podílelo 482 respondentů z 49 zemí. Českou část dotazníku vyplnilo 113 respondentů z 26 zemí, z nichž více než třetina studuje jako hlavní obor češtinu pro cizince na FF UK, pro další respondenty čeština není hlavním oborem studia. Sociolingvistický parametr pohlaví není bohužel vyvážen: šetření se zúčastnilo 17 mužů a 95 žen, čili 15 % mužů a 85 % žen (jeden respondent odmítl uvést pohlaví). Průměrný věk respondenta je 27 let (při rozpětí od 17 do 67 let), průměrná délka studia češtiny všech respondentů je 5 let. Z hlediska kontextu užívání češtiny 38 % respondentů uvedlo, že češtinu užívá v akademickém prostředí, 48 % v poloformálních situacích a 14 % mezi přáteli.

Česká verze dotazníků vykazuje největší pestrost co do počtu mateřských jazyků respondentů:

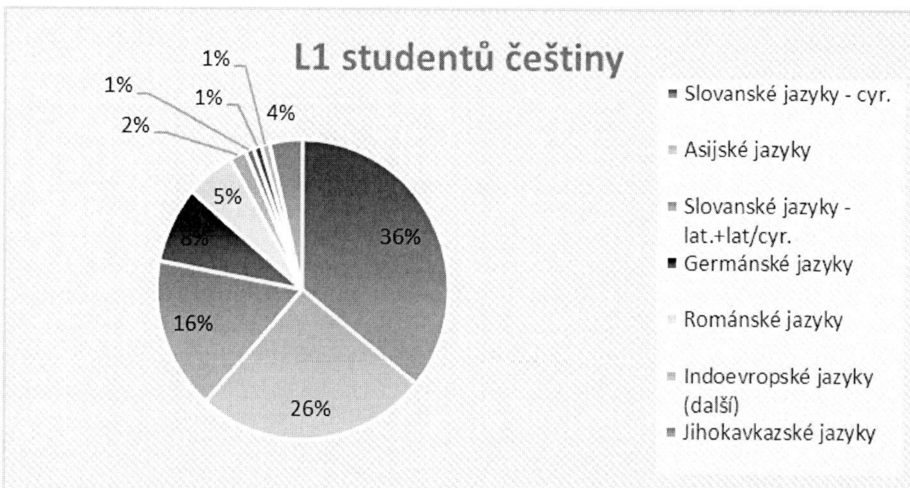

Graf 1: Mateřský jazyk respondentů

Zhruba polovina respondentů má tedy za mateřský jazyk některý ze slovanských jazyků (ruštinu, ukrajinštinu, polštinu, srbštinu a slovinštinu), čtvrtina asijské jazyky (především korejštinu, čínštinu a japonštinu). Poslední čtvrtinu tvoří nejrůznější mateřské jazyky, dominují v ní respondenti, jejichž mateřštinou jsou germánské jazyky (8 %), 5 % respondentů má jako mateřský jazyk některý z románských jazyků, 4 % respondentů jsou bilingvní (ruština/ukrajinština, angličtina/španělština, čeština/němčina, italština/čeština) a 5 % respondentů má za mateřský jazyk perštinu, albánštinu, finštinu, gruzínštinu a arabštinu. Dvě třetiny respondentů uvedly, že je čeština pro ně druhým jazykem. Studenti druhého jazyka jej používají v autentickém kontextu v různých sférách komunikace (osobní, veřejná, učební). Třetina respondentů uvedla češtinu jako cizí jazyk – studenti cizího jazyka používají jazyk pouze v oblasti učební v kontaktu s učitelem jako jeho hlavním zdrojem.

1.1.2 Výsledky šetření

Odpověď na otázku, jak respondenti vnímají **obtížnost psaní**, není nikterak překvapivá: zatímco 16 % respondentů považuje psaní i ve své mateřštině za obtížné, celých 37 % respondentů se domnívá, že je psaní v cizím jazyce náročnější. Pouze pro 29 % respondentů psaní v cizím jazyce není obtížnější než psaní v mateřštině:

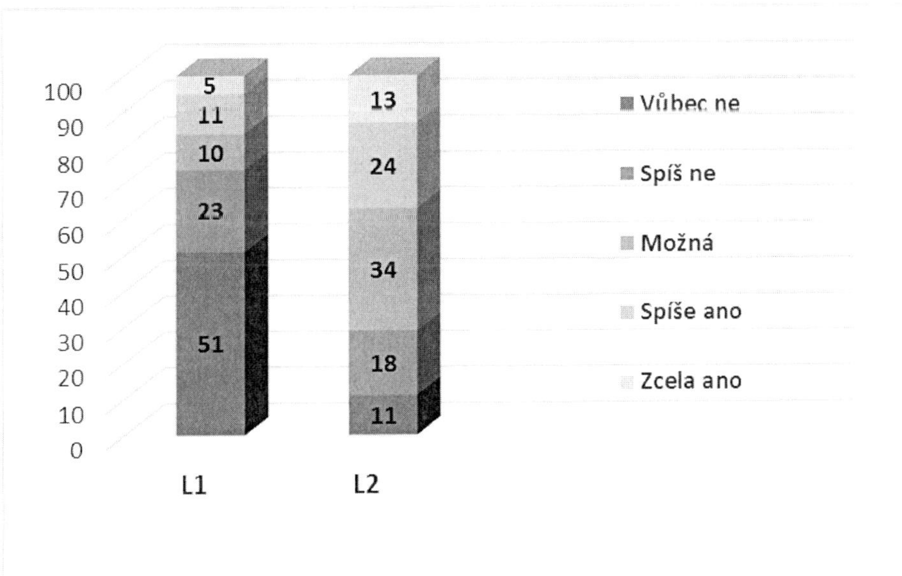

Graf 2: Názor na obtížnost psaní v L1 a L2 (údaje v procentech)

Nyní představíme, kterým faktorům respondenti přisuzují největší obtížnost při psaní ve své mateřštině a v druhém jazyce:

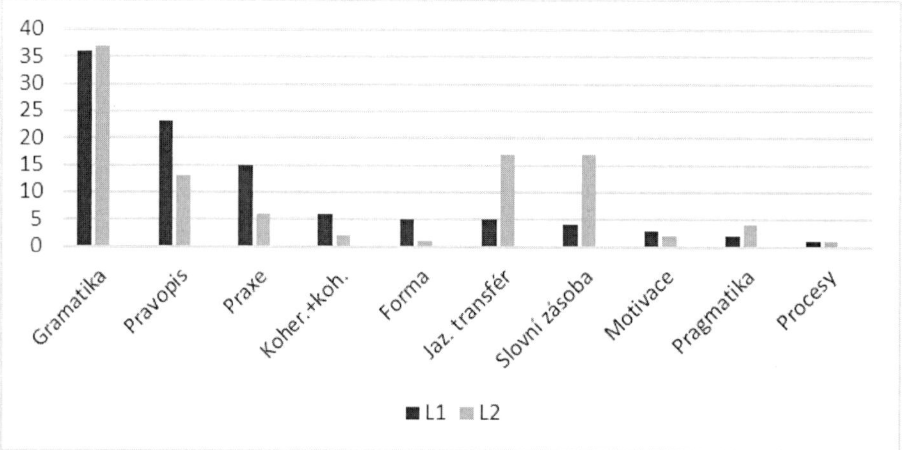

Graf 3: Faktory obtížnosti psaní v L1 a L2 (údaje v procentech)

Nejčastější odpovědi ohledně obtížnosti psaní v mateřštině se týkají gramatiky (36 %), pravopisu (23 %) a praxe (15 %). Porovnáme-li tyto odpovědi s tím, kterým faktorům respondenti přisuzují nejvyšší náročnost při psaní v cizím jazyce, zjistíme, že je pouze gramatika dle frekvence obtížnosti naprosto stejně vnímána bez ohledu na to, zda jde o mateřštinu (36 %) či cizí jazyk (37 %). Pravopis se jako faktor obtížnosti při psaní v cizím jazyce kupodivu vyskytuje až na čtvrtém místě (13 %). Na druhém, respektive třetím místě se rovnocenně vyskytují slovní zásoba a jazykový transfer (17 %). Dalším překvapivým zjištěním je skutečnost, že většina studentů uvádí, že jim textové rysy – **forma, struktura, koheze a koherence textu** nedělají při psaní téměř žádné problémy. Musíme zde však podotknout, že nám analýza studentských esejí toto přesvědčení studentů do značné míry vyvrátila, jak ještě ukážeme dále, a tudíž se lze domnívat, že vysoký stupeň sebejistoty zde nejspíš souvisí s faktem, že respondenti pravděpodobně nevěděli, co tyto pojmy přesně znamenají.

Dále nás zajímaly **zkušenosti studentů se psaním v cizím jazyce**: minimum studentů používá český výkladový slovník, hlavní oporou je jim naopak internet a dvojjazyčný slovník. Většina též uvádí, že po zadání tématu nikdy nepíše koncept ve své mateřštině, což je jistě chvályhodné, ale také si nepřipravují seznam slov, mapu nápadů a nežádají kolegy o pomoc.

Je též zajímavé, kterým **faktorům studenti přisuzují nejdůležitější** roli při snaze stát se dobrým pisatelem: mnohem častěji odpověděli, že je to silná motivace a rozšiřování slovní zásoby než znalost gramatiky a cvičení (tento faktor považují za nejméně důležitý). Ze šetření také vyplynulo, že se studenti nejvíce věnují psaní poznámek a kratších textů. Pokud jde o **žánry**, kterým by se v budoucnu rádi více věnovali, vyskytuje se na prvním místě jak v mateřštině, tak v cizím jazyce přání psát více formálních žádostí a životopisů. Zatímco u mateřského jazyka poměrně vysokou příčku zaujímá akademické psaní, u cizího jazyka jsou to kromě akademických abstraktů především eseje, zprávy a poznámky. Obecně preferovanými **tematickými okruhy** jsou: osobní život (můj volný čas, moje země, jak žít), dále jídlo, sport, hudba, životní styl; u studentů češtiny pak zejména životní styl a vzdělávání (literatura, historie, umění, film, divadlo, hudba, fotografie, rodina, cestování, sport, příroda, vyučovací metody, lingvistika, politika, filozofie, astrologie).

Nakonec dotazník obsahoval otázku, jakému **typu hodnocení** a zpětné vazby studenti dávají přednost. Drtivá většina studentů si myslí, že jim nejvíce pomůžou označení chyby, navržení lepší formulace a uvedení správné verze s případným komentářem. Doporučení vhodných cvičení a úloh šitých na míru či rozboru příčin chybování již nepřikládají tak velkou váhu. Většina studentů nejméně preferuje známku jako způsob získání zpětné vazby.

1.2 Druhá fáze projektu – výběr žánrů

Na základě zpracování dotazníků proběhl výběr textových žánrů pro Moodle. Výsledky dotazníkového šetření byly pro nás velmi důležité, proto jsme k nim přihlédly při sestavování témat didaktických jednotek, které jsou součástí online kurzu psaní. Vzniklo 12 lekcí pro jazykové úrovně B1, B2 a C1, čili 4 jednotky pro každou úroveň. Jednotky se věnují následujícím žánrům:

Úroveň B1

- anotace knihy
- životopis (CV)
- powerpointová prezentace (Univerzita Karlova)
- formální žádost (e-mail)

Úroveň B2

- zpráva ze studijního pobytu
- argumentační esej
- abstrakt
- článek (publicistický referát)

Úroveň C1

- formální dopis
- zpráva o projektu
- recenze
- výkladová esej

Jak je patrné z přehledu žánrů, při sestavování tematických okruhů jsme kromě přání studentů zaznamenaných v dotazníku zároveň vzaly v potaz nejen jazykovou kompetenci studentů a z ní plynoucí možnosti sebevyjádření na té které úrovni, ale i jejich skutečné potřeby. Všichni studenti píšou zprávy, referáty, recenze, eseje, shrnutí (abstrakty), formální dopisy, připravují se na psaní závěrečných vědeckých prací apod. Pro nižší úrovně je vhodné psaní kratších textů (anotace, e-mail), vyšší úrovně by se měly vypořádat i s delšími texty. Na rozdíl od přání studentů, plynoucího z dotazníkového šetření, všechny didaktické jednotky jsou opatřeny cvičeními vycházejícími z modelových textů a jsou úzce spjaté jednak s typickými druhy chyb, které jsme průběžně mapovaly, jednak s tematickými okruhy a žánrovými formami. Domníváme se, že zvládnutí jistého gramatického jevu a souboru prostředků typických pro jednotlivé žánry a obecně pro český psaný diskurs nesporně povede k vyšší jistotě studenta, který se pak více soustředí na obsah, strukturu a plynulé rozvíjení myšlenek v cizím jazyce.

1.3 Třetí fáze projektu – sběr a analýza kontrolních esejí

Po zpracování výsledků dotazníků jsme zhruba polovině studentů češtiny pro cizince (kolem 30 jich studuje češtinu jako hlavní obor, druhá polovina jako vedlejší obor) zadaly vypracování výkladových a argumentačních esejí. Studenti úrovně B1 a B2 psali většinou výkladové eseje a měli na výběr více témat – *Televize a její role v současném světě, Moderní formy zábavy, Jak by měla vypadat ideální práce, Co se mi líbí či nelíbí na vzdělávacím systému, Co je lepší – mít staré, nebo mladé rodiče?*. Studenti na úrovni C1 psali argumentační eseje a mohli si vybrat pouze mezi dvěma tématy: *Automobil, nebo MHD?, Pes, nebo kočka?*. Podmínky psaní se také různily. Zatímco studenti na úrovních B1 a B2 psali eseje jak v hodině bez pomůcek, tak je také vypracovávali jako domácí úkoly (kde přítomnost pomůcek nelze zcela vyloučit), studenti na úrovni C1 vypracovali eseje výlučně v hodině bez žádných pomůcek. Studenti nejvyšší úrovně navíc před psaním absolvovali teoreticko-metodologickou průpravu na psaní argumentačních esejí. Získaly jsme tak celkem 60 esejí (20 pro každou úroveň) a následně jsme je podrobily zevrubné analýze zaměřené obecně na typologii chyb, detailněji pak na obsah, strukturu, formu, textové rysy apod. Studentské práce na všech úrovních prokázaly nedostatky **v rovině gramatické a**

pravopisné (v nižší míře u C1), **lexikální** (častá záměna významově blízkých sloves (např. *dozvědět se x poznat; myslet x myslet si x přemýšlet*), v nižší míře stylové (výskyt obecněčeských výrazů vedle stylově neutrálních). V porovnání s výsledky dotazníku se jednoznačně nejvíc nedostatků vyskytuje právě v **koherenci** a **kohezi** textu, nejvýrazněji právě na úrovni C1. Pro to je jednoduché vysvětlení: text odpovídající tak vysoké úrovni již neoplývá řadou morfologicko-pravopisných chyb, je celkem čitelný, avšak pořád mu něco „chybí" – a to je právě ona myšlenková a logická soudržnost vyjádřená adekvátními výrazovými prostředky.

Analýza studentských prací jednoznačně potvrdila nutnost zahrnout do on-line kurzu psaní též gramaticko-pravopisná, lexikální a stylistická cvičení pro všechny úrovně, stejně jako cvičení zaměřená na výběr vhodných konektorů, postojových, epistemických partikulí a dalších výrazových prostředků charakteristických pro český psaný diskurs.

2 Psaní jako proces a didaktický rámec projektu

V zahraniční didaktice psaní (v mateřském, cizím i druhém jazyku) se během 90. let 20. století prosadil procesně orientovaný přístup (viz např. Dreyfürst & Sennewald 2014; Jakobs & Perrin 2014) podložený a od 80. let 20. stol. podněcovaný kognitivně psychologickými a neurovědeckými výzkumy (např. Flower & Hayes 2014: 35pp; Kästner 1997). Spolu s nimi byly modelovány i procesy psaní. Za základní model procesu psaní v cizím jazyce je považován kognitivní model Hayse a Flowerové z r. 1980 a 1981 (Flower & Hayes 2014: 35pp). Ten pojímá psaní jako proces řešení problémů vedoucí k cíli, jenž sestává z dílčích a rekursivních subprocesů. Pisatel se totiž při psaní stále navrací k již proběhnutým dílčím procesům, permanentně psaní plánuje a napsané přepracovává. Těmto činnostem odpovídají i naše on-line kurzy, mezi jejichž jednotlivými částmi může student libovolně a podle potřeby procházet.

V návaznosti na model Hayese a Flowerové se vyčleňují tři základní fáze procesu psaní (Ruhmann & Kruse 2014: 24–25): plánování a generování obsahů (*prewriting activities*), jejich převedení do jazyka a písma (*drafting*), přepracování a editování (*revising*). Tyto jednotlivé fáze do sebe mohou vzájemně zasahovat a přecházet, navíc existují rozdíly mezi jednotlivými pisateli a strategiemi, jež preferují a jež by měly být zohledněny. U každé fáze psaní je třeba osvětlit procedury, k nimž dochází, aby si je pisatelé lépe uvědomili a uměli je sami řídit. Reflexe podporuje autorovo vlastní vnímání i jeho promyšlené užití jazykových prostředků. Zpětná vazba a přepracovávání textu jsou tedy základními strategiemi textové produkce a měly by být systematicky nacvičovány.

Naše kurzy výše uvedené fáze respektují. Každá lekce je také ukončena fází reflexe a sebereflexe prostřednictvím fóra, přičemž k reflexi vlastního textu dochází již dříve při psaní konceptu. Této strategii je věnována důsledná pozornost minimálně dvakrát v každé lekci. Studenti mohou vnímat své pokroky, úspěchy i mezery s ohledem na ostatní účastníky kurzu, mohou vkládat do fór komentáře k druhým i k sobě.

V dnešním pojetí procesně orientované didaktiky psaní dále platí důležitost instrukcí učitele/lektora, které se týkají znalostí textových žánrů, jazykových norem, rétorických obratů a strukturovaného postupu při psaní, kontextu psaní, domén a diskurzu. V našich kurzech podáváme přehled o žánrech několika způsoby, a to využitím modelových textů a odkazů na další obdobné texty téhož žánru na jiných webových stránkách, přehledem typických jazykových prostředků v těchto žánrech, charakteristikou žánrů, jejich funkce i popisem jejich struktury a nakonec prostřednictvím návodných otázek ve fórech. Studenti mohou z modelových textů implicitně vyvozovat znaky žánrů, explicitně jsou jim pak na různých místech lekcí průběžně přibližovány. Pro výuku bez lektora v rámci klasického e-learningu tedy získávají rozmanitý přehled o žánrech a kontextech jejich psaní a mohou samostatně pracovat, v případě práce s lektorem (blended learning) lze navíc klást doplňující otázky, ať už ze strany studenta, či lektora. Strukturovaný postup při psaní jako úspěšná strategie potvrzená výzkumem je studentům neustále připomínán samotnou podobou lekcí, totiž jejich členěním.

S ohledem na didaktický rámec celého projektu byly vybrány autentické a situované písemné úkoly: žánry v lekcích vycházejí z požadavků kladených v českém kulturním prostředí na středoškolské i vysokoškolské studenty (a to i jejich potenciálními zaměstnavateli). Dále zohledňují, jak bylo uvedeno výše, výsledky dotazníkového šetření z druhé fáze projektu a Společný evropský referenční rámec pro dané úrovně. Též se v lekcích nacházejí autentické modelové texty, někdy částečně pozměněné s ohledem na autorská práva, a poté odkazy na podobné texty téhož žánru vyskytující se na českých webových stránkách. Tyto odkazy jen podtrhují praktičnost znalosti zvolených žánrů. Situovanost žánrů lze také podpořit provázáním lekcí jedním příběhem – do samotných lekcí jsme jej však nevčlenily, aby si jednotliví lektoři mohli individuálně různé lekce různými způsoby propojit. Zde ilustrujeme jednu z variant: modelový student plánuje stáž v zahraničí, a proto píše e-mailem žádost o stipendium, k níž připojuje svůj životopis a zamýšlený projekt, který by v zahraničí rád řešil a na jehož základě se o stipendium uchází; v průběhu stáže na partnerské univerzitě musí vytvořit PPT prezentaci na jeden ze seminářů; po návratu do své země odevzdává závěrečnou zprávu o studijní stáži a o svých zážitcích nakonec informuje ostatní spolužáky článkem o městě, v němž pobýval…). Dále lekce vždy zahrnují cvičení pro dvě úrovně ovládání jazyka, podporují tak rozvoj studenta a jeho přechod z nižší úrovně ovládání jazyka do úrovně vyšší. Studenti si přitom svobodně volí, jaká cvičení absolvují, a jaká ne.

Co se týče blended learningové podoby kurzu, má lektor více možností, jak studenty hodnotit. Pokud se zcela oprostí od klasického známkování, či známkování v procentech, zbaví pisatele potenciálních bloků a strachů z psaní a špatné známky. Pro hodnocení se totiž nabízejí další nástroje: slovní komentář nebo vkládání souborů (obrázku, dokumentu s poznámkami a komentáři), záleží tedy na lektorovi, jaký z postupů využije či jak je zkombinuje.

3 Struktura lekcí on-line kurzu

Každá lekce je členěna do pěti, respektive šesti částí a je uvozena tříminutovým videem *Jak pracovat s lekcí?* se stručnými informacemi ke struktuře lekcí a o možnostech, jak jimi procházet. Před každou lekcí se nalézá také fórum *Novinky*, kam lektoři mohou psát rozmanité informace k lekci (nové aktivity, změnu termínů ukončení lekce, úkoly pro studenty aj.), anebo si prostřednictvím fóra mohou mezi sebou vyměňovat informace i studenti. Dále se zde nachází *Chat se studenty*. Ten je určený pro komunikaci mezi lektorem a účastníky kurzu v přesně stanovený čas, případně se k němu mohou všichni vracet i později, neboť veškerá komunikace zůstává uložena. Zde mohou být prodiskutovány znaky žánru, jeho styl, typická doména či znaky diskurzu, v němž se jednotlivé žánry realizují, gramaticko-lexikální jevy a další otázky, na něž studenti jinde nenalezli odpověď.

Vstupní část každé lekce tvoří *Databáze textů* a poté začíná vlastní lekce rozdělená na *Úvod*, *Přípravu*, *Strukturu*, *Revizi* a *Sebehodnocení*. Tyto části lze procházet v libovolném pořadí, chronologicky, výběrově, nebo rekursivně.

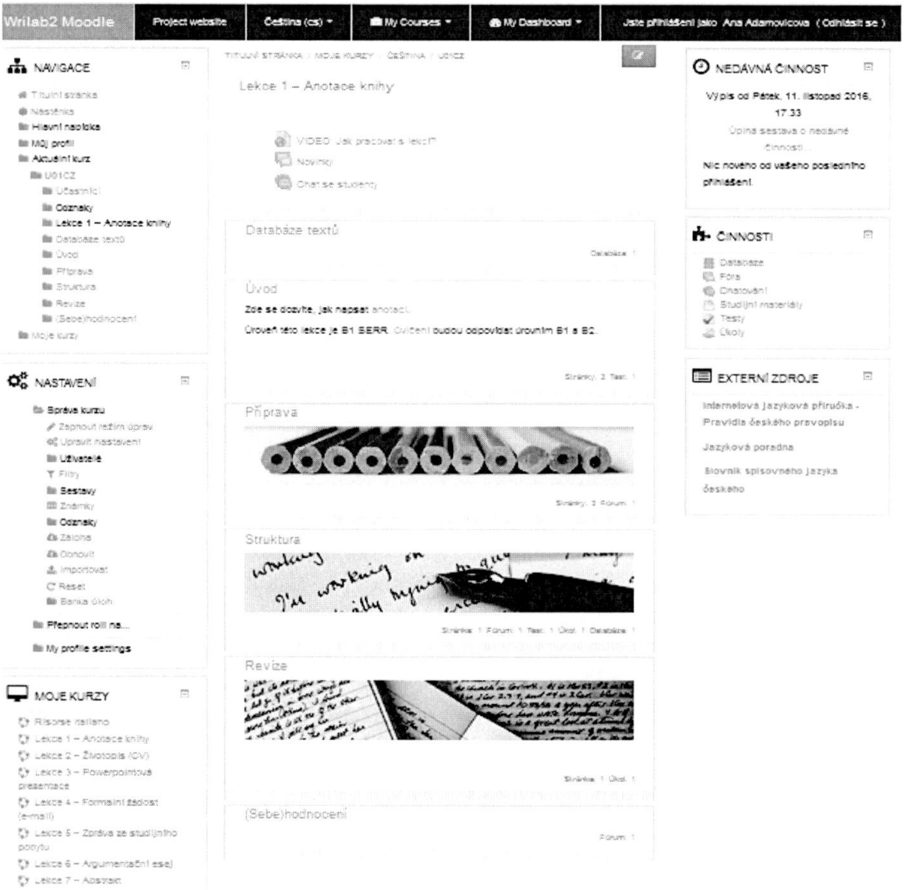

Obrázek 1: Jednotlivé části didaktických jednotek

Databáze textů je určena ke vkládání písemných prací daného žánru, které účastníci e-lekcí již dříve napsali. Tato část slouží jako databanka: účastníci kurzu po jeho absolvování mohou a) porovnat svůj nový text se starším, který do této části vložili, nebo b) v databázi vyhledat text jiného autora – nerodilého mluvčího, c) také lektor zde může vyhledat autentický text nerodilého mluvčího a dále s ním libovolně pracovat (nabízí se například jeho využití pro nový typ cvičení uzpůsobený pro potřeby konkrétní skupiny, kterou lektor vede v rámci tzv. blended learningového kurzu, upozornění lektora na úskalí žánru dokladovaná v konkrétním textu apod.).

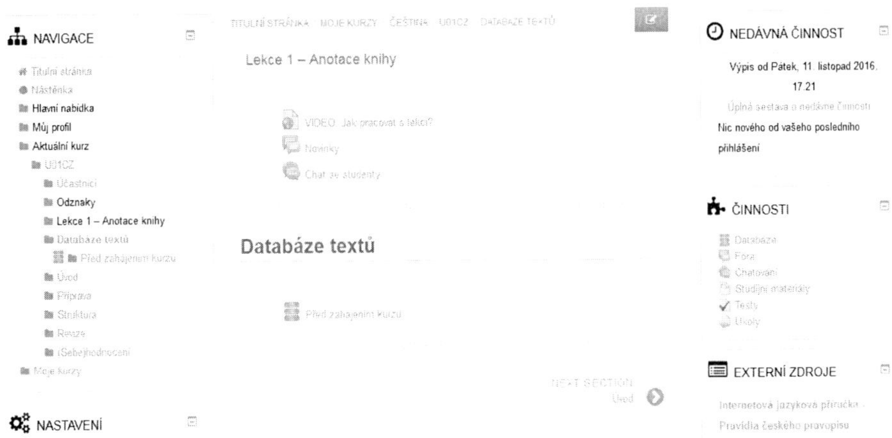

Obrázek 2: Databáze textů

V *Úvodu* se nachází stručná informace o úrovni lekce podle Společného evropského referenčního rámce a dále jeden, či dva, případně i více modelových textů, soubor jazykových prostředků gramaticko-lexikálních a sada cvičení, jež vychází z modelových textů. Cvičení mohou být využita podle potřeb účastníků kurzu a nacházejí se v nich jevy, které jsou pro daný žánr příznačné či by mohly být problematické. Gramatická cvičení jsou zároveň opatřena různými poznámkami týkajícími se probíraného jevu a odkazy na příručky, v nichž student může získat více informací. Ve cvičeních se též věnuje pozornost lexikálním jevům. Typy úloh jsou dlouhá tvořená odpověď, doplňovací úloha, krátká tvořená odpověď, pravda/nepravda, přiřazování a výběr z možných odpovědí.

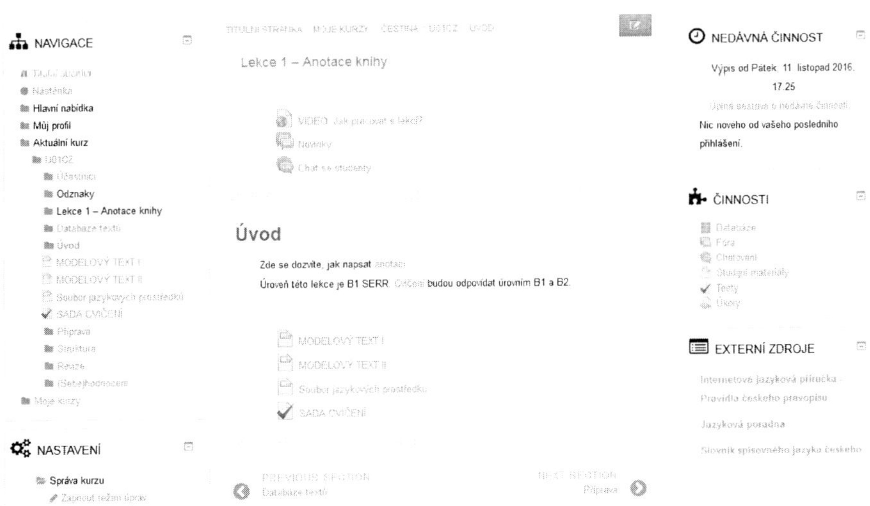

Obrázek 3: Úvod

V Přípravě jsou k dispozici popis žánru, tipy na další obdobné texty na internetu (odkazy na internetové stránky) a na vytváření vlastních nápadů a postupů pro psaní textu (tzv. *Generování nápadů*). Mezi tipy se nalézají jak pokyny k tvorbě osnovy, tak popis technik pro hledání témat a motivů vycházejících z tvůrčího psaní (viz Fišer, 2001), např. abecedáře, akrostichu, clusteru, mentální mapy, automatického textu, schématu plus/mínus, a to včetně ilustrativní fotografie. Pestrost umožňuje, aby se účastníci kurzů seznámili s různými možnostmi a zvolili si techniku, která jim nejvíce vyhovuje, navíc je tak zamezeno stereotypu. Též jsou zde uvedeny odkazy na využití softwarů, jež jsou na internetu volně ke stažení (např. Software FreeMind na http://www.xmind.net/download/win/).

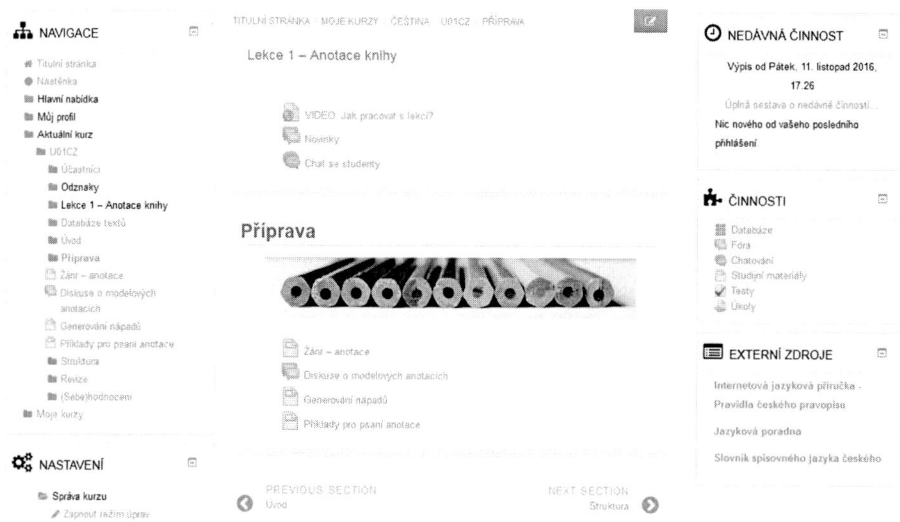

Obrázek 4: Příprava

Ve *Struktuře* účastníci najdou informaci o struktuře daného žánru. Dále se zde nachází několik cvičení na rozčlenění informací v úvodních modelových textech, a to na rozdělení textu do odstavců, uspořádání odstavců do správného pořadí a uspořádání vět v rámci odstavce. Smyslem opětovného navracení se k modelovým textům je, aby si studenti lépe vštípili znaky žánru. Další aktivitu v této části představuje *Úkol*, tedy ikona listu s rukou, sloužící k napsání a nahrání prvního konceptu textu. Text se odešle lektorovi, který k němu poskytne zpětnou vazbu (známkou, komentářem, nahraným souborem s opravami a poznámkami). Do databáze *Porovnejte svou práci s ostatními* je možné nahrát text znovu, aby ho viděli i ostatní účastníci kurzu a pisateli poslali nějaký komentář. Jejich názor může být užitečný pro vylepšení textu.

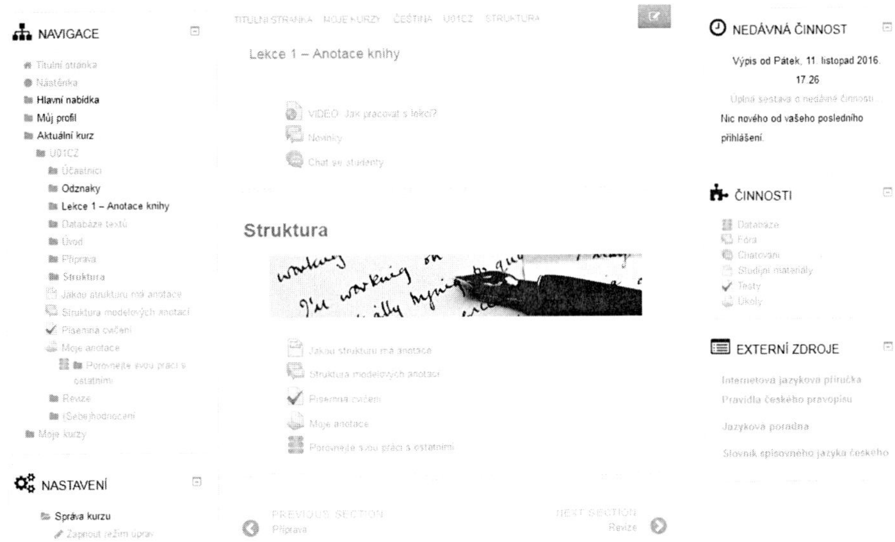

Obrázek 5: Struktura

V *Revizi* se nalézají návody k autokorektuře konceptu pod názvem *Jak revidovat text?*[18] Tyto návody se mírně liší. Též účastníky odkazují na práci s *externími zdroji*, jež jsou umístěny v pravém sloupci každé lekce. Jsou jimi *Internetová jazyková příručka – Pravidla českého pravopisu, Jazyková poradna* a *Slovník spisovného jazyka českého*. Další možností, jak si opravit pravopis, je využití volně dostupného programu *Spell Checker* (např. na https://www.spell checker.net/czech_spell_checker.html). Nakonec se tu nachází ikona *Úkolu* (v ukázkovém obrázku pod názvem *Opravená anotace*), do níž vkládají účastníci svou upravenou, finální verzi textu.

[18] Mezi tipy na revizi textu se nacházejí např. takovéto instrukce: Nechte text odležet a vraťte se k němu nejdříve po 24 hodinách. Zaměřte se na obsah a strukturu textu: obsahuje název knihy, jméno autora, nakladatelství a rok vydání? Nechte si text také okomentovat od někoho dalšího z kurzu. Poté znovu zkontrolujte dodržení žánru, tématu a rozsahu, obsah (jsou uvedeny všechny informace?, jsou relevantní?), výstavbu textu a přehlednost členění, jazykovou stránku (spisovnost a adekvátnost slov, gramatiku a pravopis). Zjistěte, zda se ve větách shodují podměty s přísudky (on byl; ona byla; ono bylo; oni byli; ony byly; ona byla; on + ona byli; ona + ona byly). Zaměřte se na slovesa z hlediska času a vidu, který jste použil/a. Podívejte se ještě jednou na slovesné vazby, předložková a pádová doplnění jednotlivých sloves. Zkontrolujte také, zdali osobní zájmena svou formou odpovídají jevům, které zastupují, a zda se vztažná zájmena svou formou vztahují ke správným slovům v textu. Nezapomeňte na spojovací výrazy a konektory. Mají logickou návaznost? Zkontrolujte, jestli jste před všemi vedlejšími a hlavními větami, které nejsou ve slučovacím poměru (spojky a, i), napsal/a čárky.

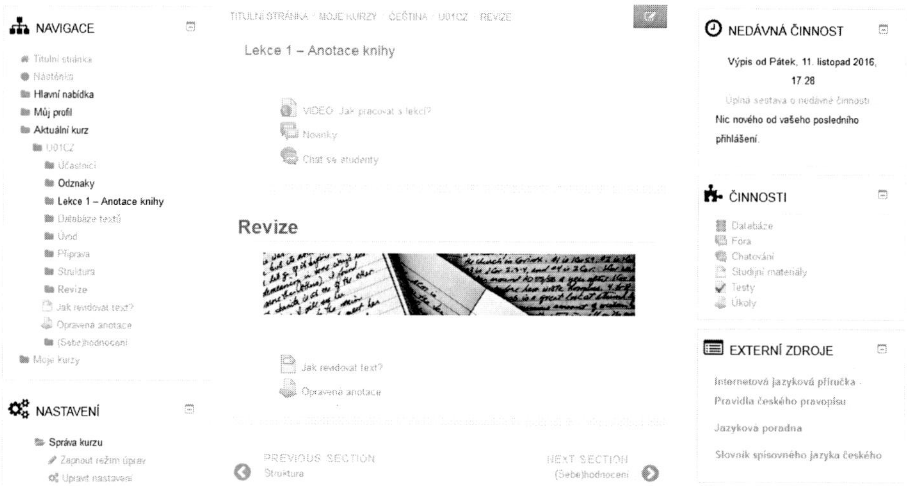

Obrázek 6: Revize

V *(Sebe)hodnocení* reflektují účastníci svůj pokrok, svoje potíže či úspěšnost a vyjadřují se k celé lekci. Tato fáze tedy slouží k reflexi i sebereflexi.

V různých částech lekcí lze najít i další *fóra*, která se specificky vztahují k daným sekcím. V nich jsou již formulovány otázky, o nichž mohou účastníci společně diskutovat a které by měly napomoci uvědomit si různé fáze psaní textu, či si upevnit/ozřejmit jeho dílčí charakteristiky.

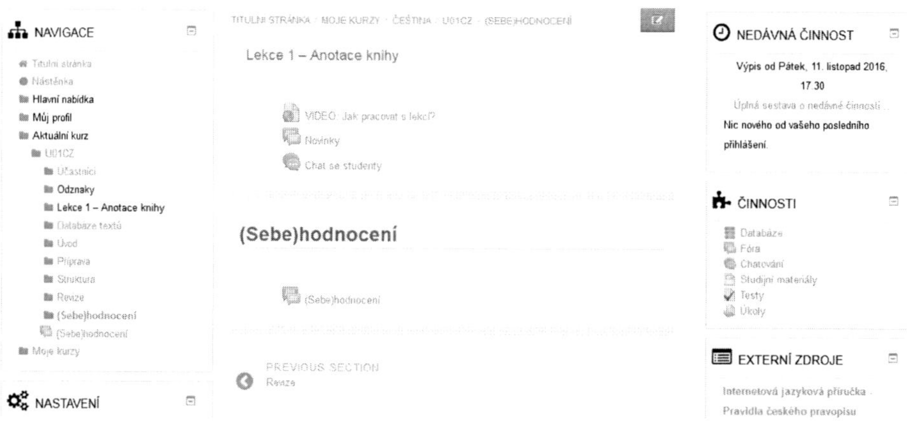

Obrázek 7: (Sebe)hodnocení

4 Zhodnocení on-line kurzů

V letním semestru akademického roku 2015/16 probíhaly na Ústavu bohemistických studií FF UK dva on-line kurzy psaní. První kurz pro studenty úrovně B1-B2 obsahoval prvních šest lekcí, v rámci druhého kurzu pro úroveň B2-C1 se probíraly didaktické jednotky 7-12. Do prvního kurzu se zapsalo 11 studentů, do druhého 10 studentů; první kurz absolvovalo 9 studentů a druhý studentů 8.

Mezi frekventanty byli studenti vyšších ročníků bakalářského studia a navazujícího magisterského studia oboru Čeština pro cizince a studenti kurzů pro stážisty a postgraduanty. Národnostní složení frekventantů bylo především slovanské (první jazyk ruština, chorvatština, polština, bulharština), menšinu tvořili Neslované (první jazyk čínština, dále japonština a korejština). V prvním kurzu studenti prošli lekce 1, 3, 5 a 6 a poté si mohli volit mezi lekcí 2 (životopis) a 4 (formální žádost – e-mail). Ve vyšším kurzu se začínalo lekcí 8 – článkem čili publicistickým referátem (témata se na výslovné přání studentů netýkala pouze Prahy, jak je doporučeno v lekci), následovaly lekce 9 – formální dopis (žádost, stížnost, omluva apod.), 10 – zpráva o projektu, 7 – abstrakt (studenti měli možnost napsat abstrakt k už vypracovanému vlastnímu textu včetně textu, který odevzdali v lekci 8), 11 – recenze a 12 – výkladová esej. V rámci pilotního on-line kurzu pro úroveň B1-B2 bylo odevzdáno 55 písemných prací, v kurzu pro úroveň B2-C1 pak 57.

Brzy se ukázalo, že je časová dotace dva týdny na jednu didaktickou jednotku příliš rychlé tempo. Studenti v tomto kurzu pracovali mnohem více než v jakémkoli dalším prezenčním kurzu, protože se mu během celého semestru věnovali maximálně aktivně – studovali teoretické východisko každé lekce, četli modelové texty, vypracovávali řadu gramatických, lexikálních a textových cvičení, připravovali se na vlastní psaní a do konce druhého týdne měli odevzdat hotový text. Každý týden jsme zhruba hodinu trávili na *chatu*, během něhož jsme společně řešili aktuální problémy a jednotlivá témata. Během semestru jsme se sešli dvakrát – na začátku a na konci kurzu. Studenti za kurz přitom nezískali více kreditů než za jakýkoli další kurz, který nevyžaduje permanentní nasazení. Hned po ukončení první didaktické jednotky byl termín na odevzdání prací u každé lekce prodloužen o týden, od půlky kurzu jsme na žádost studentů zrušily jakékoli termíny, neboť jsme si uvědomily, že je mnohem důležitější lekci vstřebat a odevzdat kvalitní práce. Bylo evidentní, že by snaha o dodržení termínu byla na úkor kvality a mohla by také vést k rezignaci na kurz. Musíme konstatovat, že studenti byli velice vytrvalí a že většině z nich na kurzu velmi záleželo. Třetina prací byla odevzdána po ukončení semestru, čtyři z nich až o celý měsíc později.

Na základě zkušeností z pilotního kurzu je zřejmé, že by jedna didaktická jednotka měla mít časovou dotaci tři týdny. První týden se student seznamuje s žánrem a tématem, druhý týden sbírá a vyměňuje si zkušenosti, vypracovává cvičení a první koncept svého textu a třetí týden by měl věnovat psaní konečné podoby textu. Optimální je tedy probrat 4 témata za semestr. Lekce je také možno procházet výběrově, rozdělit je podle preferencí studentů, žánrů, náročnosti probíraných gramatických prostředků apod.

5 Vyhodnocení zpětné vazby od studentů

Na konci on-line kurzu studenti vyplňovali dotazník – zajímal nás celkový dojem z jednotlivých lekcí, názor na materiály, cvičení a různé aktivity, dále co v kurzu postrádali, zda se vyskytovaly technické problémy apod. Celkový dojem z didaktických jednotek je vesměs pozitivní – mezi hodnotícími adjektivy se nejčastěji vyskytlo slovo „užitečný". Stejně kladně studenti hodnotili studijní materiály (modelové texty, popis žánrů, soubor jazykových prostředků). Negativní slovní hodnocení se dvakrát vyskytlo pouze u mind-mapping („nepomohlo mi v ničem", „nesplňují svůj účel") – tuto část jsme po skončení kurzu více rozpracovaly. Dále všichni shodně pozitivně hodnotili chat. Pokud jde o sadu gramaticko-lexikálních cvičení – třetina studentů je hodnotí jednoznačně kladně, třetina si myslí, že jsou užitečná, ale příliš dlouhá, třetina zastává názor, že jsou cvičení nudná a otravná. Nutnost zařadit cvičení jsme již na několika místech zmiňovaly, zde bychom chtěly ještě jednou zdůraznit, že je cvičení možné dělat výběrově. V jedné odpovědi si student stěžoval, že Moodle jen označí nesprávné řešení, nevysvětlí mu ale, v čem chyboval. Právě proto máme chat, během něhož je možné též probrat chyby. Na otázku, co by se mělo odstranit, doplnit, či změnit studenti odpovídali celkem shodně: lepší uspořádání webové stránky, zařazení více modelových textů, odstranění písemných cvičení na doplňování slov z modelových textů. Na první doporučení jsme již reagovaly, více modelových textů by však znamenalo podstatně delší kurz (navíc každá lekce obsahuje odkazy na další texty korespondující s jednotlivými žánry). Pokud jde o poslední přání – jednalo se o tzv. Cloze test, který se využívá v didaktice druhého a cizího jazyka a studentům umožňuje doplňovat chybějící slova podle kontextu. Jde tedy o test slovní zásoby. Uživatelé kurzu Wrilab2 byli upozorněni na to, že v případě Cloze testu mají své odpovědi kontrolovat s modelovým textem. Jiné varianty, o kterých se domnívali, že jsou také korektní, pak mohli konzultovat v chatu s lektorem. Jednalo se o typ cvičení, který jsme využily výjimečně: kontrolu studentských řešení s modelovým textem ovšem chápeme jako výhodu – opakovaným čtením si studenti upevňují gramaticko-lexikální struktury i znaky žánru. Nejvíce negativních odpovědí v dotazníku se týkalo technické stránky věci – špatného připojení apod., což je bohužel faktor, který nemůžeme ovlivnit a s kterým je nutno počítat v jakémkoli online kurzu.

6 Porovnání výsledků analýzy studentských kontrolních esejí a e-esejí (úroveň B1-B2)

Pro vyhodnocení písemných prací jsme zvolily s ohledem na počet respondentů 10 prací pro úroveň B1 a 10 prací pro úroveň B2, a to konkrétně eseje napsané v lekci 1 a 2 (anotace, CV – klasické a strukturované), respektive z lekce 5 a 6 (zpráva ze studijního pobytu, argumentační esej). Při analýze textů jsme využily metodiku Sylvie del Longo (del Longo & Cisotto 2014) a sledovaly informativnost textu (tvrzení, důkaz, protiargument, případný odkaz na zdroj, schopnost shrnutí), koherenci (logickou organizaci myšlenek v textu), strukturu (členění na věty a odstavce) a kohezi (prostředky textové návaznosti na všech úrovních textu). Za každou proměnnou bylo možné obdržet maximálně 4 body, tj. celkem 16 bodů.

Kvalita textů zhotovených v on-line kurzu pro úroveň B1 se ve všech sledovaných položkách oproti esejím kontrolním mírně zvýšila, a sice průměrně o 2,5 bodu, tj. o 16 % – viz Tab. 2. K nejvyššímu nárůstu došlo v informativnosti (o celý bod, tedy v této položce o 25 %) – viz Tab. 1. U textů v on-line kurzu úrovně B2 došlo také ke zvýšení počtu bodů ve všech sledovaných položkách, zejména však ve struktuře a kohezi a již jen mírně v informativnosti a koherenci (v těchto proměnných totiž vykazovaly kontrolní eseje dobrou úroveň), a sice průměrně o 4,3 bodů, tedy došlo ke kvalitativnímu nárůstu o 27 % vůči kontrolním esejím. Z níže uvedené tabulky je patrné, že pisatelé esejí z on line kurzů pro úroveň B2 získali téměř plný počet bodů. Co se týče jednotlivých jazykových rovin, u úrovně B1 přetrvávaly v nízkém počtu nedostatky pravopisné (v diakritice a interpunkci, případně v typografických konvencích – psaní jednohláskových předložek a spojek na konci řádku), lexikální (záměna blízkých slov, např. *společenství* versus *společnost*, chybná spojení, např. *otočit zaměření* versus *změnit*), ve slovesné valenci (například *chápat* plus dativ), v koncovkách substantiv a ve slovosledu (postavení enklitik). U úrovně B2 se velmi zřídka vyskytly pravopisné nedostatky v diakritice a interpunkci, případně v typografických konvencích (obdobně jako u úrovně B1) a ve slovosledu (postavení enklitik, výjimečně aktuální větné členění).

Podmínky psaní kontrolních esejí a esejí v on-line kurzu byly částečně odlišné, čímž lze rozdílné výsledky vysvětlit. V kontrolních esejích mohli respondenti částečně využít slovníky a další pomůcky (při psaní textu jako domácího úkolu), částečně museli psát bez použití jakékoliv opory – vždy však psali pouze jednu variantu textu, který dále neupravovali. V on-line kurzech bylo možné využívat on-line pomůcky (internetový slovník, pravidla pravopisu, jazykovou poradnu), radu lektora či spolužáka prostřednictvím *chatu* a diskusních fór, navíc v souladu s principy procesně pojaté didaktiky psaní zhotovovali vždy výchozí koncept, k němuž od lektora obdrželi zpětnou vazbu a na jejímž základě vytvářeli druhou, finální verzi. Je tedy patrné, že se tento postup kladně projevil na kvalitě výsledného textu. Složení respondentů s ohledem na typologii výchozího jazyka bylo shodné: výrazně převažovali Slované, tedy nositelé jazyků flektivních. Kontrolní eseje úrovně B1 a B2 psali 33 Slovani, 4 Japonci, 1 Němec, 1 Rakušan a 1 Vietnamec; e-eseje psalo 6 Slovanů, 1 Japonec, 1 Číňanka a 1 Korejka. Kontrolní eseje úrovně B1 byly psány na následující témata: *Co nám automobil dal a vzal?*, *Jak by měla vypadat ideální práce?*, *Co se mi líbí či nelíbí na vzdělávacím systému?*, *Co mi přinesl pobyt v Praze?*, *Co je lepší – mít staré, nebo mladé rodiče?* K jejich sběru došlo v březnu a dubnu 2015 a autory byli zahraniční studenti ČZU v Praze. Kontrolní eseje úrovně B2 byly psány na témata: *Televize a její role v současném světě?*, *Moderní formy zábavy?*, *Recenze výstavy Josefa Váchala?*, *Esej o češtině – důvody studia?*, *Fejeton o češtině a tzv. falešných přátelích?*. Sběr proběhl v říjnu 2014 až březnu 2015 mezi studenty Ústavu bohemistických studií FF UK v bakalářském studijním programu, případně navazujícím magisterském, v kurzech pro zahraniční stážisty a postgraduanty a v programu Česká studia.

Níže uvedená tabulka zachycuje průměrné výsledky ve čtyřech sledovaných parametrech v kontrolních esejích a esejích psaných v on-line kurzech (e-eseje) pro jednotlivé úrovně B1 a B2:

Eseje	**Informativnost**	**Koherence**	**Struktura**	**Koheze**
B1 kontrolní eseje	2,25	2,55	1,7	1,9
B1 e-eseje	3,2	2,9	2,2	2,6
B2 kontrolní eseje	3,65	3,4	2,4	2,3
B2 e-eseje	4	3,8	3,5	3,9

Tab. 1: Výsledky v jednotlivých parametrech

Úroveň	**Průměrný počet bodů (max. 16)** **Kontrolní eseje**	**Průměrný počet bodů (max. 16)** **E-eseje**	**Nárůst (body)**	**Nárůst (procenta)**
B1	8,4	10,9	2,5	16 %
B2	11,7	15,2	4,3	27 %

Tab. 2: Celkové výsledky

7 Porovnání výsledků analýzy studentských kontrolních esejí a e-esejí (úroveň B2-C1)

7.1 Kontrolní eseje: první a druhý sběr

V letním semestru akademického roku 2014/15 proběhla prezenční obdoba druhé půlky on-line kurzu, výběrově lekce 7-12 (pracovali jsme se vznikajícími materiály, což autorům kurzu poskytlo velmi cennou zpětnou vazbu). Kurzu se zúčastnilo 26 studentů: 3 studenti navazujícího magisterského programu Čeština pro cizince (2 Slované: mateřský jazyk ukrajinština a polština; 1 Neslovan: mateřský jazyk čínština), 11 studentů vyšších úrovní (B1-C1) programu pro stážisty a postgraduanty (7 Slovanů: mateřský jazyk polština – 5 studentů, bulharština a slovinština); 4 Neslované: mateřský jazyk němčina) a 12 studentů bakalářského studia oboru Čeština pro cizince (7 Slovanů: mateřský jazyk ruština – 4 studenti, makedonština – 2 studenti, a polština; 5 Neslovanů: mateřský jazyk čínština – 2 studenti, korejština, vietnamština a gagauzština /moldavština). Většina studentů dosahovala úrovně B2 s mírným přesahem k C1.

Na začátku a v polovině kurzu dvakrát proběhl sběr studentských esejí psaných na hodině: první sběr se věnoval žánru oficiální zpráva (téma: *Zpráva po návratu z výměnného pobytu*), druhý sběr argumentačnímu eseji – studenti si mohli vybrat ze dvou témat *Kočka, nebo pes?*, *Automobil, nebo MHD?* Při druhém sběru bylo odevzdáno 23 esejí. Jen třetina studentů si zvolila téma domácích mazlíčků, většina prací se věnovala tématu výhod a nevýhod užití dopravního prostředku ve městě (drtivá většina studentů dala přednost MHD). Následně 20 esejí z druhého sběru bylo podrobeno detailní analýze (byly vyřazeny eseje 3 studentů, jejichž jazyková úroveň zaostávala za průměrnou úrovní frekventantů, tj. úrovní B2).

Ačkoli všechny eseje vznikly na hodině bez žádných pomůcek, je mezi nimi značný rozdíl: zatímco v první vlně sběru psali studenti bez jakékoli přípravy, doporučení či rady, před psaním druhé eseje absolvovali krátkou teoreticko-metodologickou průpravu na psaní argumentačních textů. Přestože jak první, tak druhé eseje vykazují nejvíc nedostatků v kohezi, u prvních byla výrazně vyšší chybovost v samotném uspořádání textu, v členění na jednotlivé segmenty a odstavce, patrný byl nedostatek zkušeností s žánrem (oficiální zpráva splývala s neformálním popisem pobytu v cizí zemi apod.) Z toho jasně plyne, že se struktuře textu, uspořádání myšlenek a požadavkům v rámci jednotlivých žánrů pisatelé dají snadno naučit, obzvlášť jde-li o žánr, při kterém se respektují daná pravidla (zpráva z cesty, zpráva o projektu, formální dopis, abstrakt apod.). Široce pojatá gramatika (zahrnující pravopis a slovosled), stylistika, koherence a koheze jsou nejtěžšími úskalími, která se při procesu psaní budou nejdéle tříbit.

7.2 E-eseje

V rámci pilotního on-line kurzu bylo odevzdáno 57 písemných prací. Všechny eseje studenti psali po důkladném obeznámení s obsahem lekce – modelovými texty počínaje, vypracováním nejrůznějších typů cvičení vycházejících z modelových textů, zahrnujících lexikální a morfologicko-syntaktický repertoár prostředků relevantních pro dané téma, až po důkladné seznámení s typem a strukturou jednotlivých žánrů. Dalším důležitým momentem, do jisté míry ztěžujícím statistické porovnání typu chyb s chybami, které se vyskytly v předchozích dvou sběrech, je fakt, že během on-line kurzu studenti vypracovávali eseje v domácím prostředí, a měli tudíž k dispozici veškeré pomůcky. K analýze pro úroveň B2-C1 jsme si náhodně vybraly první verzi 20 odevzdaných esejí – 10 z žánru článek a po 5 z žánrů recenze a výkladová esej. Výběr žánrů byl podložen zajímavým a zřejmě obecně platným zjištěním: pokud jde o samotnou analýzu chyb, nejméně chyb se vyskytovalo v žánrech nejméně kreativních – ve formálním dopisu, abstraktu, powerpointové prezentaci či zprávě o projektu. U těchto žánrů jde o zvládnutí ustáleného výraziva a často hotových bloků, které do textu pouze dosazujeme. U všech dalších kreativnějších žánrů – esejů, článků či recenzí – je počet chyb mnohem vyšší. Celkově však lze říci, že je v porovnání s předchozími esejemi, v nově analyzovaných esejích mnohem více zapojena koheze, což jen svědčí o tom, že se správným dávkováním látky – výběrem modelových textů a cvičeními zaměřenými na spojovací prostředky – tento jev vcelku dá úspěšně zvládnout.

7.3 Kritéria hodnocení

Jak již bylo řečeno, při analýze chyb v rámci projektu jsme hodnotily 4 aspekty textů: informativnost, strukturu textu, koherenci a kohezi. První tři sledované aspekty byly ve větší, nebo menší míře splněny, nejvíce chyb se vyskytlo v kohezi.

Tato klasifikace však, jako jakákoli klasifikace založená na známkování, může do jisté míry obsahovat i prvky subjektivity. Navíc je založena na univerzálním vnímání chybovosti – podobné výsledky by se zřejmě vyskytly i při sledování těchto aspektů v L1. Jelikož ze čtyř sledovaných aspektů studenti získali nejméně bodů z koheze, rozhodly jsme se dál sledovat kohezi a do další analýzy studentských prací jsme též zahrnuly specifické aspekty, tj. gramatiku, pravopis a stylistiku, přičemž jsme vycházely z absolutního počtu a typů chyb na esej. V úhrnu se v obou sběrech vyskytlo přes 300 chyb, čili v průměru cca 15 chyb na esej při průměrné délce eseje 450 slov. Domníváme se, že pouze takto můžeme získat víceméně objektivní přehled o problémech, se kterými se studenti potýkají a na které je potřeba při přípravě doprovodných cvičení k psaní textů klást největší důraz.

Zde jsou navíc hodnoceny první, „neučesané“ verze odevzdaných esejů (na rozdíl od analýzy, která proběhla pro nižší jazykovou úroveň), takže jsou výskyty chyb autentičtější.

7.4 Výsledky šetření

Níže uvedený graf (Graf 4) znázorňuje typy chyb v kontrolních esejích (druhý sběr) a v e-esejích:

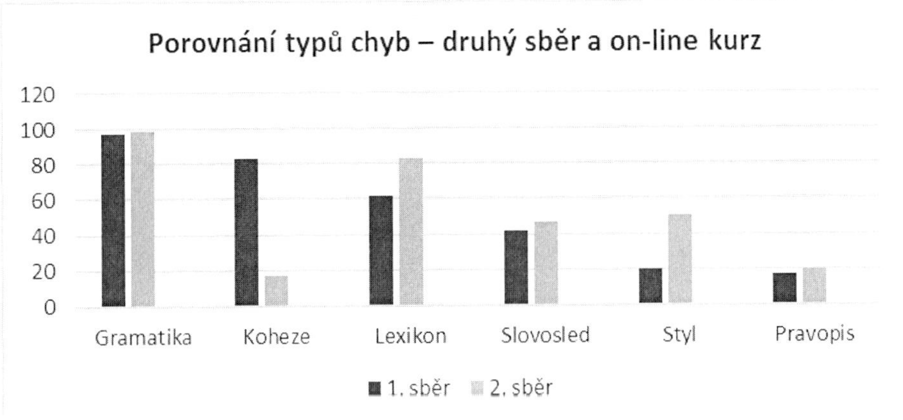

Graf 4: Porovnání typů chyb – absolutní počet chyb

Vidíme tedy, že sledované typy chyb při obou sběrech vykazují odlišné hodnoty u koheze, lexikonu a stylu. Morfologické, slovosledné a pravopisné chyby v obou případech vykazují podobné hodnoty. Nejvyšší výkyv je právě v kohezi – před absolvováním on-line kurzu bylo v esejích výrazně nízké zastoupení adekvátních spojovacích výrazů včetně deiktik a partikulí (*výše / níže zmíněný, tento, takovýto; však, zřejmě, nejspíš, tedy* apod.) vyjadřujících postojovo-logické vztahy mezi větami a odstavci. Do oddílu *Sada cvičení* jsme zapojili řadu cvičení zaměřených na tyto prostředky, což studentům v on-line kurzu zřejmě pomohlo.

Vyšší podíl chybovosti v lexikonu a stylu, ovšem také mírně v gramatice a slovosledu při druhém sběru, je celkem snadno pochopitelný: za ním se skrývá jednak žánrová pestrost, jednak studenti přihlášení do on-line kurzu měli celkově o něco nižší jazykovou úroveň než studenti, kteří psali kontrolní eseje.

7.4.1 Struktura gramatických chyb

Níže uvedený graf (Graf 5) znázorňuje strukturu gramatických chyb v e-esejích:

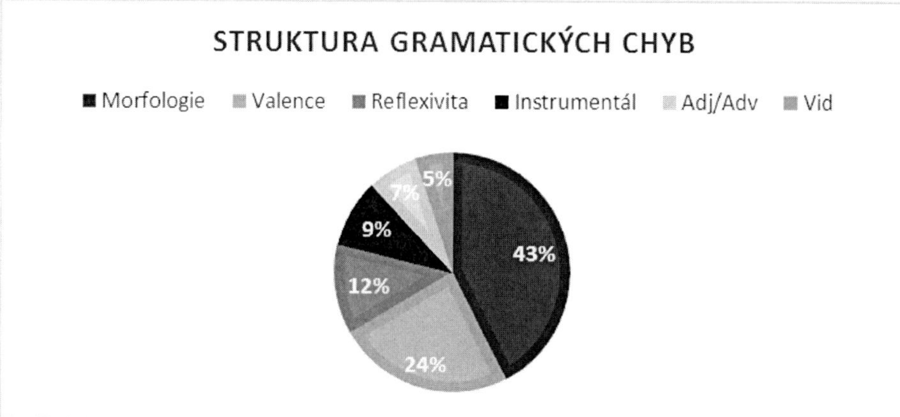

Graf 5: Struktura gramatických chyb v e-esejích

Nejčetnější morfologické chyby zahrnují měkkou deklinaci substantiv (*oddán svému cíle, názor na poezie, z jeho biografii, v kostelích, pro Nemesa, na báze, od této instituci, s minulosti*), lokál singuláru a akuzativ plurálu (*v úvodě, v takovém smysle, pro všechny spisovately, pro členové, pro některých*), deklinaci vztažných zájmen *který* (zde je častou chybou neshoda v rodě) a *jenž* a deklinaci cizích slov.

Valenční chyby zahrnují jak nedodržení vazby, tak vyšinutí z vazeb (např. *chodila sem po cestě z redakce časopisu, neodpovídá současností, podobná ve své metodě popisu reality, lákaly nejlepších hudebníků, těšit se skvělými koncerty, které u napodobování různých zvířecích zvuků zesilují celkový pocit, tkví u organizace scény, nechybí skvělých nápadů, působila vnímání člověka jako předmět, strach od, zájem k, v internetu, ve většině kolejích, ve většině případech* atd.).

Problém s reflexivitou (stejně jako se slovosledem, který s reflexivitou vytváří komplexní bod) většinou mají rusky a polsky mluvící studenti. Jedná se o dvojí porušení pravidla: buď o vynechání reflexivní částice, anebo naopak o její nadbytečnost: *hra stála atrakcí, stala první abstraktní malbou, filmy týkající koncentračních táborů, musíte zasloužit, pokusit přiblížit*; *převládají se tendence, platí se pro všechny, báseň se začínala.*

Další poměrně typickou chybou je nepoužívání instrumentálu, jenž se v písemném projevu hojně vyskytuje: *je vězeň, ještě větší problém jsou, nejlepší příklad je, není její cíl ve vyjádření emocí* (zde se také vyskytla valenční chyba), nebo naopak chybný výskyt instrumentálu ve jmenné části přísudku vyjádřené adjektivem: *tento proces nemůže být rychlým či snadným.*

Překvapivě často dochází k záměně adjektiv a adverbií: *psychický nemocná, estetické špatná, není jasně, těžké srozumitelný, prodávají se rychlé* apod.

Nejméně chyb se vyskytuje v použití vidu, ve všech případech se jedná o imperfektivní verbum namísto perfektivního: *doporučujeme vám včas vyhledávat/vyhledat si vstupenky, není těžce/těžké si nevšímat/nepovšimnout* apod.

7.4.2 Lexikon

U lexikálních chyb někdy splývá více aspektů (za lomítkem je uvedena správná varianta):

- interference často v kombinaci s neznalostí verbonominální fráze anebo vazby (např.: *povzbudit otázku, pocit/vyvolat; prkna se nadchnou uměním/jsou prodchnuta uměním; necítí soustrasti pro osud/nesoucítí s osudem; zaměnit/nahradit, kruh/prostředí, štítit/chránit, obecenstvo/ obyvatelstvo, příčina/důvod, holé/nahé tělo*);
- záměna slova podobného významu či slova podobně znějícího svědčící o neznalosti významového rozsahu slova, jeho kolokabilitě, případně úzu (např.: *výběr/volba, úmysl/záměr, číslo/počet, znít/zdát se, vypadat/ zdát se, poprvé/napřed, popisovat/znázorňovat, skončit/přestat, jedinečný/ojedinělý, uvidět/zjistit, v některém/jistém smyslu, létavý/ prchající, konečně/nakonec, pochopení/chápání, dům/domov*);
- neadekvátně použité slovo v kontextu nebo nevhodnost jeho stylové charakteristiky (např.: *flámování, noční konverzace, dát dohromady/ podnítit*);
- neznalost termínů a úzu (např.: *odrážení/odraz reality, kvalita vykonání/výkon, vytrhnutý/vytržený z kontextu, edice/ročník festivalu, renovovaná činohra/obnovené představení, proces přijetí/schvalovací proces, sociální média/sítě, hlad/hladomor, krátkost a délka samohlasek/kvantita, personální/osobní cíl*);
- výskyt zkomoleného nebo málo používaného slova (např.: *přestěhovalec/přistěhovalec, přijatá lexéma/přejaté slovo, všudepřítomný/všudypří to-mný, podařilý/zdařilý, informant/respondent, nadanost/ nadání*).

7.4.3 Stylistika

Za stylistické chyby jsme považovaly nedodržení běžného úzu, jistou šroubovanost ve vyjadřování včetně přílišné kondenzace textu či výskyt obecněčeských koncovek: *Praha každý rok láká miliony turistů; z jedné strany, z druhé strany; škola jeho zájmu; s postupem času; kdo je předkem té idey; přinucen k péči o sebe sama; přístup k uvedení známé Čapkovy hry široké veřejnosti; tímto odvážným řešením se režisér v podstatě zbavuje hlavního protikladu všem „hmyzím“ vlastnostem; doporučuji si předem hru přečíst; je to něco minulého; musí být položeno na zadnější místo; takový pocity jsou jasný, ve společenským životě, teda* apod.

7.4.4 Slovosled

Chyby v slovosledu se týkají hlavně postavení příklonek – reflexivních částic, nepřízvučných tvarů zájmen, pomocných sloves, ale také pozice částic, adjektiv nebo adverbií, anebo se vyskytují po koordinačních spojkách či souvisí s aktuálním větným členěním: *když přestaneme se na to dívat, ku příkladu si vezměme, když takové osoby setkají se, často končí to, aby přivezl mi, možná měli byste vyzkoušet, avšak je neméně zajímavý, nemá každý totiž to štěstí, některé další mosty mají zajímavou výzdobu také, z jakých ještě důvodů se jezdí do Prahy, zajímavé je to, že právě přízvuk Češi žijící na Sibiři považují za...* apod.

7.4.5 Pravopis

Pravopisné chyby na úrovni B2-C1 obsahují minimum chyb v kvantitě. Hlavní odchylky se týkají psaní čárek před spojkami *než* a *nebo* (*porucha nebo příznak; umírá víc lidí, než v autonehodách*), dále kladení čárek za slova jako *samozřejmě, nicméně, zároveň,* oddělené psaní spřežek např. *v celku, tak zvaný, na příklad* apod.

7.4.6 Koheze

Identifikace chybné koheze spočívá buď v neadekvátně užitých spojovacích a deiktických prostředcích či partikulí vyjadřujících postojovo-logické vztahy mezi větami a odstavci, anebo naopak v absenci jakéhokoli kohezního identifikátoru (v prvním případě je za lomítkem uveden správný tvar, v druhém je chybějící slovo zvýrazněno: *co/což správně ukazuje, nesmíme tak/takto myslet/ uvažovat, díky tomu/takovémuto, tím/tímto způsobem; život tohoto génia, i ta nejkrutší kritika, znamená to sice, že do svých filmů většinou zapojují výše uvedené motivy, avšak to..., ...které s výše uvedeným nemají moc společného, ...zároveň je však již zmíněná posedlost ztracenými postavami a neexistencí (toho světějšího) jistého <u>posvátna</u> či jakéhosi vyššího <u>principu</u> skoro všudypřítomná* (v tomto textu bylo při opravě adjektivum „světější" nahrazeno substantivem posvátno a bylo přidáno slovo princip). Dále bychom rády upozornily, že studenti málo využívají synonymních spojek, např. ale/avšak/přesto/; když/pokud/-li; přestože/ačkoli(v)/navzdory tomu že apod. První z uvedených spojek má výrazně nejvyšší frekvenci, další se vyskytují zcela sporadicky, anebo vůbec ne.

8 Závěr

V kurzu psaní studenty postupně vedeme k tomu, aby byli schopni v cizím jazyce vyjádřit obsah, aby dokázali adekvátně uchopit myšlenku, což samozřejmě nejde bez zvládnutí různých výrazových prostředků, ať už lexikálních či gramatických, použití adekvátního stylu a úzu běžného pro psaný diskurs a daný žánr.

Pohybujeme se tedy na ose, na jejímž pomyslném začátku je to, CO CHCI ŘÍCT, a postupně se dostáváme k tomu, JAK TYTO MYŠLENKY VYJÁDŘIT. Na základě analýzy chyb jsme zjistily, že při kreativnějších žánrech pisatelé v druhém jazyce těžko opouštějí myšlenkové pochody doprovázené gramatickými konstrukcemi, vazbami a frázemi typickými pro jejich mateřštinu. Zde myšlenka rozvíjená v mateřském jazyce jakoby „dusí" schopnost projevu v cizím jazyce, a tak se překvapivě i studenti na pokročilejší úrovni dopouštějí v těchto žánrech někdy i začátečnických chyb. Toto pozorování jen podporuje naši úvodní hypotézu, že techniku psaní nelze zcela uspokojivě zvládnout bez soustavného procvičování všech stavebních komponentů podílejících se na výsledném textu. Věříme, že naše poznatky v rámci projektu Wrilab2 napomohou lektorům češtiny jako cizího/druhého jazyka v jejich vlastní výuce psaní a zároveň že námi vytvořené lekce v prostředí Moodle přispějí k prohloubení dovednosti psaní v řadách studentů a dalších zájemců osvojujících si tento cílový jazyk.

Literatura

Albertini, John. (2008): Teaching of writing and diversity: access, identity, and achievement. In: Bazerman, Charles (Ed.). Handbook of research on writing. History, society, school, individual, text. New York: Routledge, 387–397.

Del Longo, Silvia & Cisotto, Lerida (2014): Writing to argue: Writing as a tool for oral and written argumentation. In: Klein, Perry D., Boscolo, Pietro, Kirkpatrick, Lori D. & Gelati, Carmen (Eds.): Studies in Writing. Vol. 28, Writing as a learning activity. Brill: Leiden, 15–43.

Dreyfürst, Stephanie & Sennewald, Nadja (Hrsg.): Schreiben. Grundlagentexte zur Theorie, Didaktik und Beratung. Opladen, Toronto: Barbara Budrich.

Fišer, Zbyněk 2001: Tvůrčí psaní: malá učebnice technik tvůrčího psaní. Brno: Paido.

Flower, Linda & Hayes, John R. (2014): Schreiben als kognitiver Prozess. Eine Theorie. In: Dreyfürst, Stephanie & Sennewald, Nadja (Hrsg.): Schreiben. Grundlagentexte zur Theorie, Didaktik und Beratung. Opladen / Toronto: Verlag Barbara Budrich, 35–56.

Hyland, Ken (2007): Genre pedagogy: Language, literacy and L2 writing instruction. *Journal of Second Language Writing*, roč. 16, č. 1, s. 148–164.

Hyland, Ken (2009): Academic discourse. English in a global context. London: Continuum.

Hyland, Ken (2013): Second language writing: The manufacture of a social fact. In: *Journal of Second Language Writing*, roč. 22, č. 4, 426–427.

Jakobs, Eva-Maria & Perrin, Daniel (Eds.) (2014): Handbook of Writing and Text Production. Handbook of Applied Linguistics, Vol. 10. Berlin, Boston: De Gruyter.

Kästner, Uwe (1997): Freies Schreiben in der Fremdsprache: Prozesse und ihre Didaktik. Untersuchung zur Textproduktion im fremdsprachlichen Deutschunterricht auf dem Hintergrund neuropsychologischer Theorien. Fremdsprachen in Lehre und Forschung 19. Bochum: AKS-Verlag.

Kobayashi, Hiroe & Rinnert, Carol (2013): Second language writing: Is it a separate entity? In: *Journal of Second Language Writing*, roč. 22, č. 4, 442–443.

Kormos, Judit (2012): The role of individual differences in L2 writing. In: *Journal of Second Language Writing*, roč. 21, č. 4, 390–403.

Ruhmann, Gabriela & Kruse, Otto (2014): Prozessorientierte Schreibdidaktik: Grundlagen, Arbeitsformen, Perspektiven. In: Dreyfürst, Stephanie & Sennewald, Nadja (Hrsg.): Schreiben. Grundlagentexte zur Theorie, Didaktik und Beratung. Opladen, Toronto: Barbara Budrich, 15–34.

Společný evropský referenční rámec pro jazyky: jak se učíme jazykům, jak je vyučujeme a jak v jazycích hodnotíme 2006: Council for Cultural Co-operation, Education Committee, Modern Languages Division; Olomouc: Univerzita Palackého.

Sonja Kuri, Ursula Doleschal

Zwölf Module für die Entwicklung von Textkompetenz in DaF/DaZ Didaktische Anmerkungen für Unterrichtende

1 Einleitung

Das vorliegende Kapitel stellt die didaktischen Module zum Schreiben in der Zweit- und Fremdsprache Deutsch vor: Es handelt sich dabei um zwölf verschiedene *Moodle*-Kurse zu jeweils einer Textsorte oder Textsortengruppe.

Das Ziel des dargestellten Projekts ist es, über die Lernplattform *Moodle* Material und Räume zur Entwicklung von Textsortenkompetenz ab der Sprachlernstufe B1 des Europäischen Referenzrahmens anzubieten. Das Schreiben von Texten erfassen wir dabei als lehr- und lernbar, aber nicht einfach als Technik, sondern vor allem als kognitiven Prozess.

Während des institutionalisierten Zweit- und Fremdsprachenerwerbs wird viel gelesen und viel geschrieben. Dabei ist zu konstatieren, dass seit den 1970er Jahren neben die *Mittler*funktion des Schreibens immer stärker die *Mitteilungs*funktion tritt. Kontextualisierte Schreibszenarien sind heute fester Bestandteil des institutionellen Sprachunterrichts, diese bleiben jedoch größtenteils auf wenige kürzere Textgenres beschränkt. Die *heuristische, wissensgenerierende* Funktion des Schreibens wird erst ab der Niveaustufe C1 für das wissenschaftliche Schreiben im universitären Kontext behandelt. Und auch das Lesen bezieht sich vornehmlich auf den Inhalt und den Themenwortschatz, während sprachliche Mittel der Kohärenzherstellung und Leser_innenführung[19] auf den unteren Sprachniveaustufen meist unbeachtet bleiben. Konnektoren, also die expliziten sprachlichen Verknüpfungsmittel, und Rekurrenzen, also die Wiederaufnahmen bestimmter Elemente, werden im Sprachunterricht als grammatische oder lexikalische Phänomene auf Syntaxebene, aber kaum auf Textebene behandelt, dies gilt u.a. auch für die Stellung von Syntagmen am Satzanfang zur Hervorhebung und zur Verbindung von Sätzen und Absätzen. Ansätze, dass bestimmte dieser sprachlichen Mittel in gehäufter Form in Verbindung mit bestimmten Textsorten, Textfunktionen und Textmustern vorkommen, sind vorhanden, werden aber nicht konsequent verfolgt. In diesem Bereich werden in den meisten Lehr-/Lernmaterialien Erkenntnisse der Text(sorten)linguistik nicht ausreichend berücksichtigt.

---

19 Wir halten uns hier an den geschlechtergerechten Sprachgebrauch, wie er vom Zentrum für Frauen- und Geschlechterstudien und der ÖH der Universität Klagenfurt und der WU Wien vorgeschlagen wird. Vgl. „Geschlechtergerechter Sprachgebrauch – Ein Leitfaden von Studierenden" Klagenfurt 2014 und https://www.wu.ac.at/fileadmin/wu/h/structure/about/publications/aktuelle_Brosch%C3%BCren/fair_und_inklusiv.pdf [letzter Zugriff 13.12.2016].

Müssen L2-Lernende andere, komplexere und/oder längere Textgenres wie bspw. eine Bewerbung oder einen Essay verfassen, liegen die Schwierigkeiten dann oft im Übergang „von der persönlichen Perspektive zu einer allgemeinen Perspektive“ (Schmölzer-Eibinger 2008: 144) und „vom kreativen, anschuborientierten Schreiben zum geplanten Wissen verarbeitenden und Wissen generierenden Schreiben“ (Ortner 2002: 242). Als wesentliche Teilfähigkeiten für das erfolgreiche Schreiben werden jedoch gerade Perspektivenübernahme, Adressatenorientierung, Wortschatz und morpho-syntaktische Versiertheit zur Herstellung von Kohärenz angesehen, also Komponenten, die eine umfassende Textplanung erforderlich machen. Es handelt sich dabei um transversale, textsortenunabhängige Teilkomponenten, die auch als solche erfolgreich eingeübt werden können (vgl. Becker-Mrotzek 2015: 177ff, Bräuer & Schindler 2010, Sändig 2009: 164ff). Neben dem mangelnden kulturellen Textsortenwissen und den textsortenspezifischen Vertextungsstrategien wird bei den Schreibstrategien teils erheblicher Nachholbedarf festgestellt (vgl. u.a. Ortner 2002, 2007, Kuri 2005, Steinhoff 2007, Hornung 2009, Kruse 2013)[20].

An den Feststellungen zu den erhobenen Defiziten wird manifest, dass Sprachkompetenz und Textkompetenz nicht dasselbe sind, sondern dass Textkompetenz sich aus mehreren Teilkomponenten zusammensetzt, unter denen die Sprachbasis (Wortschatz und Grammatik) nur eine ist. Wortschatz- und Grammatikarbeit wiederum muss von Texten ausgehen und wieder zu Texten hinführen, um die Lernenden deren situations-, intentions- und adressatenspezifische Verwendung bewusst erfahren zu lassen (vgl. u.a. Kuri 2005: 81f, Kühn 2013: 158f).

In der Konzeption der Module wurden diese und weitere Erkenntnisse aus der Text(sorten)linguistik (u.a. Fandrych & Thurmayr 2013, Hauser, Kleinberger & Roth 2014, Doleschal & Kuri sowie Perissutti in diesem Band) und der Schreibprozessforschung (vgl. Flower & Hayes 1980; Bräuer und Doleschal & Kuri in diesem Band) mit Ansätzen aus der Zweit- und Fremdsprachendidaktik (Feld-Knapp 2009: 116ff; Knorr & Nardi 2011, Schmidt 2005: 142ff, Kuri im Druck) zusammengeführt. In kritischer Auseinandersetzung mit verschiedenen Modellierungen von Textproduktionsprozessen (Doleschal & Kuri in diesem Band) und den teils kritischen Anmerkungen dazu wurden weiters folgende Prämissen der Konzeption der zwölf Module zugrunde gelegt (Skiba 2013: 145, Bräuer in diesem Band, Doleschal & Kuri in diesem Band):

1. Das Schreiben ist keine einsame, sondern eine umfassend kommunikative Aktivität - sowohl während des Erwerbs, als auch später in der Praxis.

---

20 Alle zitierten Beiträge beziehen sich auf den Hochschulbereich, wo diese Phänomene im Zuge der Abfassung von Seminar- und Abschlussarbeiten festgestellt wurden. Vgl. auch Perrin et al. (2003): Schreiben. Der Untertitel der Publikation zum Schreiben in verschiedenen Domänen lautet „Von intuitiven zu professionellen Schreibstrategien“.

2. Unterschiedliche Texte erfordern unterschiedliche Planungs-, Formulierungs- und Umarbeitungsschritte.

3. Während des Schreibprozess braucht es Raum für die Reflexion über unterschiedliche Text- und Schreiberfahrungen und Ausprägungen von individuellen Schreibstrategien und die Möglichkeit, weitere Strategien auszuprobieren.

2 Zwölf Module zu zwölf Textsorten

Die zwölf Module repräsentieren zwölf Textsorten in einigen ihrer möglichen Varianten. Es sind alles sogenannte Sachtexte, die sich von literarischen Gattungen insofern stark unterscheiden, als dass in Sachtexten die wesentlichen Inhalte und deren Beziehungen auf der Textoberfläche explizit versprachlicht werden sollten, während bei literarischen Texten die Kohärenzleistung von den Leser_innen zu leisten ist.[21]

Unter Textsorten verstehen wir historisch gewachsene Einheiten der kommunikativen Praxis einer Gesellschaft, die einem natürlichen Wandel unterliegen und kulturell geprägt sind (vgl. Eßer 1997, Hufeisen 2002, Adamzik 2004, Riehl 2014: 165ff, Fix 2008: 73, Doleschal & Kuri in diesem Band).[22] Um Texte verstehen und selbst herstellen zu können, müssen wir ihre Muster erkennen, also: Wie sind sie aufgebaut? Wie erfolgt die Themenentfaltung? Welche sprachlichen Charakteristika sind typisch?

Textmusterwissen und sprachliches Repertoire sind gleichermaßen an der erfolgreichen Bewältigung von Schreibanforderungen einer bestimmten Textsorte beteiligt. „[D]as Textmusterwissen ist der Rahmen für die Textentfaltung", stellt Ortner (2007: 24) hierzu fest. Dieses Textmusterwissen baut sich graduell auf, der Prozess benötigt Steuerung und Bewusstmachung. Im Laufe der Lernkarriere sollten Lernende ein umfassendes Repertoire von unterschiedlichen Textmustern erwerben (vgl. Feld-Knapp 2009: 124). Damit sind aber nicht Muster im Sinne von Normvorgaben gemeint, sondern „im Sinne der kognitiven Psychologie [als] Möglichkeitsfelder, in denen es sowohl einige überindividuelle Handlungsorientierungen gibt als auch Ermessensspielräume" (Fix 2008: 67), also einerseits Vorgaben und Konventionen, die es einzuhalten gilt, und andererseits Freiräume für individuelle Gestaltung. Es gilt aber, dass man zuerst die

---

21 Damit soll keineswegs das Potenzial von literarischen Texten und das kreative Schreiben für die intellektuelle, sprachliche und interkulturelle Bildung abgewertet werden. Sie wurden nur für das gegenständliche Projekt nicht in Betracht gezogen, weil sie das Projektziel und den Projektrahmen gesprengt hätten. Außerdem besteht in diesem Bereich wenig Nachholbedarf.

22 Es existiert keine einheitliche Definition von Textsorten. Auch wird bspw. diskutiert, ob eine *Zusammenfassung* überhaupt eine Textsorte ist. Vgl. dazu Fix, Poethe & Yos (2003: 73).

Muster erwirbt, um dann mit den Normen bzw. Konventionen bewusst spielen zu können.

Die von uns gewählten und bearbeiteten Textsorten sind:

Modul 01: *Bewerbungsschreiben*

Modul 02: *Reise-/Exkursionsbericht*

Modul 03: *Rezension*

Modul 04: *Leserbrief*

Modul 05: *Werbebroschüre/Werbebrief*

Modul 06: *Beschwerde/Reklamation*

Modul 07: *Motivationsschreiben*

Modul 08: *Kommentar*

Modul 09: *Essay/Erörterung*

Modul 10: *Gutachten*

Modul 11: *Exposé/Erwartungshorizont*

Modul 12: *Inhaltsangabe/Zusammenfassung/Abstract*

Mit diesen zwölf verschiedenen Textsorten wird eine große Bandbreite an verschiedenen Aspekten abgedeckt:

- Die gewählten Textsorten entsprechen programmatisch den Zielgruppen, denen mit der Lernplattform Schreibhilfen angeboten werden sollen: Lernende und Lehrende an Schule und Universität, Journalist_innen, Diplomat_innen, Migrant_innen und Schreibende in der öffentlichen Verwaltung, im Tourismus, in Organisationen und Unternehmen.
- Diese Textsorten haben individuellen und institutionellen Gebrauchswert[23], sie sind konzeptionell schriftliche Textsorten mit expositorischem und argumentativem[24] Charakter, sie repräsentieren ein breites Spektrum an Text-

23 In einer Fragebogenerhebung zu den Schreiberfahrungen und Schreibbedürfnissen von L2-Lernenden, die wir im Rahmen des Projekts durchgeführt haben, wurden fürs Deutsche ein paar wenige Textsorten genannt, für die Übungsbedarf bestehe: *Curriculum vitae, formelle Schreiben/Anfragen, Essay, Bericht, Zusammenfassung*. Diese wurden hier berücksichtigt. Die genannten Textsorten sind Indikatoren, welche Schreiberfahrungen Lernende im gelenkten Zweit- und Fremdsprachenunterricht machen.

24 Becker-Mrotzek et al. (2010) nennen als Beispiele für überwiegend argumentierende Texte *Kommentare, Leserbriefe, Beschwerden/Reklamation, Bittbriefe* und *Anträge, Rezensionen/Besprechungen, Thesenpapiere* und *Statements*. Für die Schule nennen sie die *Erörterung* sowie die *Textanalyse* und *-interpretation*.

funktionen und berücksichtigen notwendigerweise auch die mediale und modale Vielfalt.

- Diese Textsorten sollen in der Lebenswelt der Schreibenden bedeutsam sein oder in der Zukunft bedeutsam werden. So kommt die Wahl den kommunikativen Bedürfnissen von Studien- und Berufs- sowie Freizeitmobilen entgegen, andere Textsorten wiederum eröffnen die Möglichkeit zur direkten gesellschaftlichen Teilhabe wie der *Leserbrief*, der *Kommentar* oder der *Essay*; *Gutachten* sind außer im universitären Bereich auch in anderen Branchen zu finden.
- Die Textsorten sind wissensbereitstellende Texte für unterschiedliche Kontexte und Verwendungsbereiche. Als Beispiel nennen wir hier *Kommentar*, *Rezension* und *Gutachten*.
- Ihre Bandbreite reicht von stark konventionalisierten, wie den Briefen, (gleich drei Module nehmen Textsorten aus der Textsortenklasse Brief auf: Modul 01: *Bewerbungsschreiben*, Modul 04: *Leserbrief*; Modul 06: *Beschwerdebrief/Reklamation*) bis wenig konventionalisierte Textsorten wie die *Werbebroschüre* oder der *Essay*. Es gibt aber auch Textsorten, wie im Modul 07 das *Motivationsschreiben*, das für den Antrag auf Stipendien oder für die Zulassung zu spezifischen Praktika verlangt wird, auf der Textoberfläche entweder eine Briefform, oder aber auch eine essay-ähnliche Form aufweisen kann. Dies hat aber nur unwesentlichen Einfluss auf dessen notwendige Textbausteine.
- Jede dieser Textsorten nimmt entweder explizit Bezug auf andere Texte und/oder verarbeitet diese. Sie tun dies jedoch auf unterschiedliche Weise: So nimmt bspw. ein Leserbrief anders Bezug auf seinen Vortext als eine Rezension, in einem Essay wird anders zitiert als in einem Exposée – aber nicht nur formal, sondern auch in der Art der Vertextung.
- Die gewählten Textsorten sind auf unterschiedliche Weise konfliktträchtig, denn sie involvieren in ihren Inhalten die schreibende Person: Diese stellt sich in den Texten als Ich mit ihrem Wissen und ihrer Meinung dar. Dabei tritt jedoch das schreibende Ich meist nicht als Ich, sondern in unpersönlicher Form auf. Dies stellt für Schreibnoviz_innen eine besondere Schwierigkeit dar: Wie kann ich meine Meinung äußern, ohne *ich* zu sagen? Welche sprachlichen Mittel stehen hierfür zur Verfügung?
- Die Textsorten haben eine interkulturelle Dimension, weil sie zur Auseinandersetzung mit Kommunikationskonventionen sowohl in der Zielkultur als auch in der Ausgangskultur auffordern. Höflichkeit und der Grad von Direktheit und Indirektheit kommen da ebenso in den Fokus, wie Vertextungsmuster oder mögliche vorherrschende Vertextungsmuster. In mehrsprachigen Gesellschaften wie in Südtirol bspw. entwickeln junge deutschsprechende und -lernende Erwachsene im Gegensatz zu ihren Gleichaltrigen im deutschsprachigen Raum viel später das argumentative Textmuster, weil

die Narration eine wesentliche Strategie zur Versicherung der Identität darstellt; auch in argumentativen Texten zu diesem Themenbereich treten oft längere narrative Abschnitte auf, hinzu kommt noch das höhere Prestige narrativer Texte im romanischen Sprachraum. (vgl. Riehl 2014: 141). Wie Kuri (2005) für Italien gezeigt hat, kann das heuristische Schreiben durch unterschiedliche Lehrtraditionen auch an Universitäten schwach entwickelt sein, was mittlerweile durch die Internationalisierung im starken Umbruch ist (vgl. auch Knorr & Nardi 2011).

- Für ihre Abfassung erfordern diese Textsorten Schreibformen und Strategien, die in ihren Variationen zur Ausbildung jener transversalen Fähigkeiten beitragen, die in der Einleitung zu diesem Artikel als wesentlich für gelungenes Schreiben angeführt wurden: *Perspektivenübernahme, Adressatenorientierung, Wortschatz und morpho-syntaktische Versiertheit zur Herstellung von Kohärenz.*

Die Lehr- und Lernmaterialien sollen sowohl zum Erwerb von Schreibkompetenz als auch zum Erwerb geeigneter sprachlicher Mittel führen. Die vorgeschlagenen didaktischen Herangehensweisen sind somit geeignet, bei den Lernenden Kompetenzen auszubilden, die sie auch in der Zukunft auf andere Verwendungssituation übertragen können. In ihrer Vielfältigkeit sind die Schreibaufgaben – von der Planung über den ersten Entwurf bis zur Endredaktion – propädeutisch für weitere komplexe Textsorten und Schreibformen, haben aber auch positiven Einfluss auf komplexere mündlichsprachliche Handlungen, wie das Halten eines Vortrags oder Referats oder die aktive Beteiligung an einer Diskussion.

3 Zum Aufbau der zwölf Module

Jedes Modul besteht aus folgenden Teilen:

- Einleitung
- Tool Pool
- Planungsphase
- Schreibphase
- Selbstevaluation

Mit dieser expliziten Phaseneinteilung wird die Komplexität des Schreibprozesses in überschaubare Schritte zerlegt. Die Phasen veranschaulichen die wesentlichen Teilschritte auf dem Weg zu einem guten Text. Damit soll das Bewusstsein geschaffen werden, dass das Verfassen eines Textes ein komplexer Prozess ist, dass man aber beim Schreiben auf vielfältige Ressourcen und Strategien zurückgreifen und sich diese lesend, schreibend, diskutierend und reflektierend erarbeiten kann.

Als Einstieg gibt es ein Video, in dem der Aufbau des Moduls erklärt wird. Weiters wird interessierten Schreibenden ein Plan vorgeschlagen, wie man mit dem Modul erfolgreich arbeiten kann. Dies ist aber nur ein Angebot. Man kann an jedem Punkt in das Modul einsteigen und jene Aspekte bearbeiten, die man für den eigenen Lernprozess und die eigenen Bedürfnisse als notwendig und wichtig erachtet, und später bei Bedarf auf übersprungene Aspekte zurückgreifen. Wichtig dabei ist nur, dass man sich zuerst im Modul orientiert, um die für den eigenen Bedarf adäquaten Materialien zu wählen und Schritte setzen zu können.

3.1 Die Einleitung

Unter „**Einleitung**" findet man eine umfassende Beschreibung der Textsorte: die Kommunikationssituation mit den Rollen von Produzent_in und Rezipient_in und Textfunktion, die Produktionssituation, die Kommunikationsform / das Medium. In eigenen Rubriken werden jeweils die Entfaltung des Textthemas auf Makro- und Mikrostruktur beschrieben und die sprachlichen Charakteristika wie typische Formulierungen, Konnektoren und morpho-syntaktische Besonderheiten aufgeführt.

Leserbrief

Es handelt sich dabei um **eine Form der öffentlichen Meinungsäußerung** in den entsprechenden Rubriken von Tageszeitungen oder Zeitschriften. Sie bieten ein Forum für alle, aber es besteht kein Anrecht, dass der Leserbrief auch veröffentlicht wird. **Mehr..**

INHALTSVERZEICHNIS

Textbeschreibung

Textstruktur

Argumentationsstrategien

Sprachliche Charakteristika

Literatur

3.2 Der Tool Pool

Unter „**Tool Pool**" finden sich die notwendigen Werkzeuge: Authentische Beispieltexte, jeweils ohne und mit Kommentierungen, illustrieren mögliche Realisierungen dieser Textsorte. Diese Bearbeitung wurde gewählt, um einerseits zu zeigen, wie der Text im Original aussieht, andererseits zu zeigen, welche spezifischen Charakteristika der Textsorte man hier wie realisiert findet. Es handelt sich dabei nicht um sogenannte Prototypen, sondern um authentische Texte; aus diesem Grunde werden pro Textsorte jeweils mindestens 2 Beispiele mit und ohne Kommentierungen angeboten. So lernen Lernende an authentischen

Modellen, wie die thematische Entfaltung innerhalb der Teiltexte einer Textsorte erfolgen und sprachlich umgesetzt werden kann.

Aufgaben und Übungen rund um diese Materialien haben die Funktion, das Textmusterwissen aufzubauen und damit die Basis für das Schreiben der jeweiligen Textsorte zu schaffen. Das Zusammenspiel von Textfunktion, Textarchitektur und sprachlicher Ausgestaltung kann mit den angebotenen Rezeptionsstrategien erkundet und nachvollzogen werden, und mit den angebotenen Übungen können textsortenspezifische Aspekte geübt werden.

Weiterführendes Material und Literaturangaben bieten Interessierten Vertiefungsmöglichkeiten.

Das Lesen spielt bei der Erarbeitung der notwendigen Grundlagen und somit für das Schreiben eine wesentliche Rolle (vgl. dazu bspw. Kruse 2015). Lesend werden die Materialien erkundet und erarbeitet; das Lesen wird in weiterer Folge von Schreibaktivitäten begleitet, wie bspw. dem Notizenmachen beim Ausfüllen des Steckbriefs zur jeweiligen Textsorte.

Überlegt haben wir, wie man den verschiedenen Schreibtypen und Schreibbedürfnissen nachkommen kann, wie das Verfassen eines Textes in Schreibphasen aufgegliedert und wie für die unterschiedlichen Textsorten die einzelnen Phasen inhaltlich und technisch gestaltet werden können und müssen, um den besonderen Bedürfnissen von Schreibenden in der Zweit- und Fremdsprache zu entsprechen.

Wir haben die eigentliche/n Schreibaufgabe/n in Teilschritte zerlegt: in eine *Planungsphase* mit Materialsuche und themen- und textsortenspezifischer sprachlicher Vorbereitung, in eine *Schreibphase* von der Erarbeitung eines Entwurfs über die *Überarbeitungsphase* des Entwurfs bis zur Erstellung eines redaktionsfähigen Textes und die Redaktion des Textes und abschließend die Evaluation des Arbeits- und Lernprozesses.

Sollte es für eine Textsorte verschiedene Ausprägungen geben, werden für jede dieser Ausprägungen differenzierte Schreibaufgaben angeboten: z.B. in Modul 03: Es sind hier für die *Produkt*rezension, die *literarische/filmische* Rezension in Printmedien und Internet und die *wissenschaftliche* Rezension jeweils eigene Schreibaufgaben von der Planung bis zum fertigen Text vorgesehen.

3.3 Die Planungsphase

Unter „**Planungsphase**" werden für die Bewältigung der spezifischen Schreibaufgabe Strategien angeboten, wie man sich der Textsorte nähern kann. Hier werden sie auch nach ihren bisherigen Erfahrungen mit der jeweiligen Textsorte in ihren Sprachen gefragt und welche Phänomene, z.B. kulturelle Ausprägungen, sie bemerkt haben. Und hier finden sie Planungsinstrumente für die inhaltliche, die sprachliche sowie die strukturelle Planung. Diese Instrumente sollen helfen, die Dimensionen der jeweiligen Textsorte in ihren vielfältigen Aspekten erfassen. Damit erfolgt die thematische Planung und die Reflexion, welche thematischen Aspekte für die Zielgruppe relevant und/oder interessant wären, welche eigentlich bekannten thematischen Aspekte in ein neues Licht gerückt werden sollen usw. Hierzu gehört auch die Erarbeitung des Themenwortschatzes. Mittels Tabellen und/oder Leitfragen, aber auch Mindmap und anderen Organisationsschemata können die Schreibenden Planungsschritte ausprobieren und schrittweise ihr Repertoire erweitern.

Planungsphase

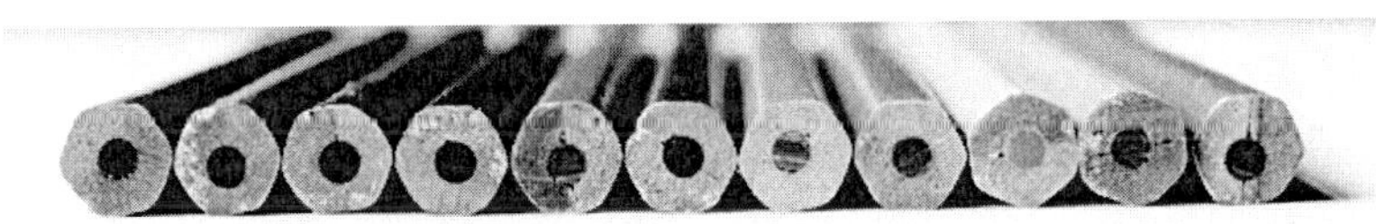

In der *Planungsphase* geht es um einen eigenen Text, den Sie schreiben sollen. Der Abschnitt *Planungsphase* enthält Materialien und Übungen, die Sie bei der Themenfindung unterstützen, die Ihnen helfen, Ideen, Informationen und Quellen zu finden und einen Plan und eine Struktur für Ihren Text zu entwickeln. Sie finden Aufgaben und Übungen zum Schreiben von Skizzen und Entwürfen als Vorarbeiten für den eigentlichen Text.

Planung eines Leserbriefes

Kooperative Ideen- und Themensammlung

Auch hier spielt das Lesen eine gewichtige Rolle, ob bei der genauen Lektüre einer Stellenausschreibung, ob beim Lesen des Referenztextes für einen Leserbrief oder bei der thematischen und sprachlichen Vorbereitung einer Werbebroschüre oder eines Exkursionsberichts. Auch hier werden Notizen gemacht und Exzerpte als Vorbereitung des Schreibens erstellt.

Wie in jeder Phase gibt es auch hier ein *Forum* für kollaborative Aktivitäten.[25]

3.4 Die Schreibphase

Unter „**Schreibphase**" finden Schreibende je nach Charakteristik und Komplexität der Textsorte unterschiedlich viele Schreibschritte; Textfelder geben Hilfestellung zur Strukturierung und inhaltliche Entfaltung des Themas vor und bieten Hilfestellung für das Formulieren der ersten Fassung, die man einer ersten Umarbeitung und daraufhin einem Feedback unterziehen möchte.

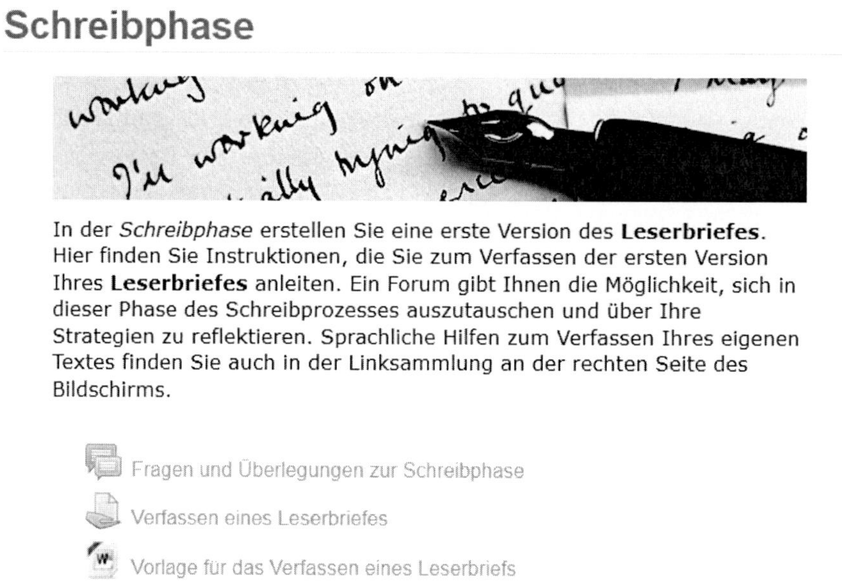

Dass Schreibende unterschiedlich vorgehen und dass unterschiedliche Strategien zu einem guten Text führen können, weiß man spätestens seit Ortners umfassender Studie *Schreiben und Denken* (2000). Zwischen den Strategien sogenannter Strukturfolger und jener von Strukturschaffern (Bräuer und Doleschal & Kuri in diesem Band) gibt es eine große Bandbreite an Strategien, die selten in ihrer Reinform auftreten. In WRILAB2 sollen Schreibende ihre präferierten und/oder habitualisierten Vorgehensweisen anwenden können, ohne auf die bisher vertrauten und/oder persönlich erfolgreichen Strategien verzichten zu müssen. Sie sollen ihre Vorgehensweisen aber reflektieren und überprüfen, ob sie

25 Hier verweisen wir auf Abschnitte 4, 5 und 6 dieses Beitrags, in denen wir auf verschiedene Aspekte des kollaborativen Arbeitens im Rahmen des Verfassens von Texten näher eingehen.

für das jeweilige Schreibprojekt angemessen sind und dann jene Schritte und Strategien in ihre Arbeitsweise integrieren, die ihr Schreiben unterstützen. Sie sollen erkennen, dass es nicht *die* richtige Vorgehensweise gibt, sondern nur eine in Hinblick auf die Textsorte adäquatere oder weniger adäquate. Wie schon in der Planungsphase gibt es auch hier ein *Forum* für den Austausch mit anderen.

Die Schreibphase erscheint im Vergleich zur vorhergehenden Planungsphase und zur nachfolgenden Überarbeitungsphase eher kurz. Sie wurde aber ganz bewusst so gestaltet, um die beiden anderen Aspekte beim Verfassen eines Textes stärker zu betonen, nämlich die Notwendigkeit einer guten Planung und die wichtige Funktion verschiedener Schritte der Überarbeitung (vgl. Doleschal & Kuri in diesem Band).

3.5 Die Überarbeitungsphase

Unter „**Überarbeitungsphase**" finden die Schreibenden je nach Komplexität und Länge der Textsorte zwei bis mehrere Schritte. Einer davon ist immer die eigene *Überarbeitung nach Vorgaben*, d.h. anhand von Leitfragen, die nochmals die wesentlichen Aspekte des Schreibprojekts in Erinnerung rufen, und die *Überarbeitung nach Feedback*.

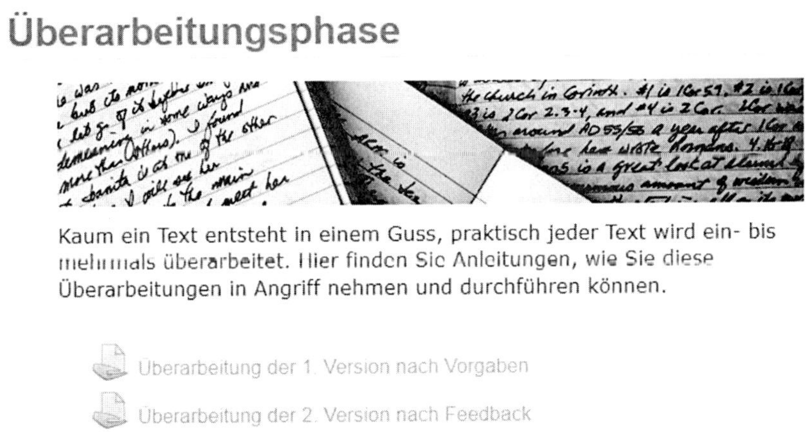

Am Ende der Überarbeitungsphase werden die Schreiber_innen aufgefordert, ihre „fertigen" Texte auf die Plattform hochzuladen, wo sie einer breiteren Leserschaft zugänglich sind. Dies kann die persönliche Bedeutsamkeit erhöhen und sie dazu motivieren, verstärkt an ihren individuellen Ausdrucksmöglichkeiten zu arbeiten.

3.6 Die Selbstevaluation

Jedes Modul schließt mit der „**Selbstevaluation**" ab. Hier sollen die Schreiber_innen nochmals auf ihren Lernweg zurückblicken und über das Material, dessen Verwendung und den Lernzuwachs reflektieren.

Selbstevaluation

In dieser Phase schauen Sie nochmals zurück und reflektieren Ihren Lernweg und Ihre Lernzuwächse auf verschiedenen Ebenen: über die Textsorte und ihre Charakteristika und über die Materialien und Aufgaben und Übungen dieses Moduls.

Die Textsorte Leserbrief im interkulturellen Vergleich

Was ich in diesem Modul gelernt habe

Reflexion des Moduls

3.7 Die Hilfsmittel

In jeder Phase hat man in der rechten Spalte des Bildschirms Zugriff auf empfehlenswerte **Online-Ressourcen** wie Wörterbücher und Datenbanken; sie bieten sprachliche Hilfestellungen und unterstützen die Autonomie der Lesenden, Übenden und Schreibenden. Damit sollen sie ermuntert werden, sich selbständig sprachliche Mittel zu erschließen und Formulierungen auf ihre Adäquatheit und Richtigkeit zu überprüfen.

ALLGEMEINE LINKSAMMLUNG

Das Deutsche Wörterbuch von Jakob und Wilhelm Grimm

Wortschatz Uni Leipzig

Das Digitale Wörterbuch der Deutschen Sprache

Elexiko Online-Wörterbuch zur deutschen Gegenwartssprache

Wörterbuch Duden Online

Grammatisches Wörterbuch des Instituts für deutsche Sprache (ids)

Neben den bisher beschriebenen Aspekten wird besonderes Augenmerk auf Feedback gelegt. Dies ist ein alle Phasen des Schreibens begleitendes Instrumentarium, das im nächsten Abschnitt behandelt wird.

4 Feedback und Bewertung

Die didaktischen Einheiten von WRILAB2 orientieren sich wie oben ausgeführt an einer prozessorientierten Schreibdidaktik. Das heißt, dass ein Text nicht in einem Guss niedergeschrieben wird, sondern mehrere Phasen durchläuft, bis er als fertig angesehen werden kann. In jeder dieser Phasen kommt dem Feedback eine besondere Rolle zu. Feedback sollte also nicht erst zum praktisch fertigen Text gegeben werden, sondern in jeder Phase auf dem Weg zum fertigen Text: So wurde in den Modulen in jeder Phase ein Forum vorgesehen, mittels dessen Schreibende Feedback von Peers und/oder von Lehrenden einholen können.

Aus schreibdidaktischen Untersuchungen geht hervor, dass Schreibende Rückmeldungen zu ihren Texten in der Regel schätzen (vgl. dazu Doleschal & Kuri in diesem Band). Auch in einer Fragebogenerhebung zu den Schreiberfahrungen und Schreibbedürfnissen von L2-Lernenden, die wir im Rahmen des Projekts durchgeführt haben, hat gezeigt, dass sich die Befragten Kommentare zu ihren Texten wünschen und mit Korrekturen ohne Kommentar weniger zufrieden sind.

Egal ob das Feedback von Peers oder von Lehrenden kommt – es muss ihm ein Kriterienkatalog zugrunde liegen. Ansonsten können die Schreibenden das Feedback nicht eindeutig einordnen und in eine Überarbeitung umsetzen. Dasselbe gilt für die abschließende Bewertung von Texten. Dieser Kriterienkatalog, der sich aus der jeweiligen Textbeschreibung mit ihren spezifischen Charakteristika ergibt, soll schon vor der Schreibaufgabe vermittelt werden und es soll klar sein, dass sich Feedback und Bewertung daran orientieren werden.

Wenn Peerfeedback durch Mitlernende geplant ist, ist es wichtig, die Peers darauf hinzuweisen, dass auch ihr Beitrag unter Beobachtung steht und es daher nicht egal ist, ob sie sich an den Kriterienkatalog halten. Die Anwendung der Kriterien ist keine reine Formalität oder eine Frage des guten Tons, sondern das Feedbackgeben hat auch eine Lernfunktion. Durch das Anwenden der Kriterien auf die Texte anderer lernt man die Identifizierung der wichtigen Punkte.

Betrachten wir dazu als Beispiele das Exposé von Modul 11, und dabei wieder zwei Kriterien – Struktur und inhaltliche Füllung.

<u>1. Struktur:</u>

Jedes Exposé hat ein Deckblatt und ein Inhaltsverzeichnis. Das Inhaltsverzeichnis sollte folgende Punkte umfassen:

- das Thema Ihres Projekts
- eine Einordnung in den wissenschaftlichen Diskurs (Abriss des Forschungsstandes und Identifizierung der Forschungslücke)
- die Fragestellung (Forschungsfrage)

- die Zielsetzung des Projekts und die erwarteten Ergebnisse
- die geplante Vorgehensweise (Methode) und das verwendete Material (Daten)
- die Arbeitsschritte und die Zeitplanung
- Wenn es bei dem Exposé oder Konzept um einen Antrag auf Förderung geht, muss es auch einen Finanzierungsplan beinhalten.

Anhand einer solchen Strukturvorgabe lässt sich die Struktur des Textes beurteilen. Allerdings muss dieses Inhaltsverzeichnis auch ein Pendant im tatsächlichen Text finden. Daher brauchen wir für den Kriterienkatalog auch minimale Vorgaben zur inhaltlichen Füllung:

<u>2. inhaltliche Füllung</u>

- Im ersten Abschnitt führen Sie in das Thema Ihrer Arbeit ein: Was wird behandelt?
- Im zweiten Abschnitt skizzieren Sie den Forschungsstand zu Ihrem Thema und wie sich dieses darin einordnen lässt. Wenn es eine Forschungslücke gibt, so nennen Sie diese und erklären, wie Sie sie füllen wollen.
- Dann erklären Sie Ihre Forschungsfrage bzw. Fragestellung. Sie können die Fragestellung in Form von Fragen darstellen.
- Anschließend formulieren Sie, welche Ziele Sie mit Ihrer Arbeit verfolgen und welche Ergebnisse Sie erwarten können. Dieser Teil kann unter Umständen fehlen oder wird schon am Anfang des Exposés genannt.
- Einer der wichtigsten Teile des Exposés ist die Darstellung des Materials und der Methode und ihre Begründung. Hier müssen Sie argumentieren und erklären, wieso gerade dieses Material und diese Methode am geeignetsten für die Beantwortung Ihrer Forschungsfrage sind und zum Erreichen Ihrer Ziele beitragen.
- Arbeitsschritte und Zeitplanung sollten in Form einer Tabelle übersichtlich dargestellt werden (vgl. Frank, Haacke & Lahm 2007, Huemer, Rheindorf & Gruber 2012).

Die Feedbackgeber_innen müssen also prüfen, ob der Text 1) formal dem geforderten Aufbau entspricht und 2) ob auch „drin ist, was drauf steht", das heißt, ob die inhaltliche Füllung tatsächlich den Überschriften entspricht. Und das soll beurteilt und rückgemeldet werden.

Beim Geben von Feedback ist es allerdings wichtig, nicht zu viele Punkte auf einmal anzusprechen: Z.B. finden Sie drei Punkte, die Ihnen besonders gefallen haben und drei Punkte, die Sie verbesserungswürdig finden.

Damit das Feedback angenommen werden kann, muss es erstens wertschätzend sein und zweitens nachvollziehbar, also konkret begründet.

Oft ist es hilfreich, offene Fragen zu stellen anstatt Feststellungen zu treffen, Wahrnehmungen zu formulieren und nicht zu interpretieren. Damit wird der Dialog mit den Schreibenden über ihre Gedanken und Reflexionen eröffnet und führt bei diesen zu weiteren Reflexionen. Den Lehrenden wird damit auch die Möglichkeit eröffnet zu verstehen, was zu den Entscheidungen geführt hat und worin mögliche Schwierigkeiten wirklich liegen könnten. Die Hilfestellungen werden damit personalisierter und zielgerichteter; die Schreibenden bekommen Angebote, einen eigenen Weg zu gehen. Feedback erfordert eine umfassende Sensibilität gegenüber den Produkten.

Daraus ergeben sich die Kriterien für gutes Feedback. Diese Kriterien sollten sein:

- exemplarisch (bei vielen Mängeln)
- beschränkte Anzahl von positiven und weniger positiven Rückmeldungen (bei Peerfeedback)
- Peerfeedback sollte argumentativ sein
- Feedback sollte verarbeitet werden
- Überarbeitung muss folgen, damit es Sinn hat und zu einem Lerneffekt führt

Zum Feedback sollen Texte in ihren unterschiedlichen Phasen der Entstehung vorgelegt werden können, also auch schon in der Planungsphase als Skizzen. WRILAB2 sieht daher in jeder Phase explizit ein ***Forum*** für Austausch und Feedback vor. Diese Textversionen können Mängel und Lücken auf allen Ebenen, strukturell/formal, inhaltlich und sprachlich, aufweisen. Hier muss die_der Feedbackgeber_in in jeder Phase entscheiden, zu welchen Aspekten zu einem bestimmten Zeitpunkt welches Feedback notwendig und zielführend ist: Damit treten in den ersten Phasen morpho-syntaktische Fehler weit in den Hintergrund, denn durch inhaltliche und strukturelle Umarbeitungen werden diese eliminiert und treten an anderer Stelle in anderer Weise wieder auf. Natürlich muss man Schreibende auf eklatante sprachliche Mängel, die der Textsorte und dem Textmuster nicht entsprechen, aufmerksam machen. Und natürlich kann man die Lernenden dazu anhalten, jeweils vor der Abgabe einer Version auf die Verständlichkeit der Ausführungen zu achten und sie auf die Hilfsmittel und Online-Ressourcen aufmerksam zu machen. Aber Feedback bedeutet nicht Fehlerkorrektur.

Feedback sollte somit auch angeben, was zuerst und was später angegangen werden soll, also zuerst die inhaltliche Vertiefung, das Textmuster und die textsortenspezifische Entfaltung des Themas mit Fokus auf Adressatenorientierung und Kohäsionsherstellung bzw. Leser_innenführung, und abschließend die sprachlich korrekte Ausführung.

Feedback ist also nicht Beurteilung. Lehrende verstehen wir hier als Begleitpersonen auf dem Weg zu einer textsortenadäquaten persönlichen Ausdrucksweise. Zur Beurteilung verweisen wir hier auf den Beitrag von Vedder in diesem Band.

5 Zu den Sprachniveaus der einzelnen Module

Es ist heutzutage praktisch unerlässlich, dass sich Sprachlehr-/-lernmaterialien am *Gemeinsamen europäischen Referenzrahmen für Sprachen* (GER) orientieren. Wie in Doleschal, Gindl & Kuri (2016) angeführt und in Kuri (im Druck) ausgeführt, ist der GER, der in seiner Konzeption noch dem kommunikativem, also dem mündlichen Paradigma verpflichtet ist, im Bereich des Schreibens nicht sehr aussagekräftig: Es sind nur wenige Textsorten explizit angeführt, der Fokus liegt auf den kognitiven Operationen, die auf den einzelnen Stufen schriftsprachlich bewältigt werden sollen. Auch sind wir mit der Zuordnung der Rezension zum Kreativen Schreiben nicht einverstanden (siehe Niveau B2.1), da die Rezension eine funktionale Textsorte mit genau definierten Funktionen und Ansprüchen ist. Hier verweisen wir auf die Textsortenbeschreibung, die Beschreibung des Aufbaus und die sprachlichen Charakteristika in Modul 03 auf der WRILAB2-Plattform.

Für die vorliegenden zwölf Module geben wir in der folgenden Tabelle eine Grobzuordnung, ab welcher Niveaustufe man mit welcher Textsorte beginnen kann, auch wenn die angebotenen Materialien in ihrer Konzeption und ihrem Umfang stufenübergreifend angelegt sind. Innerhalb der einzelnen Module, wie bspw. bei Rezension, Beschwerde/Reklamation, Leserbrief oder auch Zusammenfassung/Inhaltsangabe/Abstract sind jeweils mehrere Schreibaufgaben vorgesehen, die unterschiedlich komplex und damit auch schon problemlos ab einem konsolidiertem B1-Niveau angegangen werden können: Die Zusammenfassung des Inhalts eines Films kann bereits auf der B1-Stufe gelingen, während die Zusammenfassung eines wissenschaftlichen Berichts auch auf C1-Niveau eine unüberwindliche Schwierigkeit sein kann.

Die Bewältigung einer spezifischen Schreibaufgabe hängt, wie wir oben bereits ausgeführt haben, nicht nur von den allgemeinen Sprachkenntnissen ab, sondern von vielen weiteren Faktoren. Diese wären

- das zu behandelnde Thema mit seinem spezifischen Themenwortschatz
- die Erfahrungen mit verschiedenen Formen von Sprache

- mentale Konzepte, die durch vorangegangene Lese- und Schreiberfahrungen entwickelt werden konnten (vgl. Doleschal/Kuri in diesem Band)
- die spezifische Aufgabenstellung für das Schreibprojekt
- die zur Verfügung stehenden Ausgangsmaterialien für die thematische und sprachliche Bewältigung, wie themenspezifische Texte, Textsortenmodelle, Textsortenbeschreibungen mit deren sprachlichen Charakteristika
- eine gute Schreibbegleitung und Feedback-Kultur
- und nicht zuletzt die Relevanz des zu erstellenden Textes für den_die Schreiber_in zum Erstellungszeitraum (vgl. Bräuer in diesem Band)

Mit der folgenden Tabelle wird eine Grobzuordnung der einzelnen Einheiten und Materialien zu den Niveaubeschreibungen des Gemeinsamen europäischen Referenzrahmens für Sprachen (GER) vorgenommen. Die linke Spalte führt an, welche der Textsorten und Textoperationen auf dieser Stufe bereits sprachlich bewältigt werden können.[26] Dies impliziert, dass für das Erreichen der jeweiligen Stufe man mit der Arbeit an den verschiedenen Aspekten der nächsthöheren Stufe schon auf der niedrigeren beginnen muss.

Unsere Probekurse haben ergeben, dass Mithilfe der verfügbaren Online-Ressourcen und der notwendigen didaktischen Begleitung im Rahmen von Klassenunterricht oder *Blended-learning*-Kursen die Materialien erfolgreich auf den hier angegebenen Niveaustufen eingesetzt werden können. Wie dies organisiert werden kann, behandelt der nächste Abschnitt.

---

26 Die Tabelle stellt eine Zusammenstellung der drei Tabellen im GER S. 67-68 dar. Die Hervorhebungen wurden von uns vorgenommen.

	GER			Modul
B1	Schriftliche Produktion allgemein Kann unkomplizierte, **zusammenhängende Texte** zu mehreren vertrauten Themen aus seinem/ihrem Interessengebiet verfassen, wobei einzelne kürzere Teile in linearer Abfolge verbunden werden.	Kreatives Schreiben Kann **unkomplizierte, detaillierte Beschreibungen** zu einer Reihe verschiedener Themen aus seinem/ihrem Interessengebiet verfassen. Kann **Erfahrungsberichte** schreiben, in denen Gefühle und Reaktion in einem einfachen, zusammenhängenden Text beschrieben werden. Kann eine **Beschreibung eines realen oder fiktiven Ereignisses** oder einer kürzlich unternommenen Reise verfassen. Kann eine **Geschichte erzählen.**	Berichte und Aufsätze schreiben B1.1 Kann **in einem üblichen Standardformat sehr kurze Berichte** schreiben, in denen Sachinformationen weitergegeben und Gründe für Handlungen angegeben werden. B1.2 Kann einen kurzen, einfachen Aufsatz[i] zu Themen von allgemeinem Interesse schreiben. Kann im eigenen Sachgebiet mit einer gewissen Sicherheit größere Mengen von Sachinformationen über vertraute Routineangelegenheiten und über weniger routinemäßige **Dinge zusammenfassen,** darüber **berichten** und dazu **Stellung nehmen.**	Modul 01: **Bewerbungsschreiben** Modul 02: **Reise-/Exkursionsbericht** Modul 03: **Rezension** Modul 04: **Leserbrief** Modul 05: **Werbebroschüre/-brief** Modul 12: **Inhaltsangabe/Zusammenfassung/Abstract**
B2	Schriftliche Produktion allgemein Kann **klare detaillierte Texte** zu verschiedenen Themen aus seinem/ihrem Interessengebiet verfassen und dabei **Informationen und Argumente aus verschiedenen Quellen zusammenführen** und **gegeneinander abwägen.**	Kreatives Schreiben B2.1 Kann **klare detaillierte Beschreibungen** zu verschiedenen Themen aus seinem/ihrem Interessengebiet verfassen. Kann eine **Rezension**[ii] eines Films, eines Buchs oder Theaterstücks schreiben. B2.2 Kann klare, detaillierte zusammenhängende **Beschreibungen** realer oder fiktiver Ereignisse und Erfahrungen verfassen, dabei den Zusammenhang zwischen verschiedenen Ideen deutlich machen und die **für das betreffende Genre geltenden Konventionen** beachten.	Berichte und Aufsätze schreiben B2.1 Kann in einem **Aufsatz** oder **Bericht etwas erörtern,** dabei Gründe für oder gegen einen bestimmten Standpunkt angeben und die Vor- und Nachteile verschiedener Optionen erläutern. Kann **Informationen und Argumente aus verschiedenen Quellen zusammenführen.** B2.2 Kann einen **Aufsatz** oder **Bericht** schreiben, in dem etwas systematisch **erörtert** wird, wobei entscheidende Punkte angemessen hervorgehoben und stützende Details angeführt werden. Kann verschiedene **Ideen oder Problemlösungen gegeneinander abwägen.**	Modul 06: **Beschwerde/Reklamation** Modul 07: **Motivationsschreiben** Modul 08: **Kommentar** Modul 09: **Essay/Erörterung** Modul 12: **Inhaltsangabe/Zusammenfassung/Abstract**
C1	Schriftliche Produktion allgemein Kann **klare, gut strukturierte Texte zu komplexen Themen** verfassen und dabei die entscheidenden Punkte hervorheben, Standpunkte ausführlich darstellen und durch Unterpunkte oder geeignete Beispiele oder Begründungen stützen und den Text durch einen angemessenen Schluss abrunden.	Kreatives Schreiben Kann **klare, detaillierte, gut strukturierte und ausführliche Beschreibungen** oder auch **eigene fiktionale Texte** in **lesergerechtem, überzeugendem, persönlichem und natürlichem Stil** verfassen.	Berichte und Aufsätze schreiben Kann **klare, gut strukturierte Ausführungen zu komplexen Themen** schreiben und dabei zentrale Punkte hervorheben. Kann **Standpunkte ausführlich darstellen** und durch Unterpunkte, geeignete Beispiele oder Begründungen stützen.	Modul 10: **Gutachten** Modul 11: **Exposé/Erwartungshorizont**

[i] Das englische *essay* wird in der deutschen Übersetzung des Referenzrahmens als *Aufsatz* bezeichnet. Das Modul 09: *Essay/Erörterung* in WRILAB2 nimmt mit *Erörterung* die Aspekte eines typischen deutschsprachigen Schulaufsatzes auf, wie auch den *Essay* als journalistische Textsorte.

[ii] Es ist interessant, dass im GER die Abfassung einer *Rezension* unter Kreatives Schreiben angeführt wird.

6 Wie die Module im Unterricht eingesetzt werden können

Jedes Modul ist gleich aufgebaut und man findet vielfältige Materialien, um das Schreiben der spezifischen Textsorte zu erlernen. Damit kann jedes Modul einzeln und unabhängig von anderen verwendet werden.

Die Module sind für das Selbststudium geeignet; Lernende finden hier für ihr individuelles Studium zum Schreiben umfassende Unterstützung, aber auch Muttersprachler_innen, die textstrukturelle und/oder sprachliche Zweifel haben, können Gewinn daraus ziehen.[27] Besonders erfolgreich sind die Module in gesteuerten Lernsettings wie *Blended Learning* oder Klassenunterricht einsetzbar, wie die Kurse in unserer Testphase gezeigt haben.

Der Aufbau jeder Einheit ist so gestaltet, dass sowohl induktive als auch deduktive Vorgehensweisen möglich sind: Man kann systematisch die Materialien durcharbeiten und dann das Schreiben angehen, oder man beginnt mit dem Schreiben und greift bei Bedarf auf die Materialien zurück. Die Aufgaben müssen nicht alle abgearbeitet werden: Sie sind als modulares Angebot zu verstehen, aus denen Unterrichtende und Lernende je nach Bedarf schöpfen können. In unserer Testphase hat sich in einem Kurs jedoch gezeigt, dass alle unsere Proband_innen beim 1. zu erstellendem Text sofort mit dem Schreiben begannen und die Angebote im Tool Pool nicht benutzten sowie die Planungsphase gänzlich übersprangen. Sie begründeten dies mit Zeitmangel. Die Ergebnisse zeigten große Abweichungen von der Textsorte und deren spezifischen Vertextungsstrategien; die Sätze waren kaum durch entsprechende sprachliche Mittel kohärent miteinander verbunden. In Kursen der Testphase mit starker Begleitung durch die Unterrichtenden zeigten sich hingegen bessere Resultate. Eine genaue Analyse ist in Vorbereitung.

Mit den Modulen lassen sich in heterogenen Gruppen damit problemlos Differenzierungen vornehmen. So kann durch die sprachniveau-orientierte Auswahl von Aufgaben und Übungen und/oder durch unterschiedliche Themen und Textsortenvarianten den Bedürfnissen Einzelner entsprochen werden. Als Beispiel kann hier wieder das Modul 04 *Rezension* herangezogen werden: Einige verfassen eine Produktrezension, andere eine Rezension zu einem Buch oder einen Film.

Den besonderen Interessen und Bedürfnissen kann aber auch durch die parallele Bearbeitung unterschiedlicher Module entgegengekommen werden. So könnten einige ein Bewerbungsschreiben (Modul 01), andere ein Motivationsschreiben (Modul 10) verfassen.

Mittels einer sogenannten *story-line* (vgl. dazu Bräuer in diesem Band) können mehrere Module zu längeren Schreibkursen zusammengefügt werden.

---

27 Vgl. dazu bspw. Sändig (2010: 220f), die über die Schwierigkeiten von Muttersprachler_innen berichtet.

Hier ein Beispiel:[28]

> Die Studierenden planen ein fiktives Auslandssemester für die Erstellung einer wissenschaftlichen Arbeit. Zu Beginn müssen sie sich für ein Stipendium für dieses Auslandssemester bewerben, das ein Motivationsschreiben (Modul 07) verlangt. In der Gastuniversität sollen sie in schriftlicher und mündlicher Form ihr Thema vorstellen. Dafür erstellen sie einen Essay (Modul 09), in dem sie die wichtigsten Quellen zu ihrem Thema gegenüberstellen (Kontroversenreferat). Für das Gespräch mit der_dem Betreuer_in müssen die Studierenden ein Exposé (Modul 11) vorlegen. Die Informationen, die sie für den Essay gesammelt haben, können hierfür hilfreich sein. Bei einer Tagung sollen sie ihre Arbeit vorstellen. Die Tagungsorganisation möchte ein Abstract (Paper Abstract, Modul 12) für die Homepage.
>
> Dauer: 4 Einheiten über 10 Wochen

Wenn gewünscht, kann das Schreibprojekt noch mit Modul 02: *Reisebericht* erweitert werden. Aus Erfahrung sollten jedoch nicht mehr als 4 Module in so einem Schreibprojekt vorgesehen werden, da die Dauer des Projekts zu lang wird.

Schreiben soll durch persönliche aktive Beteiligung als kommunikativ, wissensgenerierend und lustfördernd erlebt werden. Die Mitglieder von Lerngruppen müssen, wie dies WRILAB2 vorsieht, nicht gemeinsam vor Ort sein, sondern können auf der Moodle-Plattform zusammengeführt und begleitet werden, sodass die Lernenden orts- und zeitunabhängig an ihren Aufgaben arbeiten können. Mittels Chat und Forum besteht die Möglichkeit, sich bei Bedarf praktisch jederzeit Unterstützung holen zu können, andererseits aber auch nur zu bestimmten Terminen online sein zu müssen, um sich darüber auszutauschen, wie der Arbeitsprozess verläuft; Austausch und Hilfe geben und Hilfe über Feedback zu bekommen trägt zur Sicherheit bei. Hierzu ist es natürlich notwendig, dass vorher die Spielregeln und Termine festgelegt werden und dass sich alle daran halten. Damit kann dem Zeitproblem begegnet werden, das uns gegenüber immer wieder von Sprachunterrichtenden als Argument gegen die umfassende Bearbeitung von Schreibaufgaben vorgebracht wurde. Das zeitintensive Recherchieren und Planen sowie das eigentliche Schreiben wird aus dem Präsenzunterricht ausgelagert, wo Platz geschaffen wird für die Kommunikation über die Anforderungen des Schreibens und über Texte und deren Verfasstheit.

Auch arbeitsteilige Aufgaben sind möglich, vor allem bei jenen Textsorten, die aus klar definierten Teiltexten bestehen, wie bspw. die literarische/filmische Rezension fürs Internet: Zuerst erfolgt eine gemeinsame sprachliche und inhaltliche Planung und die Verteilung der Aufgaben. Darauf folgt die individuelle[29]

---

[28] Diese *story* wurde von Michaela Gindl, Universität Klagenfurt, für einen Online-Kurs entwickelt.

[29] Man kann das Formulieren in Paar- oder Kleingruppenformation vornehmen lassen. Wir haben aber die Erfahrung gemacht, dass Lernende lieber allein formulieren,

Schreibphase: Eine Person schreibt eine Zusammenfassung eines Films, die andere beschäftigt sich mit Hintergrundinformationen und der Einordnung des Werks, eine dritte verfasst den Kritikteil. Die Umarbeitungsaktivitäten bis zum fertigen kohärenten Text erfordern dann wieder Kooperation.

Und schließlich gibt es noch die Möglichkeit der Kooperation in allen Phasen, auch des gemeinsamen Formulierens.

Es bieten sich also verschiedene Formen des kollaborativen Schreibens an: Das sogenannte *interactive writing* entspricht unserem ersten Beispiel, wo Lernende in verschiedenen Phasen miteinander interagieren und sich austauschen, aber dann jeweils für den fertigen Text die Verantwortung und die Autorschaft haben. Im zweiten und dritten Beispiel, die (wieder nach Louth in Woitkowski 2012: 16) echtes *group writing* repräsentieren, sind alle Gruppenmitglieder an allen Teilprozessen aktiv beteiligt und teilen sich die Verantwortung und die Autorschaft.

Diese kollaborativen Formen entsprechen authentischen und zeitgemäßen Schreibformen unter Ausnutzung der technischen Möglichkeiten, eben vom quasi lektorbegleiteten Verfassen eines Textes bis zur gemeinsamen Autorschaft, letzteres erfordert aber eine_n Moderator_in, die_der den Verlauf und den Fortschritt im Auge behält; auch müssen die Arbeitsgruppen klein und übersichtlich gehalten werden. (vgl. Woitkowski 2012: 135ff).

Die zwölf Module ersetzen keinen Sprachkurs, sie bereichern ihn aber nicht nur, sondern komplettieren diesen durch die konsequente Berücksichtigung textorientierter Aspekte.

Mit dem Sprechen über Textsorten und deren Charakteristika und persönliche Schreiberfahrungen und -strategien wird eine neue Kultur im Umgang mit Schreiben und Texten realisiert (vgl. Feld-Knapp 2010: 190). Die Konzentration der Unterrichtenden liegt somit nicht mehr auf dem Schreibprodukt mit seinen Defiziten, sondern auf dem Prozess als Voraussetzung für das Gelingen des Produkts. Damit wird auch der Forderung nach möglichst hoher Authentizität im Umgang mit Texten und dem Schreiben entsprochen (u.a. Bräuer 2010, Woitkowski 2012).

Die notwendigen Hilfestellungen, wie dies technisch von den Unterrichtenden eingerichtet und durchgeführt werden kann, gibt das **Technische Handbuch** auf der WRILAB2-Homepage.

7 Sich die Technik nutzbar machen

Die Module stehen sowohl in einer Online-Version als auch jedes einzeln als Download-Paket gratis zur Verfügung. Letztere Version erlaubt, jedes Modul

---

was Eßer (1997: 183) und Woitkowski (2012: 138) bestätigen. Andererseits hat sich gezeigt, dass das gemeinsame Formulieren auch sprachfördernd sein kann. Vgl. dazu Faistauers Studie *Wir müssen zusammenschreiben* von 1997.

auf die eigene Moodle-Plattform herunterzuladen und es auch spezifischen Bedürfnissen anzupassen, so kann es auch individuell weiterentwickelt werden. Hier ein Beispiel: Für die Zusammenfassung des Inhalts eines Films oder eines literarischen Werks für eine Rezension können bei Bedarf zuerst die hierfür notwendigen Aspekte aus dem Modul 12 erarbeitet werden. Zu diesem Zwecke können die entsprechenden Materialien aus Modul 12 in das Modul 04: *Rezension* kopiert werden.

Auch hierfür gibt das **Technische Handbuch** von Michaela Gindl auf der WRILAB2-Plattform Hilfestellung.

Voraussetzung für die kostenfreie Verwendbarkeit der Materialien sind die *Creative-Commons-Lizenzen*. Jede Aufgabe, jede Übung, jeder Text ist in der Fußzeile mit einem der folgenden Symbole versehen. Diese erklären, welche Materialien wie verwendet werden dürfen.

Die von uns verwendete Lizenz setzt sich aus den folgenden Symbolen zusammen:

by – Attribution / Namensnennung: Der Name der Urheberin / des Urhebers muss genannt werden.

nc – Non commercial / nicht kommerziell: Eine kommerzielle Nutzung ist nicht gestattet.

sa – Share alike / Weitergabe unter gleichen Bedingungen: Werden die Materialien bearbeitet, so muss die bearbeitete Version unter vergleichbaren Bedingungen / einer vergleichbaren Lizenz weitergegeben werden.

Diese Lizenz erlaubt also die Nutzung und die Veränderung der Materialien. Auch die veränderten Materialien dürfen weitergegeben werden, allerdings unter der Bedingung, dass die Urheberin/der Urheber des Originals genannt und die neue Version unter derselben Lizenz veröffentlicht wird. Weder die originalen noch die veränderten Materialien dürfen kommerziell genutzt werden.

Diese Symbole befinden sich auch auf den Beispieltexten mit und ohne Kommentar im Tool Pool. Nur für den Beispieltext 1 zum Leserbrief mit und ohne Kommentar gilt eine eingeschränkte und befristete Verwendungszusage seitens des Suhrkamp-Verlags als Rechteinhaberin. Wir werden uns Ende 2020 um die Verlängerung der Rechte bemühen.

Wir wünschen viel Spaß und Erfolg bei der Arbeit mit WRILAB2!

Literatur

Adamzik, Kirsten (2004): Textlinguistik. Eine einführende Darstellung. Tübingen, Niemeyer.

Becker-Mrotzek, Michel, Frank Schneider, Frank & Tetling, Klaus (2010): Argumentierendes Schreiben – lehren und lernen. Verfügbar unter: https://www.standardsicherung.schulministerium.nrw.de/cms/upload/netzwerk_NfUE/deutsch/argumentieren_einfuehrung_lang.pdf [letzter Zugriff: 13.12.2016].

Becker-Mrotzek, Michael, Brinkhaus, Moti, Grabowski, Joachim, Hennecke, Vera, Jost, Jörg, Knapp, Matthias, Schmitt, Markus, Weinzierl, Christian & Wilmsmeier, Sabine (2015): Kohärenzherstellung und Perspektivenübernahme als Teilkomponenten der Schreibkompetenz. Von der diagnostischen Absicherung zur didaktischen Implementierung. In: Redder, Angelika, Naumann, Johannes & Tracy, Rosemarie (Hrsg.): Forschungsinitiative Sprachdiagnostik und Sprachförderung – Ergebnisse. Münster: Waxmann, 177-205.

Bräuer, Gerd (2005): Schreiben verändern und durch Schreiben verändern – Potenziale moderner Schreibdidaktik für die Schul- und Hochschulentwicklung. In: Abraham, Ulf, Kupfer-Schreiner, Claudia & Maiwald, Klaus (Hrsg.): Schreibförderung und Schreiberziehung. Eine Einführung für Schule und Hochschule. Donauwörth: Auer, 213-222.

Bräuer, Gerd & Schindler, Kirsten (2010): Authentische Schreibaufgaben im schulischen Fachunterricht. In: *Zeitschrift Schreiben* 15.1. (1-6). Verfügbar unter: www.zeitschrift-schreiben.eu/2010/#braeuer_schindler [letzter Zugriff: 13.12.2016].

Bräuer, Gerd (2016): The Didactic Framework for WRILAB2, in diesem Band.

Doleschal, Ursula, Gindl, Michaela & Kuri, Sonja (2016): EU-Projekt "On-line Reading and Writing Laboratory for Czech, German, Italian and Slovenian as L2" (www.wrilab2.eu). In: *VERBAL-Newsletter* 1/2016, 7-8. Verfügbar unter: www.verbal.at [letzter Zugriff 13.12.2016].

Doleschal, Ursula & Kuri, Sonja (2016): WRILAB2: On-line Reading and Writing Laboratory for Czech, German, Italian and Slovenian L2. Insights from Theory and Application, in diesem Band.

Eßer, Ruth (1997): „Etwas ist mir geheim geblieben am deutschen Referat." Kulturelle Geprägtheit wissenschaftlicher Textproduktion und ihre Konsequenzen für den universitären Unterricht von Deutsch als Fremdsprache. München: Iudicium.

Faistauer, Renate (1997): „Wir müssen zusammenschreiben": Kooperatives Schreiben im fremdsprachlichen Deutschunterricht. Innsbruck: Studienverlag.

Fandrych, Christian & Thurmair, Maria (2011): Textsorten im Deutschen. Linguistische Analysen aus sprachdidaktischer Sicht. Tübingen: Narr.

Feld-Knapp, Ilona (2009): Textsortenspezifische Merkmale und ihre Relevanz für Spracherwerbsprozesse (DaF). In: Adamzik, Kirsten & Krause, Wolf-Dieter (Hrsg.): Text-Arbeiten. Textsorten im fremd- und muttersprachlichen Unterricht an Schule und Hochschule. (2. überarbeitete Auflage). Tübingen: Narr, 115-135.

Feld-Knapp, Ilona (2010): Texte im Fremdsprachenunterricht – alte Probleme und neue Herangehensweisen. In: Krause, Wolf-Dieter (Hrsg.): Das Fremde und der Text. Fremdsprachige Kommunikation und ihre Ergebnisse. Potsdam: Universitätsverlag Potsdam, 188-206.

Fix, Ulla (2008): Texte und Textsorten – sprachliche, kommunikative und kulturelle Phänomene. Berlin: Frank & Timme.

Fix, Ulla, Poethe, Hannelore & Yos, Gabriele (2003): Textlinguistik und Stilistik für Einsteiger. Ein Lehr- und Arbeitsbuch. Unter Mitarbeit von Ruth Geier. Frankfurt am Main: Peter Lang.

Hayes, John R. & Flower, Linda S. (1980): Identifying the Organization of Writing Processes. In: Gregg, Lee W./Steinberg, Erwin R. (Eds.): Cognitive processes in Writing. Hillsdale: Erlbaum, 3-30.

Frank, Andrea, Haacke, Stefanie & Lahm, Swantje (2013): Schlüsselkompetenzen: Schreiben in Beruf und Studium. (2. Auflage). Stuttgart: Metzler.

Gemeinsamer europäischer Referenzrahmen für Sprache: lernen, lehren, beurteilen. Niveau A1-A2-B1-B2-C1-C2 (2001): Straßburg: Europarat/Langenscheidt.

Gindl, Michaela (2016): Technisches Handbuch zu WRILAB2. Verfügbar unter: www.wrilab2.eu/moodle [letzter Zugriff: 13.12.2016].

Hauser, Stefan, Kleinberger, Ulla & Roth, Karsten Sven (Hrsg.) (2014): Musterwandel – Textsortenwandel. Aktuelle Tendenzen der diachronen Text(sorten)linguistik. Bern: Peter Lang.

Hornung, Antonie (2009): Probleme fremdsprachiger Schreibpraxis im Fokus neuer Spracherwerbsforschung. In: *gfl-journal* (No 2-3), Verfügbar unter: www.gfl-journal.de [letzter Zugriff: 13.12.2016], 128-146.

Huemer, Birgit, Rheindorf, Markus & Gruber, Helmut (2012): Abstract, Exposée und Förderantrag: Eine Schreibanleitung für Studierende und junge Forschende. Wien: Böhlau.

Hufeisen, Britta (2002): Ein deutsches *Referat* ist kein englischsprachiges *Essay*. Theoretische und praktische Überlegungen zu einem verbesserten textsortenbezogenen Schreibunterricht in der Fremdsprache Deutsch an der Universität. Innsbruck: Studienverlag.

Knorr, Dagmar & Nardi Antonella (Hrsg.) (2011): Fremdsprachliche Textkompetenz entwickeln. Frankfurt am Main: Peter Lang.

Kruse, Otto (2013): Schreiben und kritisches Denken. Systematische und didaktische Verknüpfungen. In: Doleschal, Ursula, Mertlitsch, Carmen, Rheindorf, Markus & Wetschanow, Karin (Hg.): Writing across the Curriculum at Work. Theorie, Praxis und Analyse. Wien: LIT, 39-64.

Kruse, Otto (2015): Lesen und Schreiben. Der richtige Umgang mit Texten im Studium. (2. Auflage). Wien: Verlag Huter & Roth.

Kuri, Sonja (2005): Im Spannungsfeld der Mehrsprachigkeit. Deutsch an italienischen Universitäten. In: Glaboniat, Manuela, Rastner Eva Maria & Wintersteiner, Werner (Hrsg.): Sprachbegegnungen (Heft 2 – 2005 *ide*), 74-84.

Kuri, Sonja (im Druck): www.WRILAB2.eu. Ein Online-Labor zur Entwicklung von Textkompetenz in den Sprachen Deutsch, Italienisch, Slowenisch und Tschechisch. In: Lazarescu, Ioan & Scheuringer, Hermann (Hrsg.): Akten des Kongresses Braşov/Kronstadt, 1.-4. Juni 2015. Regensburg: Pustet (16 Seiten).

Kühn, Peter (2013): Wortschatz. In: Oomen-Welke, Ingeborg & Ahrenholz, Bernt (Hrsg.): Deutsch als Fremdsprache. Baltmannsweiler: Schneider Verlag Hohengehren, 153-164.

Ortner, Hanspeter (2002): Schreiben für Fortgeschrittene – vom kreativen zum wissenschaftlichen Schreiben. In: Portmann-Tselikas, Paul R. & Sabine Schmölzer-Eibinger (Hrsg.): Textkompetenz. Neue Perspektiven für das Lernen und Lehren. Innsbruck: Studienverlag, 233-246.

Ortner, Hanspeter (2007): Die (schriftliche) Darstellung von Sachverhalten als Stimulus für die Denk-, Sprach- und Schreibentwicklung. In: Schmölzer-Eibinger, Sabine & Georg Weidacher (Hrsg.): Textkompetenz. Eine Schlüsselkompetenz und ihre Vermittlung. Tübingen: Narr, 113-139.

Ortner, Hanspeter (2000): Schreiben und Denken. Tübingen: Niemeyer.

Perissutti Anna-Maria (2016): The Use of Thematic Progression to Improve Students' Essay Structure, in diesem Band.

Perrin, Daniel, Böttcher, Ingrid, Kruse, Otto & Wrobel, Arne (2003): Schreiben. Von intuitiven zu professionellen Schreibstrategien. (2., überarbeitete Auflage). Wiesbaden: Westdeutscher Verlag.

Riehl, Claudia Maria (2014): Sprachkontaktforschung. Eine Einführung. (3. Auflage). Tübingen, Narr.

Sändig, Uta (2009): Die Textsortenvariante ‚literaturwissenschaftlicher Kurzessay' und ihre Realisierung durch fremdsprachige Lerner. In: Adamzik, Kirsten & Krause, Wolf-Dieter (Hrsg.): Text-Arbeiten. Textsorten im fremd- und muttersprachlichen Unterricht an Schule und Hochschule. (2. überarbeitete Auflage). Tübingen: Narr, 155-171.

Schmidt, Isolde (2005): Schreiben im Fremdsprachenunterricht. In: Abraham, Ulf, Kupfer-Schreiner, Claudia & Maiwald, Klaus: Schreibförderung und Schreiberziehung. Eine Einführung für Schule und Hochschule. Donauwörth: Auer, 142-151.

Schmölzer-Eibinger, Sabine (2008): Lernen in der Zweitsprache. Grundlagen und Verfahren der Förderung von Textkompetenz in mehrsprachigen Klassen. Tübingen: Narr.

Sennewald, Nadja (2014): Schreibstrategien. Ein Überblick. In: Dreyfürst, Stephanie & Sennewald, Nadja (Hrsg.) Schreiben. Opladen, Toronto: Verlag Barbara Budrich, 169-190.

Skiba, Dirk (2013): Vom Schreiben zur Textproduktion. In: Oomen-Welke, Ingeborg & Ahrenholz, Bernt (Hrsg.): Deutsch als Fremdsprache. Baltmannsweiler: Schneider Verlag Hohengehren, 141-152.

Steinhoff, Thorsten (2007): Wissenschaftliche Textkompetenz. Sprachgebrauch und Schreibentwicklung in wissenschaftlichen Texten von Studenten und Experten. Tübingen: Niemeyer.

Vedder, Ineke (2016): Assessing functional adequacy in L2 and L1 writing. Proposal of a rating scale, in diesem Band.

Woitkowski, Felix (2012): Kollaboratives und literarisches Schreiben im Internet. Berlin: LIT.

Gianluca Baldo

Guida alla sezione italiana di Wrilab2

1 Introduzione

Questo capitolo intende introdurre e presentare la sezione italiana di Wrilab2. Il fine è offrire all'utente, anche inesperto, una guida pratica, che contenga però anche un inquadramento teorico dei contenuti del portale online per la scrittura in L2. La descrizione delle attività e delle risorse presenti sul sito è pertanto di volta in volta motivata e si fonda sui principi didattici generali soggiacenti alle scelte attuate dai membri del gruppo di lavoro in fase di pianificazione e creazione dei materiali didattici.

All'avvio del progetto, già durante i primi meeting internazionali, i lineamenti descritti nel capitolo introduttivo di questo volume si sono rivelati estremamente fecondi e hanno orientato parte significativa delle scelte successive (cfr. Bräuer in questo volume, paragrafo *The didactic framework for Wrilab2*). Le teorie sulla scrittura che sono invece rimaste sullo sfondo, come esperienza condivisa, e hanno sostenuto in filigrana ogni passo dei lavori sono quella cognitivista e la successiva prospettiva socioculturale[30].

Gli studi cognitivisti hanno consentito il superamento delle idee più legate alla tradizione e fortemente indirizzate al testo finale, inteso come prodotto e risultato. La rappresentazione a tre blocchi di Flower & Hayes (1980), scomposta nei suoi elementi costitutivi e con alcune modifiche, ha infatti orientato la creazione del diagramma che è stato modello e struttura dei corsi presenti nella sezione italiana del portale.

Nell'intenzione di superare i limiti di questo approccio, che in parte sottovaluta gli aspetti sociali del processo, nonché di valorizzare al massimo le opportunità di apprendimento cooperativo offerte dal mezzo informatico e dalla rete, il punto di vista cognitivista è stato proficuamente integrato dalla prospettiva socioculturale, più attenta alla promozione della scrittura come sistema di comunica-

30 Ai fini di Wrilab2 la scrittura e i generi testuali sono intesi come un sistema di abilità e competenze connotate a livello sociale e culturale, che può e si raccomanda sia sviluppato attraverso forme di interazione con altri apprendenti. La didattica dei generi supera il livello morfosintattico di superficie e rivolge la sua attenzione alla struttura più profonda dei testi, con l'obiettivo di fornire agli utenti del portale strumenti e modi per operare scelte sociolinguistiche consapevoli (cfr. Hyland 2007: 150-154). La classe, anche virtuale, di lingua seconda diventa allora un ambiente di apprendimento cooperativo, a maggior ragione nel momento in cui ciascun allievo si fa portatore di specificità culturali che rendono l'individuo un'utile risorsa e un valore aggiunto per l'intero gruppo.

zione in situazioni il più possibili autentiche, situate e collaborative[31]. I forum, i database e il servizio di messaggi diretti offerti dalla piattaforma Moodle si sono facilmente adattati a questi scopi.

La sezione italiana di Wrilab2 offre dodici corsi, chiamati Unità Didattiche32, finalizzati all'insegnamento della scrittura funzionale in L2. Si tratta quindi di testi orientati a rispondere a specifiche esigenze di carattere anche pratico. I tipi testuali più rappresentati sono quello argomentativo ed espositivo, mentre assai più ricca è la varietà dei generi: la relazione di viaggio, il saggio breve, la lettera di reclamo, il curriculum vitae, la recensione, l'articolo di opinione, il riassunto, la relazione di tirocinio e l'introduzione alla tesi di laurea. Questo criterio di scelta si allinea e ispira alla considerazione della prima categorizzazione come universale e della seconda come culturalmente e socialmente determinata: "parlando di tipi testuali, ci si pone su una dimensione di astrazione rispetto ai testi reali, su una dimensione ancora più astratta, generale e preliminare rispetto a quella dei generi che sono invece, al di là della loro apparente universalità, storicamente e culturalmente determinati" (Lavinio 2000: 126). Una delle idee pedagogiche di fondo del gruppo di lavoro di Wrilab2 è stata proprio quella di affrontare una didattica per generi, in grado di descrivere le loro caratteristiche testuali e linguistiche, con il fine di colmare le lacune degli utenti del portale e di offrire loro la possibilità di sviluppare una maggiore consapevolezza riflessa riguardo a questi aspetti: "Genre pedagogies promise very real benefits for learners as they pull together content, and contexts" (Hyland 2007: 150).

Nel primo paragrafo di questa breve guida sarà illustrata la struttura a blocchi comune ai dodici corsi della sezione italiana di Wrilab2. Nel successivo saranno presentati i generi scelti per le attività di scrittura del sito, con maggiori dettagli rispetto anche alla prospettiva didattica adottata. Nella terza parte le necessità espresse dagli utenti durante la fase di ricerca iniziale del progetto, saranno affiancate dalla descrizione dei numerosi modelli e delle fonti, con l'intento di suggerire idee per la creazione di percorsi il più possibile reali, autentici e situati attraverso i contenuti caricati sul sito (cfr. Bräuer in questo volume, paragrafo *Authentic tasks and task arrangements*). Il paragrafo seguente, il quarto, presenterà le risorse utilizzate per offrire agli utenti del portale informazioni dirette sui testi modello, sui generi e sulla tipologia testuale. La quinta e ultima parte di questa guida mostrerà alcune delle possibilità di comunicazione messe a disposizione da Moodle, adattate al fine di stimolare la creazione di gruppi di scrittu-

---

31 Cfr. Bräuer in questo volume, paragrafo *Authentic tasks and task arrangements*, Cisotto (2015: 15-17) e Hyland (2007: 154-155).

32 È bene notare che questa terminologia si avvicina solamente in parte alle definizioni delle scienze dell'educazione e a quelle delle indicazioni ministeriali (cfr. Balboni 2012: 161-167). Con Unità Didattica su Wrilab2 è inteso principalmente un corso di Moodle, che ospita e offre risorse e attività finalizzate alla scrittura online di un testo appartenente a una tipologia e genere specifici.

ra, con forme di apprendimento e creazione della conoscenza cooperative. Tutte le scelte operative attuate saranno sostenute sul piano teorico attraverso riferimenti alle fonti e al già citato inquadramento didattico generale.

1.1 La struttura a sezioni

La struttura a sezioni delle Unità Didattiche è la soluzione che pare meglio coniugare le restrizioni imposte da Moodle, strumento adottato per la realizzazione dei corsi, e le necessità imposte dall'approccio alla scrittura che fa da cornice alle attività didattiche del portale. Le fasi di generazione delle idee e loro organizzazione, prima mentale e successivamente grafica, la trascrizione in forma di prima bozza e la revisione si dispongono in maniera lineare lungo la pagina web, scorrendola dall'alto al basso. Questa ripartizione assicura agli utenti gradualità nell' avvicinamento ai contenuti e consente così di evitare quel sovraccarico a livello cognitivo ed emotivo che potrebbe in diverso caso accompagnare dei compiti di scrittura in L2 complessi e articolati come quelli proposti (cfr. Olson 2013: 382-385). I generi presentati prevedono infatti funzioni retoriche anche complesse e risultano in parte connotati a livello socioculturale. La suddivisione in sequenze o reti organizzate di esercizi più semplici, meno impegnativi a livello di risorse mentali richieste, è uno dei principi cardine dell'inquadramento teorico di Wrilab2.[33]

La presenza di una struttura lineare come quella descritta non sancisce però in alcun modo per l'utente la necessità di seguire un ordine stabilito di svolgimento delle attività e di consultazione delle risorse. Un libro guida virtuale, posto immediatamente prima dell'inizio di ciascun corso e quindi al suo esterno, ha la funzione di introdurre i contenuti, con collegamenti verso l'interno al fine di una più semplice scelta e navigazione del sito. Le sezioni di ciascuna Unità Di-

---

33 Lo *scaffolding* in Wrilab2 è stato interpretato partendo dell'inquadramento teorico di Vygotsky (1987) e inteso come un metodo per suddividere un compito complesso in una serie di esercizi più semplici e più facilmente così alla portata degli apprendenti (cfr. Bräuer in questo volume, paragrafo *Scaffolding and transfer of competence*).

dattica italiana sono dunque sei: database, introduzione, pianificazione, trascrizione, revisione e autovalutazione.

Database

È un'area per la condivisione di testi con altri utenti. Wrilab2 invita i suoi utenti a comunicare, entrare i contatto tra di loro, scambiare buone pratiche, consigli, opinioni e giudizi sulla scrittura, nell'ottica della creazione di una comunità virtuale di creatori di testi.

Introduzione

In questa sezione è presentato per la prima volta il compito di scrittura attorno al quale si orientano tutti i contenuti del corso. Di solito questo avviene attraverso un video, nel quale sono fornite indicazioni generali sul genere testuale, e con un primo testo modello, che è analizzato sia dal punto di vista del contenuto sia della struttura.

Pianificazione

La seconda sezione di ciascun corso ospita numerose fonti, di cui solitamente almeno una è multimediale o prevede attività specifiche che invitano a sfruttare le potenzialità della rete. Gli scrittori sono guidati nella consultazione dei testi, ma anche nella loro analisi, con particolare attenzione per il livello strutturale più profondo. La didattica dei generi va difatti oltre il livello morfosintattico e lessicale, che passano in secondo piano rispetto al processo di lettura e alla capacità di operare scelte linguistiche consapevoli di grado superiore: "genre-based writing instruction offers students an explicit understanding of how target texts are structured and why they are written in the way they are" (Hyland 2007: 151).

Inoltre la varietà e diversità dei contenuti proposti invita alla riflessione sulla molteplicità delle fonti di informazione disponibili in rete: quotidiani online, blog, siti specializzati, siti di recensioni, enciclopedie, video e interviste ai protagonisti o agli autori. Ciascun utente è invitato a scegliere, nella rosa di possibilità, quella che più ritiene adatta ai suoi bisogni e necessità linguistiche (cfr. *Paragrafo 3. Modelli e fonti*, in questo capitolo). Prima di passare alla scrittura della bozza il portale propone ai suoi utenti di riorganizzare le idee raccolte in forma di mappa concettuale, disegnata liberamente su carta oppure creata grazie al programma *Freemind*, gratuito e scaricabile in rete. In questo modo, prima di passare alla successiva trascrizione, gli iscritti al sito sono invitati a dare una rappresentazione spaziale alle loro conoscenze sull'argomento del quale si apprestano a scrivere, illustrando graficamente i concetti, rendendo più evidenti i collegamenti e i passaggi logici (cfr. Cisotto 2015: 30-32).

Trascrizione

Gli studenti mostrano spesso una sensibilità limitata verso la progettazione dei testi[34]. Uno dei fini di Wrilab2 è promuovere questo genere di consapevolezza. A questo sono destinate le attività didattiche della sezione di trascrizione: oltre al compito di scrittura, affiancato da un modello con una lista di domande atte a guidare passo dopo passo il processo, è presente un libro virtuale con risorse specifiche sul genere testuale. Gli utenti del portale che, durante la pianificazione e con attività pratiche erano stati guidati alla scoperta dei primi aspetti strutturali del testo, nonché delle scelte stilistiche consapevoli degli autori e delle forme dell'argomentazione, sono ora invitati a fermarsi per un momento di riflessione e approfondimento prima di iniziare a scrivere.

Revisione

Wrilab2 desidera rendere i suoi utenti sensibili riguardo all'importanza di questa fase dell'elaborazione testuale, nell'ottica del superamento di una concezione dell'insegnamento della scrittura più tradizionale e fortemente orientata al testo come prodotto, più che al processo messo in atto durante la sua creazione: "gli studi del cognitivismo, [...] hanno condotto al superamento della concezione tradizionale dell'imparare a scrivere, a lungo caratterizzata dall'identificazione della componente scritta con il solo prodotto finale e dalla predominanza della «fisicità» del testo, valutato esclusivamente sulla base di standard di correttezza linguistica" (Cisotto 2015: 15). A questo fine ciascuno dei corsi ospita un libro virtuale che accompagna gli apprendenti nella revisione, attraverso istruzioni chiare e dirette, con pagine di domande aperte volte a indirizzare la loro attenzione anche verso gli aspetti specifici al genere testuale.

Autovalutazione

All'interno dell'ambiente didattico virtuale di Wrilab2 è spesso possibile contare sul sostegno e feedback di un docente o assistente linguistico. La presenza di insegnanti esterni di accompagnamento è difatti sostenuta e raccomandata, soprattutto nel caso di gruppi di utenti numerosi o classi intere che decidano di iscriversi e iniziare a utilizzare il portale. In questo modo la comunicazione potrà proseguire anche al di fuori dell'aula scolastica, online, attraverso le differenti applicazioni create in Moodle proprio a questo scopo.

Non minori energie sono però dedicate a incentivare forme di valutazione alternative. Attività strutturate invitano alla riflessione sul percorso svolto e alla autovalutazione dei progressi, mentre un forum dedicato favorisce lo scambio di idee e opinioni tra pari, nell'ottica dell'istituzione di una comunità virtuale di

---

34 I risultati del questionario somministrato nel 2014 dai ricercatori di Wrilab2 a un campione di circa cento apprendenti di italiano come lingua seconda o straniera hanno evidenziato che le difficoltà più comunemente percepite dai potenziali utenti del portale riguardano grammatica, sintassi, lessico e ortografia. Solamente uno degli informanti ha citato un più vago "perché per me è difficile la scrittura di un testo".

appassionati di scrittura che si sappia autosostenere anche in assenza di forme istituzionali di verifica delle competenze. L'obiettivo è forse ambizioso, ma lo strumento tecnologico adottato offre la potenzialità per la creazione di un ambiente virtuale all'interno del quale sia possibile una partecipazione più attiva, con forme di apprendimento cooperativo che si auspica possano portare a una migliore comprensione e interiorizzazione dei contenuti, oltre che allo sviluppo di competenze sociali e di una maggiore consapevolezza rispetto alla funzione comunicativa della scrittura (cfr. Novello 2012: 84-85).

1.2 L'area Risorse di Wrilab2

La maggior parte dei contenuti presenti sul sito invita a focalizzare l'attenzione sugli aspetti strutturali più profondi dei testi, mentre aree come la morfologia e il lessico ricevono una minore attenzione. Le informazioni di cui un allievo di L2 può avere bisogno sono però molte e gli studenti cercano e si aspettano di trovare un sostegno specifico a ciascuno di questi livelli[35]. La soluzione è stata quella di creare una tredicesima Unità Didattica, parallela alle dodici dedicate ad altrettanti generi testuali. Questo corso, chiamato *Area Risorse*, è raggiungibile in qualsiasi momento attraverso un collegamento visibile nel blocco laterale destro della pagina web, di modo che gli allievi possano trovarlo con facilità e aprire una nuova finestra di navigazione per raggiungere gli strumenti o i contenuti di loro interesse. I materiali presenti in quest'area sono suddivisi in tre sezioni: attività morfosintattiche, lessicali e risorse esterne.

Attività morfosintattiche

L'idea alla base di questa prima sezione, *Grammatica e dintorni*, è appunto quella di una grammatica con esercizi. La descrizione delle forme e la spiegazione degli usi sono dirette e la scelta degli argomenti è determinata dall'utilità rispetto ai contenuti e al genere testuale presentato nelle diverse Unità Didattiche. Sono perciò presenti dodici esercizi, ognuno dei quali si lega principalmente a uno dei corsi della piattaforma.

---

35 L'analisi dei dati raccolti attraverso le sezioni del questionario indirizzate a rilevare le difficoltà percepite dai potenziali utenti del portale rispetto alla scrittura in L2 hanno indicato che gli elementi più frequentemente citati dagli informanti sono proprio la grammatica, l'ortografia e il lessico.

Attività lessicali

Anche la sezione *Parole, parole, parole* ospita dodici quiz, ma l'approccio è lessicale. Si tratta di esercizi di abbinamento, scoperta e approfondimento del lessico specifico necessario ad affrontare al meglio i compiti di scrittura previsti dal portale. Anche in questo caso, quindi, gli ambiti sviluppati sono legati ai temi dei dodici corsi a cui si riferiscono e che completano.

Risorse esterne

Wrilab2 non dimentica di essere un portale per l'e-learning aperto al pubblico e proiettato verso la rete, con la quale scambia fonti, modelli e informazioni. Uno degli obiettivi del progetto consiste nello sfruttare quanto più possibile le potenzialità offerte da internet in modo da creare un ambiente di apprendimento il più possibile globale, includendo materiali autentici e multimediali, nonché collegamenti esterni in grado di rispondere alle esigenze di una tipologia di utenti il più possibile varia e stratificata (cfr. Novello 2012: 87-88). Nella sezione *Oltre Moodle: altre risorse del web* sono presenti esclusivamente collegamenti esterni a siti che si occupano di italiano per stranieri, di rilevazione o certificazione della competenza, di approfondimento a tutti il livelli linguistici, enciclopedie, dizionari e risorse multimediali.

2 I generi

Come accennato precedentemente in questo capitolo, la gran parte dei modelli e delle fonti di Wrilab2 appartiene alle tipologie testuali argomentativa ed espositiva. All'interno di queste, intese come categorie universali[36], è stato identificato un certo numero di generi più rappresentativi e adeguati rispetto alle necessità e ai bisogni dei potenziali visitatori del sito. Sul processo di scelta hanno influito sia considerazioni didattiche generali, legate all'utilità all'interno dei programmi di studio scolastici e universitari, sia considerazioni specifiche e interne alla cornice teorica di riferimento delineata dal gruppo di lavoro internazionale durante i primi incontri[37]. Non è stata trascurata però un'attenta indagine esplora-

---

36 Nella voce *Tipi di testo* dell'*Enciclopedia dell'Italiano Treccani*, consultata online il 09/12/2016: http://www.treccani.it/enciclopedia/tipi-di-testo_(Enciclopedia-dell' Italiano)/), Lala specifica che "i tipi testuali distinti dalle classificazioni tradizionali sono però categorie generali, definibili con tratti universali e reperibili in tutte le lingue e culture, i generi, al di là della loro apparente universalità, implicano l'adattamento del messaggio linguistico alle esigenze comunicative delle diverse società: essi variano quindi da una cultura all'altra, e anche nell'ambito della medesima cultura, da un'epoca storica a un'altra".

37 Si tratta in questo caso dell'idea di fondo di creare materiali il più possibile autentici e situati, per i quali l'utente sia in grado di percepire l'utilità immediata e un valore pratico reale rispetto alla sua attività scolastica o professionale e in una specifica

tiva delle reali percezioni dei potenziali utilizzatori del portale. Un gruppo campione è stato difatti raggiunto nel 2014 da un sondaggio che ha interessato più di 400 informanti, di cui circa un centinaio per la sezione italiana, con il fine di indagare gli usi, le percezioni, le paure e gli interessi dei futuri iscritti alla piattaforma rispetto ai compiti della scrittura in L1 e L2.

2.1 Le necessità espresse dagli utenti

Uno dei blocchi del questionario ha consentito di rilevare l'importanza di alcuni generi testuali, così come essa è percepita da gruppi di potenziali utenti del portale. La domanda posta agli informanti è stata: "Quanto sono importanti i seguenti generi per il tuo futuro?"

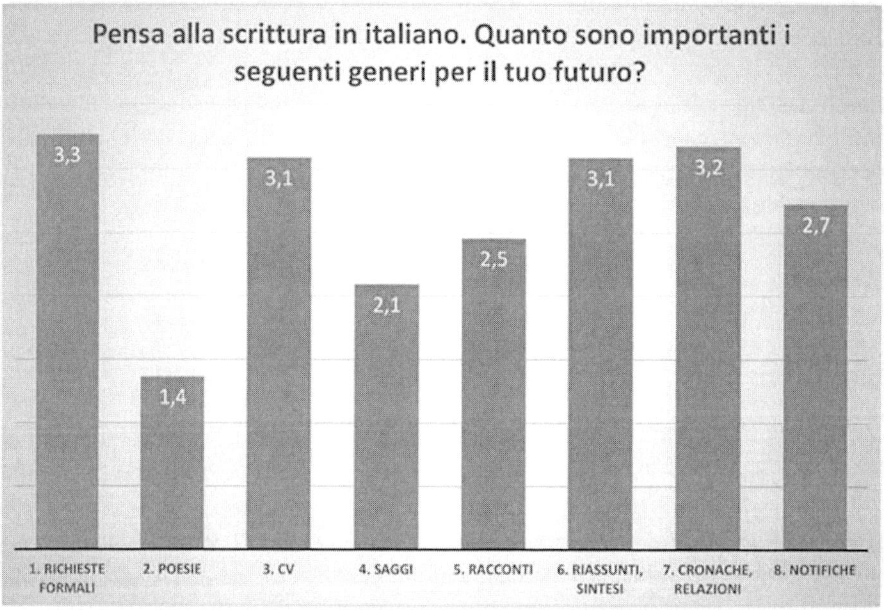

Per ciascun genere è stato chiesto di dare una misura del proprio atteggiamento individuale attraverso i valori di una scala Likert a cinque punti. I dati raccolti sono stati analizzati sia nella volontà di predisporre materiali e attività il più possibile rispondenti alle necessità reali degli apprendenti sia al fine di rilevare eventuali scostamenti tra le percezioni personali e l'importanza dei generi nell'ambito di specifici percorsi formativi, in particolare nella scuola secondaria e nell'università.

unità di tempo (cfr. Bräuer in questo volume, paragrafo *Authentic tasks and task arrangements*).

2.2 I generi scelti da Wrilab2

I dodici corsi di scrittura ospitati da Wrilab2 sono legati ai contesti accademici, professionali e sociali all'interno dei quali gli utenti del portale potrebbero trovarsi a operare. L'obiettivo è, pure nel rispetto delle scelte didattiche teoriche e delle preferenze degli utenti, quello di creare un legame tra l'ambiente di apprendimento online e il mondo reale. I generi sono stati interpretati, all'interno della cornice di riferimento già delineata nell'introduzione a questo capitolo, come modalità d'uso del linguaggio scritto ben riconoscibili e caratterizzate a livello socioculturale, in parte fondate sulle esperienze di una comunità di parlanti: "Genre refers to abstract, socially recognised ways of using a language" (Hyland 2007: 149). Sono stati così scelti i compiti di scrittura argomentativa ed espositiva per le dodici Unità Didattiche e, successivamente, sono stati attribuiti ai diversi livelli di competenza linguistica previsti dal ben noto Quadro Comune Europeo di Riferimento.

Livello B1	*Livello B2*	*Livello C1*
Relazione di un viaggio	Articolo di opinione	Relazione di un tirocinio
Recensione tecnico pratica	Introduzione alla tesi di laurea	Recensione letteraria
Curriculum vitae	Riassunto espositivo	Riassunto argomentativo
Lettera di reclamo	Saggio breve argomentativo	Saggio argomentativo

Alcuni generi si sono rivelati più vicini alle esperienze personali dei parlanti, come per esempio la recensione pratica di un oggetto tecnologico o di un ristorante, altri sono al contrario maggiormente legati alla vita professionale e culturale, come è nel caso del *curriculum vitae*, della recensione letteraria o dell'introduzione alla tesi di laurea. Dal punto di vista di un docente desideroso di iscrivere un gruppo di suoi allievi a Wrilab2, questo panorama offre la garanzia di potere scegliere i materiali, le risorse e le attività più adeguati rispetto alle necessità concrete e reali di un'ampia gamma di possibili programmi d'aula.

2.3 I livelli linguistici del QCER

I materiali presenti sul portale sono adatti ai livelli da B1 a C1 del Quadro Comune Europeo di Riferimento per le lingue, con qualche oscillazione motivata sia dalla volontà di utilizzare fonti il più possibile autentiche, testi e video reperibili su quotidiani online, attraverso blog, enciclopedie e forum, sia dalla consapevolezza che le attività e i quiz saranno utilizzati direttamente in rete e quindi con una vasta disponibilità di strumenti multimediali a supporto, come per esempio i dizionari, le grammatiche e siti tematici. È anche opportuno notare che i diversi testi ospitati da una stessa Unità Didattica si possono di fatto collocare a livelli leggermente diversi, così da offrire materiali sempre adatti ai bisogni e alle esigenze di un'utenza non uniforme e stratificata come si immagina essere quella che si rivolgerà al portale.

3 Modelli e fonti

Le attività di scrittura di Wrilab2 si orientano e sviluppano attorno a numerosi modelli e fonti. I primi, ospitati nella sezione introduttiva di ciascuna Unità Didattica, rappresentano buone pratiche di scrittura e si possono considerare in qualche modo esemplari rispetto alle caratteristiche del genere testuale presentato in quel corso. Le fonti, più numerose e nella fase di pianificazione, invece hanno una duplice funzione: da una parte sono ulteriori esempi del genere testuale, spesso in forma multimediale e tenendo conto delle risorse disponibili in rete, dall'altra mostrano come sia possibile reperire nuove idee, informazioni e punti di vista alternativi attraverso internet. In questo caso la funzione prevalente è forse la seconda, difatti è possibile incontrare voci di enciclopedie, siti settoriali, blog di esperti e specialisti, notiziari e articoli di quotidiano, recensioni tecniche, pratiche o letterarie.

Ciascun testo è analizzato grazie agli strumenti offerti dal portale Moodle, che cercano di realizzazione per via informatizzata e il più possibile automatica alcune delle tecniche glottodidattiche di uso più frequente, adattandole di volta in volta agli obiettivi specifici di Wrilab2. La scoperta delle strutture testuali avviene in maniera induttiva, partendo sempre da esempi concreti e proponendo attività che invitano e indirizzano gli apprendenti verso la scoperta delle funzioni comunicative profonde. Gli esercizi permettono quindi di operare sulle strutture più rilevanti e pertinenti rispetto a ciascuno dei generi considerati. Per esempio gli esercizi di riordino o titolazione dei paragrafi di un testo modello consentono di introiettare la conoscenza e permettono di rilevare l'importanza dell'ordine delle parti in un saggio o in un diario di viaggio.

Sia i modelli, sia le fonti, sono testi il più possibile autentici e solo ai livelli più bassi di competenza le versioni sono adattate o semplificate. La scelta dei temi e degli argomenti trattati è in parte dettata dal genere, ma tiene conto anche delle preferenze dei futuri utilizzatori del portale.

3.1 Le necessità espresse dagli utenti

Una delle domande del questionario di Wrilab2 del 2014 chiedeva una preferenza riguardo a dieci possibili temi di scrittura: "Quali sono le tematiche che ti interessano così tanto da volerci scrivere un testo?" Seppure tenendo conto del fatto che questo tipo di quesito indaga un livello del processo di scrittura più superficiale rispetto alla scelta del genere e attiva quindi funzioni mentali e linguistiche meno profonde, l'analisi delle risposte ha in parte indirizzato la selezione dei materiali successivamente caricati sul sito.

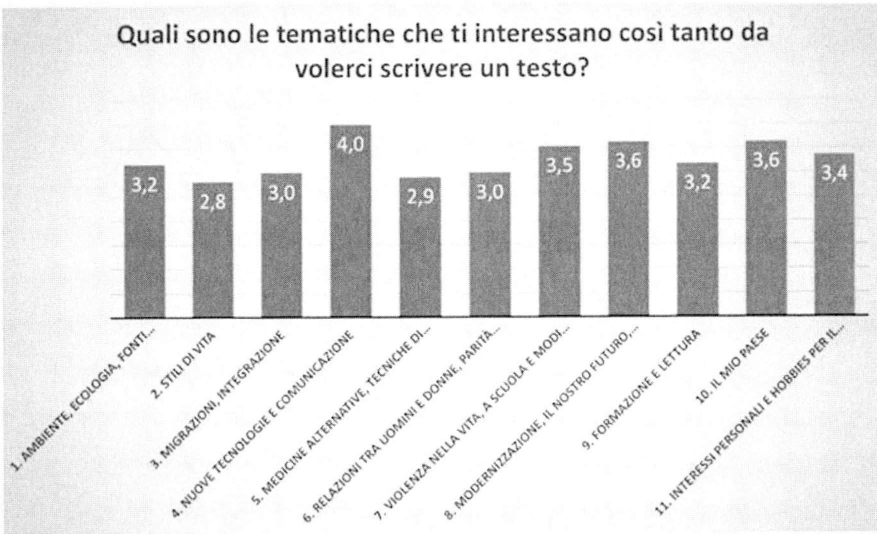

Lo studente, che in questo caso è paragonato a un vero e proprio autore e scrittore, è il soggetto attivo dell'acquisizione linguistica e come tale è posto al centro del processo. I materiali proposti cercano p di tenere nella giusta considerazione l'utilità reale e quella percepita dai diversi gruppi di utenti, allievi e insegnanti, in quanto protagonisti dell'esperienza di Wrilab2 (cfr. Balboni 2012: 95-105).

La scelta dei modelli e delle fonti ha in conclusione tenuto conto sia delle necessità imposte dal genere sia del tipo di utenza ipotizzato per il sito, con le sue esigenze ed eventuali interessi specifici. Le variabili in gioco si sono rivelate di conseguenza numerose ed è stato nondimeno necessario considerare che spesso è impossibile ascrivere un testo a un'unica categoria. Gli apprendenti individuali, i gruppi, oppure i docenti che accedono alla piattaforma possono però ricorrere alle tavole riassuntive presentate in questo paragrafo e utilizzarle come guida e fonte al fine di operare una scelta ragionata e per pianificare con maggiore consapevolezza un percorso di apprendimento.

3.2 I testi modello

I modelli sono sempre autentici e talvolta multimediali, con contenuti attinti dalla rete, mentre solo in alcuni casi sono stati adattati per venire incontro alle necessità e al livello linguistico degli apprendenti. Nella progettazione delle attività di analisi e sintesi il gruppo di lavoro di Wrilab2 si è concentrato sulla creazione di esercizi finalizzati a indurre l'utente a scendere in profondità e a dare importanza agli elementi strutturali, alle scelte di registro e al destinatario, piuttosto che a generare forme di imitazione piatta e meccanica. Le attività di lettura e comprensione guidano in maniera implicita alla scoperta degli elementi specifici al genere, ma coloro i quali preferiscono un approccio più tradizionale e meno induttivo possono ricorrere a pagine in pdf che utilizzano un sistema piuttosto semplice e trasparente di annotazione e colori distintivi per dare evidenza agli aspetti più rilevanti della struttura testuale.

La tabella che segue descrive i dodici modelli, rappresentativi di altrettanti generi presenti sul sito, e offre informazioni orientative riguardo al livello linguistico suggerito per affrontare con successo le attività didattiche, alla tipologia di utenza idealmente prevista per ciascun corso e ai contenuti caricati sulla piattaforma. Il sistema di indicatori adottato è:

- *Scuola secondaria*, il materiale è adatto a studenti della scuola secondaria;
- *Università*, il testo è particolarmente adatto a studenti universitari;
- *Professionale*, la fonte o il modello sono stati pensati per utenti che si rivolgono a Wrilab2 per soddisfare necessità di tipo professionale;
- *Unione Europea*: Wrilab2 è un portale finanziato dall'Unione Europea, è sembrato quindi importante e doveroso introdurre dei materiali che in qualche maniera possano richiamare l'idea di Europa unita e siano in grado di invitare gli apprendenti a focalizzare la loro attenzione su alcune delle sfide affrontate negli anni recenti dall'Unione;
- *Materiale ludico*: il contenuto informativo passa in secondo piano rispetto all'aspetto ludico e l'attività è pensata per sostenere la motivazione degli apprendenti.

Genere testuale	*Liv.*	*Testo modello*	*Scuola secondaria*	*Università*	*Professionale*	*Unione Europea*	*Materiale ludico*
Relazione di viaggio	B1	Viaggiare in Vespa	✓	✓			✓
Recensione tecnica pratica	B1	*Bianca* di Nanni Moretti	✓	✓			
Curriculum vitae	B1	Il CV del Rag. Fantozzi		✓	✓		✓
Lettera di reclamo	B1	Reclamo di condominio		✓	✓		
Riassunto espositivo	B2	I valori dell'Unione		✓		✓	
Introduzione alla tesi di laurea	B2	Introduzione a una tesi di laurea in economia		✓	✓		
Saggio breve argomentativo	B2	USA: i *social network* fanno bene alla vita		✓			
Articolo di opinione	B2	Le sfide dell'Unione				✓	
Recensione letteraria	C1	*L'apocalisse rimandata* di Dario Fo	✓	✓			
Relazione di tirocinio	C1	Un corso in e-learning		✓	✓		
Riassunto argomentativo	C1	Tema sul motorino	✓				✓
Saggio breve argomentativo	C1	*Social network*, le spie dell'industria	✓	✓			

3.3 Le fonti e la generazione delle idee

La funzione delle fonti, nella sezione di pianificazione, si differenzia rispetto a quella dei modelli. Da una parte si tratta di testi, anche multimediali e interattivi, nei quali talvolta prevale la funzione ludica e di sostegno alla motivazione; dall'altra questi contenuti contribuiscono ad approfondire la conoscenza del genere testuale e delle sue caratteristiche specifiche. Le fonti presentano un input ricco e vario, con molteplici approcci al processo di generazione e raccolta delle idee. La strategia è anche in questo caso quella di assecondare I diversi tipi e stili di apprendimento, tenendo in questo modo conto delle esigenze reali e autentiche di ciascun utente: "learning and instruction should provide students always a chance to identify personal strengths and urgent chances for further learning and, with it, the ability to acknowledge ones' own "comfort zone" and to enable oneself to go beyond this comfort zone in a responsible manner" (cfr. Bräuer in questo volume, paragrafo *Facilitating different needs of individual learners*).

Mentre svolgono le attività gli studenti sono invitati a ricorrere a siti specializzati, voci di enciclopedia, dizionari e quotidiani online, temi svolti da altri prima di loro, recensioni letterarie o di uso pratico. Uno degli obiettivi è sviluppare così una consapevolezza dell'esistenza di risorse valide, attendibili e facilmente raggiungibili in rete, che possono rivelarsi utili a sostenere il processo di scrittura.

La tabella inclusa in questo paragrafo, non dissimile da quella del precedente, descrive le numerose e varie fonti offerte da Wrilab2 ai suoi utenti. I testi sono raggruppati in base al loro genere e livello linguistico di appartenenza, ma sono presenti anche delle informazioni aggiuntive finalizzate a facilitare una scelta consapevole dei contenuti e dei materiali da parte degli insegnanti o assistenti linguistici in fase di progettazione didattica. Il sistema di indicatori adottato è del tutto analogo a quello già presentato, con l'aggiunta di una sola voce:

- *Multimediale*: la fonte è un video, una canzone, oppure prevede attività di ricerca e rielaborazione che mettano a frutto e utilizzino le possibilità offerte dal mezzo informatico e dalla rete internet.

Dopo avere consultato testi di diverso tipo gli apprendenti sono invitati a riorganizzare le informazioni, a dare loro forma anche grafica usando il programma Freemind, liberamente disponibile in rete, oppure disegnando su carta una mappa concettuale che sarà poi fotografata con lo smartphone. L'immagine risultante potrà essere successivamente inviata a uno dei forum interni dedicato alla generazione delle idee e gli utenti potranno così ricevere l'opinione e il commento sia di un assistente linguistico sia di altri frequentatori iscritti al portale. Una scelta e un uso accorti delle fonti consentiranno idealmente di attrarre l'attenzione degli apprendenti su quella fase di pianificazione che tanto può influire sugli esiti finali del processo di scrittura.

Genere testuale	*Testo fonte*	*Scuola secondaria*	*Università*	*Professionale*	*Unione Europea*	*Materiale ludico*	*Multimediale*
Relazione di viaggio (B1)	Gita a Urbino	✓					✓
	Il carnevale di Venezia	✓	✓			✓	
	Webquest a Bologna	✓				✓	✓
Recensione tecnica o pratica (B1)	Il *Cyrano de Bergerac*	✓	✓				
	Museica di Caparezza	✓	✓			✓	
	Il *Kindle* di Amazon	✓	✓			✓	✓
Curriculum vitae (B1)	Informazioni da un sito		✓	✓			
	Il CV in formato europeo		✓	✓	✓		
	Un video di Adecco		✓	✓			✓
Lettera di reclamo (B1)	Problemi di alloggio						
	Reclami al lavoro			✓			
	Le bollette scadute						✓
Riassunto espositivo (B2)	Guida di Rimini					✓	
	La vita di Galileo Galilei	✓	✓				
	Gli ausiliari, da ALMAtv	✓	✓			✓	✓
Introduzione alla tesi di laurea (B2)	Una tesi in scienze della formazione primaria		✓				
Saggio breve argomentativo (B2)	Facebook giova all'umore	✓	✓				
	Contro i *social network*	✓	✓				
	L'amore ai tempi di Facebook		✓			✓	✓
Articolo di opinione (B2)	Anno nuovo, vita nuova					✓	
	Emergenza morti per parto	✓	✓				
	La paura dell'islam	✓	✓				
Recensione letteraria (C1)	*La discesa degli orsi* (Buzzati)	✓	✓				
	Una lama di luce (Camilleri)	✓	✓				
	Il barone rampante (Calvino)	✓	✓			✓	
Relazione di tirocinio (C1)	Scuola Montessori a Barcellona		✓				
	Tutti giù per terra ONLUS		✓	✓			
	Realizzazione di un filmato		✓				
Riassunto argomentativo (C1)	La pirateria musicale	✓	✓				
	L'idea di Unione Europea	✓	✓		✓		
	Il congiuntivo, da ALMAtv	✓	✓			✓	✓
Saggio breve argomentativo (C1)	Cercare informazioni in rete	✓	✓				
	L'attendibilità delle fonti	✓	✓				
	Citare l'informazione nel testo		✓				

3.4 Percorsi

Gli utenti che si rivolgono a Wrilab2 per perfezionare la loro abilità di scrittura di uno specifico genere non sono tenuti a svolgere tutte le attività e a consultare tutte le fonti e i modelli previsti in un corso. La ricchezza e la varietà degli stimoli e dei materiali suggeriscono la possibilità di operare scelte individuali, fondate su bisogni e necessità specifici, o anche soltanto sull'interesse e sulla preferenza per una determinata tematica. La motivazione, motore e spinta dell'apprendimento linguistico, si trova grazie a questa scelta al centro del processo di apprendimento, nella volontà di assecondare ciascun possibile visitatore del sito, adolescente o adulto, studente o professionista (cfr. Balboni 2012: 95-105). Se gli apprendenti si iscrivono come gruppo e sono accompagnati nel loro percorso da un docente, sarà per quest'ultimo possibile progettare con cura l'esperienza formativa e offrire assistenza nelle scelte, nonché una valida guida verso gli obiettivi didattici desiderati.

Una forma di pianificazione più alta, che richiede però una maggiore esperienza e frequentazione di Wrilab2, è quella che prevede la concatenazione di due o tre Unità Didattiche in un unico percorso attraverso altrettanti generi testuali. Affinché questa attività sia considerata interessante e motivante dagli studenti si suggerisce di creare percorsi tematici a tappe, selezionando con cura gli esercizi da completare e le risorse da consultare in ciascuna fase. In questo modo l'utilità dei testi potrà essere percepita con maggiore chiarezza e questo uso autentico e situato dei materiali potrà attivare un livello di apprendimento più profondo. Un esempio di questa modalità di accesso ai contenuti del portale potrebbe essere chiedere la scrittura di una relazione di viaggio, alla quale si farà seguire la recensione di un albergo o di un ristorante e, infine, una lettera di lamentela formale per un disservizio. Oppure, a una relazione di tirocinio universitario potrebbe essere richiesto di allegare un *curriculum vitae*, collegando in maniera armoniosa e significativa due generi testuali assai utili a livello accademico e professionale. In questo modo i diversi generi possono legarsi a formare una serie che rivela la sua autenticità e utilità pratica nel momento in cui si va a collocare all'interno di uno specifico ambiente socioculturale. Un valore aggiuntivo può scaturire se agli elementi della costellazione così formata si assegna un ordine di tipo cronologico (cfr. Hyland 2007: 156-158).

4 Informazione

In Wrilab2 l'informazione sui caratteri strutturali dei testi è presentata sempre in una maniera induttiva. Le attività che accompagnano i modelli e le fonti invitano alla riflessione sugli aspetti specifici ai generi. Un utente esperto e attento, che abbia svolto almeno due dei quiz previsti per ciascun corso, dovrebbe disporre già di elementi sufficienti ad avvicinarsi alla scrittura della bozza, senza ricevere ulteriori indicazioni aggiuntive secondo un approccio più formale. Ciononostante in diversi punti dell'Unità Didattica sono disposte risorse con contenuti che hanno la funzione di offrire spiegazioni dirette e chiare a beneficio di quegli apprendenti che preferiscono avvicinarsi in maniera più tradizionale e meno induttiva ai testi. Si tratta di pagine e interi libri virtuali che vanno così a costituire un riferimento costante per chi desideri un approfondimento specifico[38].

Un genere testuale prevede però l'attuazione di funzioni retoriche complesse e nella presentazione dei compiti e delle strategie esiste il rischio di un sovraccarico cognitivo per gli apprendenti. Nel caso delle lingue seconde è possibile che i parlanti abbiano sviluppato una competenza comunicativa più che sufficiente a soddisfare i bisogni quotidiani, ma ancora limitata e non del tutto adeguata rispetto alle necessità poste dalla scrittura, soprattutto accademica o se paragonata al livello dei nativi: "ELs are often cognitively overloaded, especially in mainstreamed classrooms where they are held to the same performance standards as native English speakers" (Olson 2013: 382). Al fine di limitare questo carico per unità di tempo, la cornice teorica di riferimento di Wrilab2 prevede una distribuzione dell'informazione, così come dei compiti, il più possibile graduale e rispettosa delle potenzialità effettive degli apprendenti.

4.1 Pagine e libri virtuali

La pagina permette di presentare un quantitativo di informazioni limitato rispetto al libro, ma sempre con la presenza di immagini, contenuti multimediali e collegamenti. Questa risorsa è utile a offrire indicazioni semplici e brevi, in modo da guidare gli utenti nel loro percorso. In alcuni casi le azioni richieste per svolgere un compito possono essere assai complesse, come per esempio quando un utente del sito desidera inviare un commento a un compagno iscritto al suo stesso corso. La presenza di pagine con istruzioni costituisce in questi casi la guida più efficace.

Il libro virtuale è costituito da un certo numero di pagine organizzate in capitoli e paragrafi. Quando l'apprendente inizia a sfogliare la risorsa, nella barra laterale destra della pagina web compare un sommario che

38 In una didattica fondata sui generi imparare la scrittura può richiedere spiegazioni più dirette, anche riguardo a obiettivi e aspettative: "Learning occurs more effectively if teacher are explicit about what is being studied, why it is being studied, and what will be expected of students at the end of the course" (Hyland 2007: 152). Bernstein (1975) parla in questo caso di *visible pedagogies*, che sono messe in atto rendendo espliciti agli apprendenti l'inquadramento dei compiti, gli obiettivi, i criteri e i modi di trasmissione della conoscenza.

permette uno spostamento rapido all'interno del testo. La funzione del libro è allora quella di presentare contenuti e informazioni, anche multimediali, legati tematicamente fra di loro.

4.2 Distribuzione dell'informazione nell'Unità Didattica

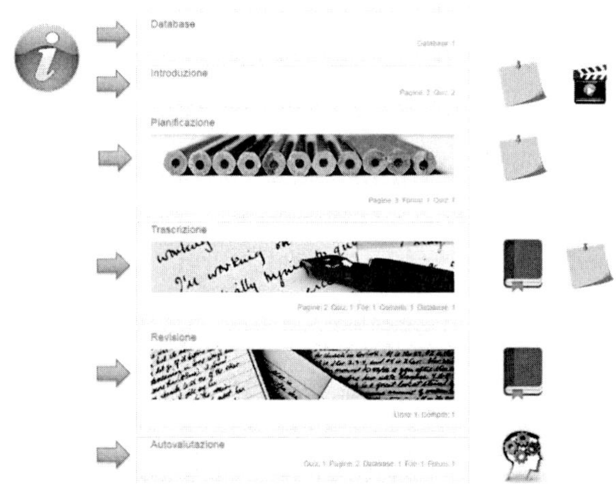

L'informazione sul genere testuale è ripartita sezione dopo sezione in tutte le fasi dell'Unità Didattica, in maniera progressiva e con ritorni e collegamenti, in un movimento di crescita a spirale che costruisce la conoscenza nuova a partire da quella già esistente. Un libro che precede il corso, come si è detto, introduce i contenuti e guida con degli opportuni collegamenti la scelta dei materiali da cui avviare ciascun percorso individuale. Nella sezione di introduzione un video multimediale presenta il genere testuale e una pagina introduce il compito di scrittura. Nella successiva pianificazione una seconda pagina offre le prime indicazioni strutturali, a un livello molto generale, al fine di orientare e indirizzare l'attenzione degli utenti mentre svolgeranno le attività di comprensione e analisi dei testi. Nella fase di trascrizione un libro virtuale presenta indicazioni più chiare e complete, in maniera diretta e strutturata, così da sistematizzare e completare le conoscenze acquisite fino a questo punto. Una pagina in formato Word con un modello della struttura del genere e liste di domande che invitano a riflettere sui possibili contenuti completa la sezione e invita alla scrittura della bozza. Nell'area di revisione un ultimo libro virtuale offre informazioni e domande che suggeriscono di focalizzare l'attenzione su questo importante momento del processo di scrittura. Infine, nella sezione di autovalutazione, un quiz ripropone gli elementi specifici principali del genere testuale, ripercorre idealmente il percorso dell'Unità Didattica e permette agli studenti di avanzare un bilancio conclusivo e autonomo del processo di apprendimento appena concluso.

5 Comunicazione

Wrilab2 non è soltanto un portale per la scrittura funzionale in L2, ma aspira anche a diventare un luogo di incontro di appassionati, un ambiente controllato

di apprendimento nel quale scambiare buone pratiche, informazioni e opinioni. Il processo di scrittura è considerato anche secondo una prospettiva di carattere socioculturale, alla pari di un sistema di competenze in parte interrelate che possono essere apprese con grande efficacia in contesti di interazione e cooperazione con altri utenti (cfr. Cisotto 2015: 17-18). Uno degli obiettivi del progetto è allora superare un'ottica più strettamente scolastica, per rivolgere l'attenzione verso forme di comunicazione nuove e per certi aspetti più autentiche. Le discussioni online possono facilitare l'apprendimento cooperativo e stimolare anche gli apprendenti più introversi; aumentando così la socialità all'interno della classe virtuale e riducendo la dipendenza dalla figura tradizionale dell'insegnante (cfr. Novello 2012: 90-91). Il portale Moodle che ospita i materiali didattici offre numerosi mezzi di comunicazione adatti a questi scopi e tutte le Unità Didattiche prevedono momenti dedicati alla condivisione delle idee tra pari. I principali strumenti utili a questo scopo sono il messaggio privato, il database e il forum.

5.1 Messaggi privati, database e forum

Moodle consente ai suoi iscritti di entrare in contatto tra loro in diversi modi. La maniera più semplice è il messaggio privato, o PM. Il blocco laterale *Utenti Online* permette di verificare con grande semplicità e immediatezza se l'utente desiderato si trova al momento all'interno del sito. In alternativa il blocco di *Navigazione* può fornire in qualsiasi momento un elenco di tutti i partecipanti a un corso. Per inviare un messaggio è sufficiente selezionare il nome della persona desiderata e, poco sotto il suo avatar, scegliere l'opzione *Invia un messaggio*. È anche consentito inoltrare una comunicazione a un gruppo formato da più utenti.

I database sono archivi di file utilizzati da Wrtilab2 per conservare le composizioni scritte in passato dagli studenti. Nel corso del tempo si potrà in questo modo creare una vera e propria biblioteca di testi, modelli e fonti a disposizione dei nuovi iscritti al portale. In ciascuna Unità Didattica sono presenti più database, per archiviare gli elaborati prodotti in ciascuno dei diversi momenti del processo di scrittura: prima di iniziare il percorso, dopo avere completato la bozza e a versione definitiva consegnata. In questo modo gli utenti sono invitati a una maggiore consapevolezza riguardo alle proprie capacità e ad avviare un processo di costante autovalutazione del proprio livello di competenza.

Il forum è lo strumento di comunicazione più usato sulla piattaforma e permette agli utenti di scambiarsi opinioni durante le diverse fasi del processo di scrittura oppure di inviare opinioni e suggerimenti sul lavoro svolto. Sono presenti due forum in ciascuna Unità Didattica. Il primo è nella sezione di pianificazione ed è dedicato allo scambio di idee prima di iniziare la scrittura. Il secondo è nella sezione di autovalutazione, al termine del processo, e può essere utile a condividere i risultati e anche a festeggiare i successi. Il *Forum News*, esterno e precedente alle sei sezioni nelle quali si articola ogni corso, è invece utilizzato esclusivamente dagli assistenti del progetto per comunicazioni tecniche o di servizio.

Il vantaggio del forum rispetto ai messaggi privati è che le domande e le risposte rimarranno visibili e potranno in seguito essere lette da altri. Quando un utente scrive sul forum, lascia una comunicazione accessibile a qualsiasi iscritto alla piattaforma, quindi pubblica. Qualora si preferisca che i messaggi siano visualizzati solo dai membri di un gruppo ristretto, sarà necessario selezionare l'opzione *Gruppi separati* prima dell'invio e, nel menu a tendina del forum, scegliere il nome del gruppo di appartenenza. In questo modo soltanto gli iscritti a quel gruppo potranno visualizzare i messaggi e dare loro risposta.

5.2 La comunicazione tra pari in Wrilab2

Gli utenti di Wrilab2 sono invitati a collaborare assieme, in una comunità di scrittori, con l'obiettivo di elaborare testi il più possibile di qualità e vicini alle caratteristiche e alla struttura dei generi scelti. Le risorse e le attività messe a disposizione sono molteplici e, qualora l'utente si sia iscritto al portale assieme a un gruppo e con un insegnante accompagnatore, in qualsiasi punto del processo è prevista la possibilità di chiedere un aiuto o il sostegno del docente o assistente linguistico esterno. Tuttavia, una diversa e non meno importante forma di aiuto, può giungere anche dagli altri iscritti al sito, che si trovano nelle medesime condizioni e affrontano difficoltà paragonabili. Il quadro teorico di riferimento del progetto considera positivamente la strategie didattiche del commento da parte dei pari, che in alcuni contesti può abbassare la tensione e l'ansia legate al processo di scrittura (cfr. Bräuer in questo volume, paragrafo *Process-oriented learning and (peer) interaction*). Il gruppo di lavoro del progetto crede quindi in questa modalità di scambio di idee, buone pratiche, consigli e opinioni. Le caratteristiche e le potenzialità offerte da Moodle, in particolare attraverso il database e il forum, consentono di lasciare tracce visibili del proprio passaggio, che potranno essere seguite e percorse nuovamente in futuro, perseguendo così potenzialmente anche obiettivi di tipo interculturale (cfr. Novello 2012: 91). Solo creando una comunità di scrittori e conservando archivi testuali ricchi di contenuti il progetto potrà in futuro essere utilizzato ancora e diventare un punto di riferimento per chi desideri avvicinarsi alla scrittura funzionale in lingua seconda, in particolare per quanto riguarda le tipologie testuali argomentativa ed espositiva.

Riferimenti bibliografici

Balboni, Paolo E. (2012): Le sfide di Babele. Torino: UTET.

Bernstein, Basil (1975): Class, Codes and Control 3: Towards a Theory of Educational Transmissions. London: Routledge & Kegan Paul.

Cisotto, Lerida & Gruppo RDL (2015): Scrivere testi in 9 mosse. Curricolo verticale di scrittura per la scuola primaria e secondaria di primo grado. Trento: Erickson.

Flower, Linda & Hayes, John R. (1980): The dynamics of composing: making plans and juggling constraints. In: Gregg Lee W. & Steinberg, Erwin Ray (Eds.) (1980): Cognitive Processes in Writing. Hillsdale N.J.: Lawrence Erlbaum, 31-50.

Hyland, Ken (2007): Genre pedagogy: Language, literacy and L2 writing instruction. In: *Journal of Second Language Writing* 16/3 (2007) 148-164.

Lala, Letizia: Tipi di testo. In: Enciclopedia dell'Italiano Treccani. Available: http://www.treccani.it/enciclopedia/tipi-di-testo_(Enciclopedia-dell'Italiano)/ [consultato il 09/12/2016].

Lavinio, Cristina (2000): Tipi testuali e processi cognitivi. In: Camponovo, Fabio & Moretti, Alessandra (2000): Didattica ed educazione linguistica. Quaderni del Giscel. Firenze: La Nuova Italia, 125-144.

Novello, Alberta (2012): «Tecnologie e cooperative learning». In: Caon, Fabio & Serragiotto, Graziano (a cura di) (2012): Tecnologia e didattica delle lingue. Teorie, risorse, sperimentazioni. Torino: UTET, 84-94.

Olson, Booth Carol, Scarcella, Robin & Matuchniak, Tina (2013): Best Practices in Teaching Writing to English Learners. Reducing Constraints to Facilitate Writing Development. In: Graham, Steve (a cura di): Writing Instruction. New York, London: The Guilford Press, 381-402.

Mihaela Knez, Damjana Kern

Razvijanje pisne zmožnosti v slovenščini kot drugem jeziku s pomočjo spletnega laboratorija za branje in pisanje (WRILAB2)

1 Uvod

Pisanje je tesno povezano s procesom izobraževanja, saj se te jezikovne dejavnosti naučimo predvsem v šoli. Pri pisanju se učenci učijo zapisane različice jezika, ki se od govorjene razlikuje tako po obliki kot po rabi. Domači govorci si pri razvijanju svoje pisne zmožnosti pomagajo s svojo že razvito govorno zmožnostjo, medtem ko začnejo govorci slovenščine kot drugega jezika zmožnost govorjenja in pisanja razvijati hkrati (Weigle 2000: 4). Učeči se pisanje potrebujejo za različne namene (Vähäpässi 1982: 9): za učenje (npr. pisanje zapiskov, izpiskov, narekov, povzetkov), izražanje čustev in občutkov (pisanje zasebnih pisem), informiranje (pisanje poročil, življenjepisa), prepričevanje (pisanje prošenj, pritožb), zabavo (kreativno pisanje), ohranjanje stikov (pismo, elektronska pošta, razglednica). Je pomembno orodje za učenje, s stopnjo izobraževanja pa se njegova pomembnost veča. Pisanje se tesno povezuje tudi z bralno zmožnostjo učenca. Hayes v zvezi s pisanjem izpostavlja zlasti zmožnost kritičnega branja oz. branja z namenom evalvacije besedila, ob katerem pisec odkrije pomanjkljivosti svojega besedila. Medtem ko se slabši bralci (in tudi govorci) osredotočajo na popravljanje lokalnih napak na ravni posameznih povedi, se boljši bralci osredotočajo na izboljšanje vsebine in organizacije besedila. Pomembno je tudi učinkovito branje izvorne literature (besedil, s katerimi si pomagamo pri pisanju ali pa jih citiramo) in branje navodil (Hayes 1996: 26–28). Napačno razumevanje izvornih besedil in navodil lahko pomembno vplivata na uspešnost pisanja.

Pisci se v drugem jeziku pri pisanju poslužujejo istih procesov kot v prvem, za to se, če dosežejo določeno stopnjo znanja, tako kot pri drugih spretnostih znanje iz prvega jezika lahko prenese v drugi jezik. Seveda pa je proces pisanja otežen, saj se mora pisec v drugem jeziku vedno znova ukvarjati z omejitvami, ki jih prinaša nižja jezikovna zmožnost v drugem jeziku in se zato med procesom pisanja bolj osredotoča na obliko kot pa na vsebino besedila. Govorci drugih jezikov načeloma manj načrtujejo pisanje, pišejo manj tekoče in z več napakami, zaradi česar so njihova besedila pogosto tudi manj učinkovita (Weigle 2000: 36). Da imajo učenci govorci drugih jezikov zaradi manjše slovnične zmožnosti težave, so pokazali tudi rezultati raziskave o pisanju[39], ki smo jo med učenci, govorci slovenščine, nemščine, češčine in italijanščine kot drugega jezika, izvedli v okviru projekta WRILAB2. Učenci govorci slovenščine kot druge-

[39] Raziskava je bila izvedena leta 2015. Vanjo je bilo vključenih 482 respondentov, od tega 87 govorcev slovenščine kot drugega jezika.

ga jezika so najbolje ocenili razumljivost svojih besedil, največ težav pa imajo po njihovem mnenju s slovnično pravilnostjo in ustreznim zapisovanjem besed (prim. graf 1).

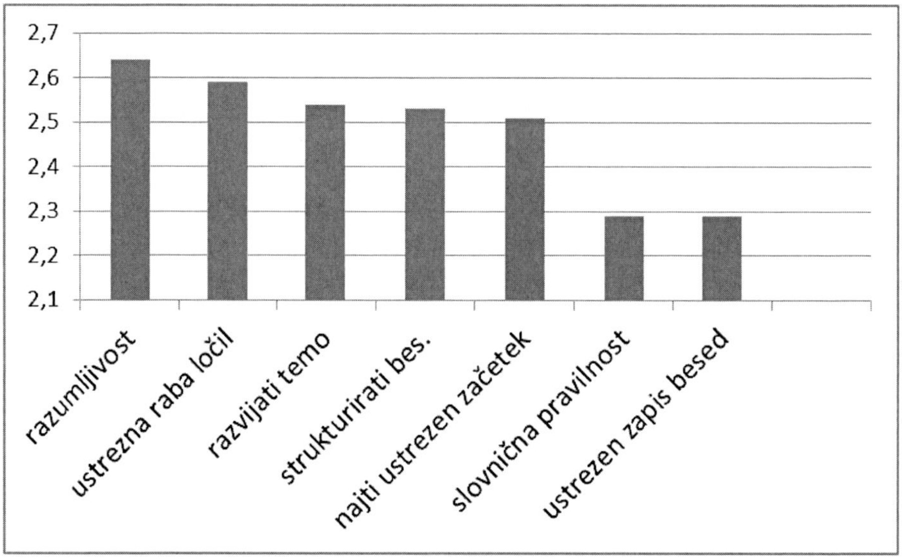

Graf 1: Samozaupanje učencev v pisanje, N = 87

Kljub zavedanju, da dobro razvita pisna zmožnost pomembno pripomore k uspešnosti izobraževanja, pa je specializiranih gradiv, ki bi bila govorcem slovenščine kot drugega jezika pri tem v pomoč, razmeroma malo oz. so večinoma del obstoječih splošnih učbenikov za učenje slovenščine kot drugega jezika. To vrzel smo skušali zapolniti s pripravo gradiva v okviru evropskega projekta »Spletni laboratorij za branje in pisanje v češčini, nemščini, italijanščini in slovenščini kot drugem jeziku«. Pomanjkanje ustreznih učnih gradiv za razvijanje pisne zmožnosti v drugem jeziku (zlasti na srednješolski in univerzitetni stopnji) se je namreč pokazalo v vseh navedenih jezikih.

2 Komu je spletni laboratorij namenjen?

Portal WRILAB2 je namenjen zlasti učencem in študentom, katerih prvi jezik ni slovenščina, vendar se šolajo v slovenskem jeziku oz. je slovenščina eden izmed jezikov njihovega šolanja, npr. učencem in študentom priseljencem, učencem v slovenskih in dvojezičnih šolah v zamejstvu, študentom na lektoratih slovenščine v tujini in tujim študentom, ki študirajo v Sloveniji, svojo pisno zmožnost pa lahko s pomočjo portala poglobijo tudi domači govorci.

Portal omogoča različne oblike učenja. Zlasti pri učencih in študentih na ravni B2 in C1 lahko poučevanje v celoti poteka na daljavo, lahko ga izvedemo v kombinirani obliki, tako da del pouka izpeljemo skupaj z učenci v razredu, del nalog (zlasti pisanje) pa učenci opravijo doma. Portal ima lahko tudi le vlogo priročnika za pisanje, s katerim si uporabniki pomagajo priložnostno.

3 Predstavitev enot

Pri izbiri enot oz. pripravi učnega gradiva smo izhajali iz dejanskih potreb učečih se[40], zato smo vanj vključili tiste besedilne vrste, s katerimi se učenci in študenti srečujejo v okviru svojega šolanja pa tudi v vsakdanjem življenju. Rezultati naše raziskave so pokazali, da učenci kot samostojni tvorci v šoli pričakovano najpogosteje pišejo akademska in funkcionalna besedila[41], nekoliko redkeje pa se lotevajo kreativnega pisanja (prim. graf 2).

Prav tako je iz rezultatov razvidno, da se zdijo učencem in študentom slovenščine kot drugega jezika navedene besedilne vrste za njihovo življenje različno pomembne. Večjo pomembnost pripisujejo obvladovanju pisanja življenjepisa, prošenj, esejev, poročil in obvestil (prim. graf 3), kar smo skušali v čim večji meri upoštevati tudi pri izboru besedilnih vrst, ki smo jih vključili v spletni portal WRILAB2.

---

[40] Specifika slovenske skupine v projektu je bila ta, da je bila med sodelujočimi šolami, ki so testirale pripravljeno gradivo, tudi Državna večstopenjska šola s slovensko-italijanskim dvojezičnim poukom v Špetru v Italiji, v katero so vključeni učenci, stari od 6 do 14 let. V testiranje gradiva so bili vključeni predvsem učenci zadnjih razredov, vendar gre kljub temu za mlajše učence kot v drugih jezikovnih skupinah, ki so bile vključene v projekt. Temu primerno smo za učenje pisanja v slovenščini prilagodili tudi učno gradivo.

[41] Pisanje akademskih besedil (npr. seminar, referat, esej, poročilo) pomeni pomemben način prikaza pridobljenega znanja in je del skoraj vsakega šolskega predmeta, medtem ko poteka učenje pisanja funkcionalnih besedil predvsem pri jezikovnem pouku, z dejanskim pisanjem funkcionalnih besedil za lastne potrebe pa se učenci srečajo predvsem proti koncu šolanja, ko komunikacijo v zvezi s svojimi potrebami namesto staršev prevzamejo sami oz. ko začnejo vstopati na trg dela.

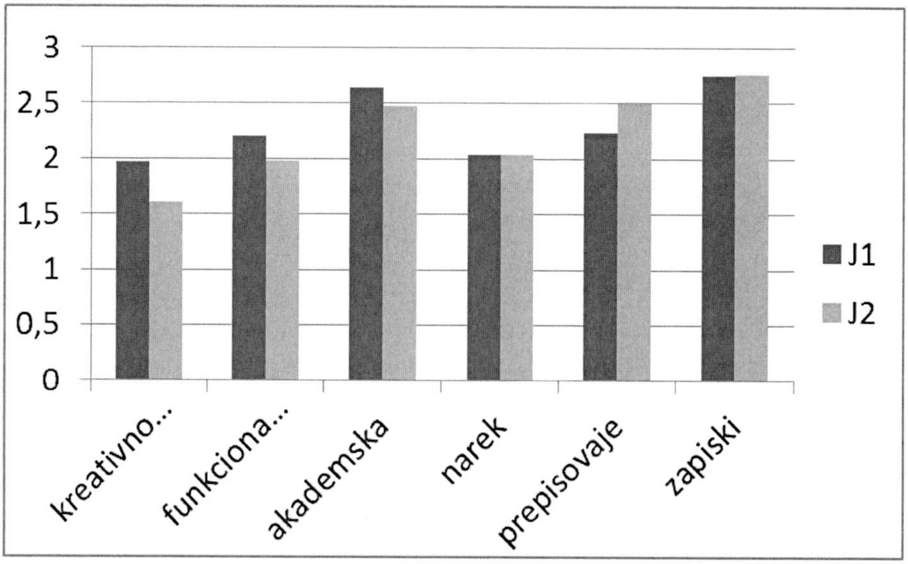

Graf 2: Vrste besedil, ki jih učenci najpogosteje pišejo v šoli v prvem (J1) in drugem (J2) jeziku, N=482

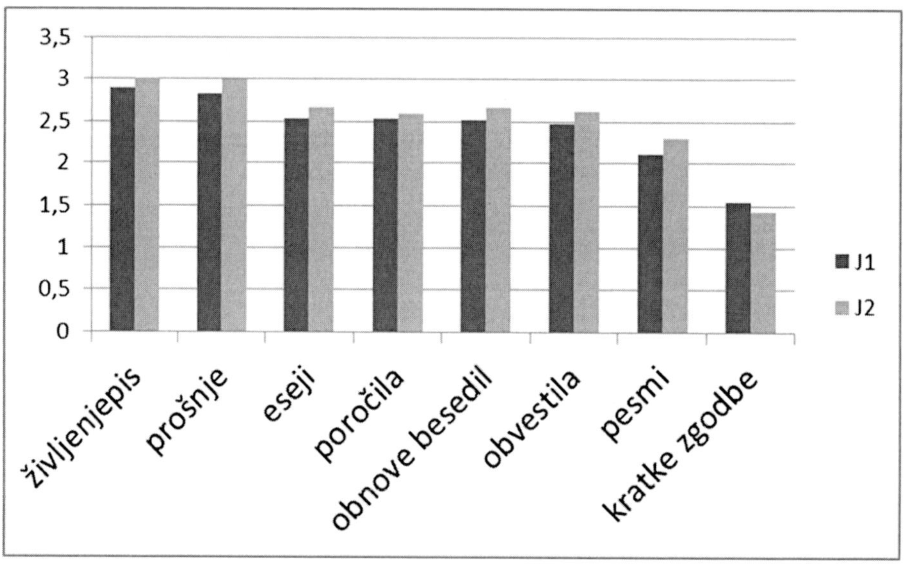

Graf 3: Besedilne vrste, ki se zdi učencem pomembne v njihovem nadaljnjem življenju, N = 87

Izbrali in didaktizirali smo dvanajst različnih besedilnih vrst – življenjepis, pritožbo, prošnjo, e-pismo, oceno knjige, filma ali predstave, predstavitev osebe ali kraja, poročilo o ekskurziji, poročilo o eksperimentu, povzetek, referat ali seminar, razpravljalni esej in idejno zasnovo šolskega projekta ali raziskave. Gre za besedilne vrste, ki se v skladu z opisniki Skupnega evropskega jezikovnega okvira praviloma uvrščajo na višje ravni jezikovnega znanja (B2–C1), seveda pa so z izborom enostavnejših sporazumevalnih in slovničnih vzorcev ter besedišča dostopne tudi govorcem na ravni B1. Tudi posamezne naloge pred pisanjem so večinoma zasnovane večnivojsko in so izbirne.

B1	B2–C1
življenjepis pritožba prošnja e-pismo	predstavitev osebe ali kraja poročilo o ekskurziji ocena knjige, filma ali predstave poročilo o delovni praksi, eksperimentu referat, seminar razpravljalni esej povzetek, izvleček, obnova besedila idejna zasnova šolskega projekta ali raziskave

Za ponazoritev zahtevnosti posamezne ravni navajamo opisnike za pisanje, kot so navedeni v Skupnem evropskem jezikovnem okviru (Ferbežar idr. 2011: 85–86, 106) in ki so učiteljem lahko v pomoč tudi pri ocenjevanju besedil.

C1	**Splošno pisno izražanje** Pisati zna jasna, dobro strukturirana besedila o kompleksnih temah, v katerih poudari bistvene prvine, svoja stališča osvetli z daljšimi pojasnili in tehtnimi primeri ter besedilo ustrezno sklene. **Ustvarjalno pisanje** Pisati zna jasne, podrobne, dobro strukturirane in razvite opise in domišljijska besedila v prepričljivem, osebnem in naravnem slogu, primernem za potencialnega bralca. **Poročila in eseji** Pisati zna jasne, dobro strukturirane prikaze kompleksnih vsebin, pri čemer poudari ustrezne pomembne prvine. Razširiti zna besedilo in podrobneje osvetliti svoja stališča z dodatnimi pojasnili, razlogi in ustreznimi primeri. **Splošna pisna interakcija** Izraža se jasno in natančno in se učinkovito in prožno prilagaja naslovniku.

<table>
<tr><td>B2</td><td>Splošno pisno izražanje
Pisati zna jasna besedila s podrobnostmi o različnih temah z znanih področij. Povezuje in vrednoti podatke in trditve iz različnih virov.
Ustvarjalno pisanje
Pisati zna jasne, podrobne opise resničnih in izmišljenih dogodkov in doživetij. Pri tem v besedilu jasno izraža razmerja med mislimi in sledi ustaljenim konvencijam izbrane zvrsti (B2+).
Pisati zna jasne, podrobne opise na različne teme, povezane z njegovim interesnim področjem. Napisati zna oceno filma, knjige ali gledališke igre (B2-).
Poročila in eseji
Pisati zna eseje in poročila, v katerih sistematično razvije argumentacijo in ustrezno poudari dodatne omejitve, navaja razloge in ustrezne primere. Ovrednotiti zna različne misli ali možne rešitve nekega problema (B2+).
Pisati zna eseje ali poročila, v katerih razvije določen argument, navede razloge za določeno stališče ali proti njemu ter pojasni prednosti in slabosti različnih možnosti. Povezati zna podatke in argumente iz več virov (B2-).
Splošna pisna interakcija
Učinkovito zna sporočati novice in izražati mnenja v pisni obliki ter sprejemati sporočila drugih.</td></tr>
<tr><td>B1</td><td>Splošno pisno izražanje
Pisati zna preprosta povezana besedila o vrsti znanih tem s področij, ki ga zanimajo. Pri tem krajše samostojne trditve poveže v linearni niz.
Ustvarjalno pisanje
Neposredno in podrobno zna opisati vrsto znanih vsebin, povezanih z njegovim interesnim področjem. Opisati zna doživetja; pri tem v preprostem povezanem besedilu opiše svoja čustva in odzive. Opisati zna dogodke, resnične ali izmišljene, ali nedavno potovanje. Napisati zna preprosto zgodbo.
Poročila in eseji
Pisati zna kratke, preproste eseje o temah, ki ga zanimajo. Precej samozavestno zna povzemati, poročati in navajati svoje mnenje o zbranih dejstvih, ki zadevajo znane vsakdanje in nevsakdanje zadeve z njemu znanega področja (B1+).
Pisati zna zelo kratka poročila v standardnih konvencionalnih oblikah (npr. na obrazcih), s katerimi posreduje vsakdanja dejstva in navaja razloge za ukrepanje (B1-).
Splošna pisna interakcija
Posredovati zna informacije in misli o abstraktnih in konkretnih temah, preverjati informacije ter dovolj natančno spraševati o problematiki ali jo razložiti. Pisati zna osebna pisma in sporočila, v katerih prosi za preproste neposredno uporabne informacije ali jih posreduje. Povedati zna, kar se mu zdi pomembno.</td></tr>
</table>

Seveda pa se je treba zavedati, da učenci in študenti niso povsem homogena publika, saj se obe ciljni skupini razlikujeta tako po kognitivnih zmožnostih in zrelosti kot tudi zanimanjih, zato vse dejavnosti v posameznih enotah niso za vse uporabnike enako ustrezne. Prav tako znotraj posamezne besedilne vrste nismo mogli povsem upoštevati potreb uporabnikov glede na njihovo študijsko usmeritev.

4 Zgradba enote

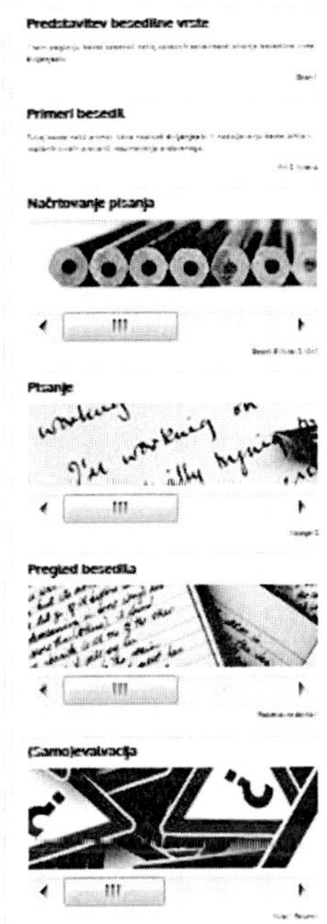

V vsaki enoti naj bi se učeči se izpopolnili v pisanju ene besedilne vrste. Izjemoma je v enoto vključenih tudi več besedilnih vrst, ki pa so si po funkciji oz. namenu sorodne (npr. povzetek, izvleček). Učne enote imajo enotno zgradbo, dejavnosti pa smo pri posamezni enoti razdelili na:

- predstavitev besedilne vrste,
- primeri besedil,
- jezikovna sredstva,
- pisanje,
- pregled besedila,
- (samo)evalvacija.

4.1 Predstavitev besedilne vrste

V tem razdelku učeči se najdejo kratek opis izbrane besedilne vrste oz. žanra in njene tipične značilnosti. Namen predstavitve je pri učečih se uzavestiti značilnosti diskurza določene besedilne vrste in kontekstualnih vidikov njene jezikovne rabe. Navedene so tudi internetne povezave in strokovna literatura, s pomočjo katerih lahko učeči se poglobijo svoje vedenje o določeni besedilni vrsti.

4.2 Primeri besedil

Na tem mestu so predstavljeni tipični vzorčni primeri izbrane besedilne vrste. Gre za besedila, ki so jih v avtentičnih situacijah napisali domači govorci. V eni od različic je besedilo tudi komentirano: izpostavljena je tipična zgradba besedila, način razvijanja teme in tipični sporazumevalni in slovnični vzorci (npr. tipično besedišče, slovnične oblike, sporazumevalni vzorci, povezani z družbenimi konvencijami). Sledijo vaje za razumevanje zapisanih besedil. Raziskave namreč kažejo, da razvijanje bralne zmožnosti v drugem jeziku pomembno vpliva na zmožnost pisanja (Krashen 1993 v Hyland 2003: 17), saj oba procesa vključujeta podobne kompleksne kognitivne in sporazumevalne zmožnosti, s pomočjo katerih rešujemo jezikovne naloge in ob katerih se aktivira obstoječe jezikovno znanje in splošno vedenje. S pomočjo branja učeči se pridobivajo novo znanje znotraj določenega predmetnega področja, predvsem pa se ob tem seznanijo s tipičnimi vzorci, besediščem in zgradbo besedila (Hyland 2003: 17-18).

4.3 Jezikovna sredstva

V razdelku Jezikovna sredstva učeče se seznanjamo z naborom sporazumevalnih vzorcev (tudi tipičnih glagolov, samostalnikov in pridevnikov), ki se pogosto pojavljajo v določeni besedilni vrsti oz. ob določeni temi. Tako se učeči se v sicer izolirani obliki brez širšega sobesedila seznanijo z večjim številom sporazumevalnih vzorcev, tudi tistih, ki v vzorčnih besedilih niso bili uporabljeni.

Sledijo vaje, s pomočjo katerih uporabniki portala razvijajo svojo leksikalno (vaje za utrjevanje specifičnega besedišča, povezanega z besedilno vrsto ali temo), oblikoslovno, skladenjsko (vaje za usvajanje oblikoslovnih in skladenjskih vzorcev), pravopisno (npr. vaje za ustrezno postavljanje ločil in pisanje velike začetnice) in pragmatično zmožnost (vaje za organiziranje in strukturiranje besedil, koherentnost besedil, slogovno ustreznost, retorično učinkovitost, poznavanje konvencij). Seveda pa je treba poudariti, da namen portala ni sistematično razvijanje slovnične zmožnosti. V ta namen mora učitelj pripraviti dodatne vaje, še posebej, če gre za govorce na nižjih ravneh jezikovnega znanja (npr. na ravni B1).

4.4 Pisanje

V tem razdelku je učečim se podana konkretna naloga za pisanje. Skušamo jih voditi skozi celoten proces pisanja:

- načrtovanje pisanja: učeče se spodbujamo k zbiranju idej za pisanje v obliki alinej ali miselnih vzorcev, priklicu informacij, ki so jih pridobili pri predstavitvi besedilne vrste in reševanju vaj v enoti, iskanju knjižnih in spletnih virov, ki bi jim bili lahko v pomoč pri pisanju;
- priprava prvega osnutka besedila;
- priprava končnega besedila.

Čeprav je večina pripravljenih dejavnosti usmerjena v sistematično vodenje učenca od začetka pisanja do končnega besedila, naj učitelj upošteva, da so nekateri učenci uspešnejši, če so lahko pri pisanju povsem svobodni in pišejo po navdihu ter besedilo uredijo šele v zaključni fazi.

Učeči se si lahko pri pisanju pomagajo tudi z različnimi spletnimi jezikovnimi viri, dostopnimi v slovenščini, npr. s slovarji Inštituta za slovenski jezik na portalu Fran, predvsem s Slovarjem slovenskega knjižnega jezika in Slovenskim pravopisom, korpusom Gigafida, z Amebisovim pregibnikom Besana in s Ponsovim prevajalnikom. Povezave z omenjenimi jezikovnimi viri so ves čas dostopne v desnem zgornjem kotu portala. Priporočljivo je, da učitelj učencem vsak jezikovni vir predstavi in jim hkrati tudi pokaže, kako se jih najučinkoviteje uporablja.

4.5 Pregled besedila

V tem razdelku pisca usmerjamo pri pregledovanju in dopolnjevanju besedila, svoje besedilo pa lahko ponudi tudi v komentar svojim sošolcem ali pa ga odda v pregled svojemu učitelju.

4.6 Samoevalvacija

Gre za sklepno fazo enote. Pisec lahko v tem razdelku ovrednoti dejavnosti v enoti in kritično razmisli o svojem pisanju in pisnem izdelku ter svojem napredku. Njegovi odgovori so v pomoč učitelju pri pripravi nadaljnjih dejavnosti, avtorjem portala pa služijo kot informacija o ustreznosti in učinkovitosti nalog.

Didaktične enote so torej sestavljene tako, da učenca vodijo skozi proces pisanja in ga učijo načrtovati posamezne faze pisanja ter upoštevati tako vsebinske (poznavanje tematike, upoštevanje sociokulturnega védenja) kot jezikovne (besedišče, sporazumevalni in slovnični vzorci, poznavanje besedilnih vrst) vidike pisanja, hkrati pa je mogoče med njimi tudi poljubno preskakovati. Tako smo se želeli približati različnim zmožnostim in potrebam posameznika.

5 Povratna informacija

Učečemu se je kakovostna povratna informacija, ki mu jo po branju oz. pregledu besedila da učitelj, pri razvijanju pisne zmožnosti v veliko pomoč. Po eni strani pisec lahko opazuje, kako se na njegovo pisanje odziva naslovnik oz. bralec, po drugi strani pa mu kritični in povedni komentarji učitelja pomagajo izboljšati pisanje. Rezultati že omenjene raziskave, ki smo jo izvedli med učenci, so pokazali, da je učencem pri učenju pisanja v veliko pomoč, če učiteljeva povratna informacija ni osredotočena zgolj na ocenjevanje njihovih pisnih izdelkov, ampak bolj na učiteljevo prizadevanje, da bi učeči se svojo zmožnost pisanja izboljšal. To pomeni, da učitelj napake označi, predlaga boljšo možnost ali rešitev, napiše komentar in se z učencem o besedilu, njegovih pomanjkljivostih in tudi pozitivnih straneh, pogovori (prim. graf 4).

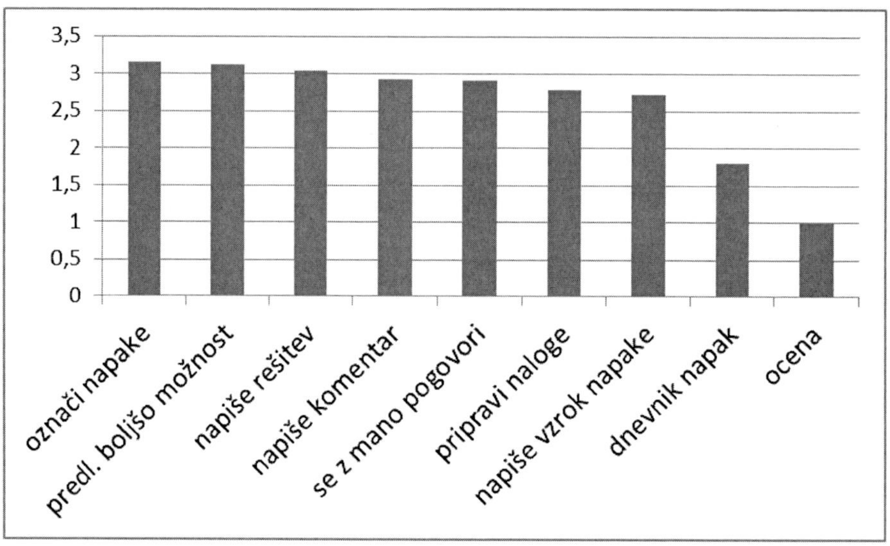

Graf 4: Učiteljeve oblike pomoči, ki učencem najbolj pomagajo pri pisanju, N = 87

Če besedilo tudi oceni, je pomembno, da učencem pove, zakaj se je za določeno oceno odločil, in svojo odločitev tudi utemelji. Izrazi naj se o vsebinski ustreznosti in namenu besedila (ali vsebina ustreza nalogi, ali ga je besedilo pritegnilo, ali je pisec prepričljiv v svojih argumentih, ali je izkazal zadostno poznavanje teme itn.), njegovi zgradbi (ustrezen začetek, zaključek, organiziranost besedila), obsegu in izbiri besedišča, slovnični in pravopisni ustreznosti. Dobro je, če je pisec vnaprej seznanjen s kriteriji ocenjevanja.

Naša anketa je tudi pokazala, da se govorci pri pisanju v slovenščini kot drugem jeziku pogosteje obračajo po pomoč k sošolcem kot pa, kadar pišejo v svojem prvem jeziku (prim. graf 5).

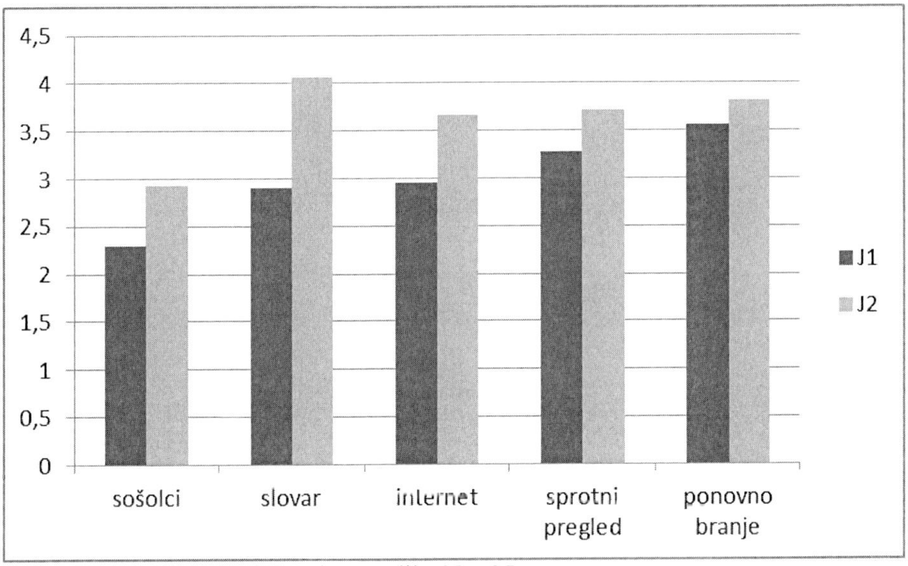

Graf 5: Vrste pomoči pri pisanju besedila, N = 87

Tudi enote portala Wrilab so pripravljene tako, da ves čas spodbujajo dialog med učencem in učiteljem in tudi dialog z vrstniki. Temu sta namenjeni rubriki »Povej, vprašaj« in »Poklepetaj«. S tem želimo učence spodbuditi, da bi aktivno poiskali pomoč, če bi jo potrebovali tudi med samim procesom pisanja in svoj končni izdelek pripeljali do želenega rezultata.

Možnost, da učeči se dobijo vmesno povratno informacijo o svojem pisnem izdelku, je podana tudi v razdelku »Pregled besedila«. Na tem mestu se lahko odločijo, da posredujejo svoje besedilo v komentar učitelju oz. vrstnikom. Ogledajo (in komentirajo) pa si lahko tudi besedila drugih učencev. Ta so jim lahko v dodatno pomoč pri oblikovanju besedila.

Seveda se je treba zavedati, da je posredovanje pisnih izdelkov v komentar vrstnikom lahko tudi neprijetna izkušnja, zato je posebna naloga učitelja, da učence opozori na spoštljivo izražanje mnenja. Izpostavi naj prednosti medvrstniške povratne informacije. Ena od teh je zagotovo ta, da lahko pisec na tak način pridobi več mnenj o svojem besedilu (brez strahu, da bi bil ob tem tudi ocenjen) in lahko tudi opazuje, kakšen učinek ima na vrstnike njegovo besedilo (torej gre za zelo avtentičen način pridobivanja povratne informacije), hkrati pa tudi sam kot kritični bralec drugih besedil razvija zmožnost presojanja besedila. Po drugi strani pa lahko ravno zato, ker še niso vešči podajanja relevantnih povratnih informacij in so še sami v procesu razvijanja pisne in tudi bralne zmožnosti, piscu podajo nerelevantno, lahko tudi napačno sporočilo (se npr. osredotočijo le na slovnično ustreznost besedila, besedilo vrednotijo z vidika svojih sociokulturnih izkušenj) ali pa ga s svojo neustrezno izraženo kritiko tudi prizadenejo. Zato naj učitelj posebej poudari, da morajo biti komentarji spoštljivi in spodbudni. V njih lahko piscu podajo nekaj predlogov za izboljšavo besedila in mu zastavijo vprašanja, ki so se jim odprla ob branju besedila. Popravki naj bodo jasni in utemeljeni. Pri branju naj se osredotočijo na to, ali so besedilo razumeli, ali so bila sporočila jasna, argumenti prepričljivi, ali je pisec v njih vzbudil zanimanje za besedilo, katera je glavna ideja, ki jo želi izpostaviti pisec, kateri del besedila se jim zdi najboljši in zakaj, v katerih delih besedila bi pričakovali podrobnejše informacije, obrazložitve, ali morda kje katera misel ni izpeljana do konca itn. Tudi pisec mora do komentarjev vrstnikov zavzeti določeno distanco in se, če je v dvomih, o ustrezni odločitvi posvetovati z učiteljem. Ustreznega komentiranja se učeči se najlažje naučijo, če vodeno pregledajo svoje besedilo, k čemur jih spodbujamo z dejavnostmi v razdelku Pregled besedila. Učenci lahko besedilo svojih vrstnikov komentirajo tako, da ga odprejo v wordovem dokumentu in svoje komentarje vpišejo s pomočjo funkcije Pregled → Nova pripomba[42], lahko pa besedilo tudi natisnejo in komentarje napišejo na roko. Učeči se si med seboj lahko pomagajo v različnih fazah pisanja – v fazi zbiranja idej, pri komentiranju prvega osnutka besedila ali končnega besedila, seveda pa je tudi pri tej dejavnosti treba upoštevati želje pisca in spoštovati tudi njegovo odločitev, da svojega pisanja ne bo dal v komentar vrstnikom.

6 Zaključek

Spletni portal WRILAB2 smo si sodelavci projekta zamislili kot laboratorij, v katerem bi učitelji in učenci s pomočjo teoretičnih in praktičnih napotkov ter vaj iskali, preizkušali in našli najučinkovitejše poti pisanja. Nove strategije, učinkovita raba podpornih gradiv in dobra povratna informacija vrstnikov in učitelja naj bi učence postopoma vodile do faze, ko bodo postali samostojni in učinkoviti pisci, ki bodo znali uspešno premostiti omejitve, s katerimi se srečujejo govorci drugih in tujih jezikov.

Literatura

Ferbežar Ina idr. (ur.) (2011): Skupni evropski jezikovni okvir: učenje, poučevanje, ocenjevanje.

Hayes, John R. (1996): A new framework for understanding cognition and affect in writing. V: Levy, C. Michael & Ransdell, Sarah (ur.): The science of writing. Mahwah, NJ: Lawrence Erlbaum Associates, 1-27.

Hyland, Ken (2003): Second language writing. Cambridge: University Press

Krashen, Stephen (1993): The power of reading: insight from the research. Englewood, CO: Libraries Unilimited.

Vähäpässi, Anneli (1982): On the specification of the domain of school writing. V: Purves, Alan C. & Takala, Sauli (ur.): An international perspective on the evaluation of written composition. Oxford: Pergamon, 265–289.

Weigle, Sara Cushing (2002): Assessing Writing. Cambridge: Cambridge University Press.

42 Funkcijo najdejo v osnovni wordovi vrstici.

Contributors

Ana Adamovičová, lektorka Ústavu bohemistických studií na Filozofické fakultě Karlovy univerzity. Pravidelně též působí na Univerzitě v Tampere ve Finsku, kde učí český jazyk, literaturu a kulturu. Je autorkou řady učebnic češtiny pro cizince. Podílela se na řadě projektů. Věnuje se výzkumu mluvené češtiny, především partikulí v mluveném jazyce.

Ana Adamovičová, is Lecturer at the Institute of Czech Studies at the Faculty of Arts, Charles University. She also periodically teaches Czech language, literature and culture at the University of Tampere in Finland. She is the author of many textbooks of Czech for foreigners. She has participated in many projects. Her activities cover research on spoken Czech, particulary on particles in spoken Czech.

Gianluca Baldo è un insegnante di italiano L2 con esperienza in scuole pubbliche, università e istituti privati, sia in Italia sia all'estero (Federazione Russa e Canada). Nel 2012 ha conseguito il dottorato di ricerca in Scienze Linguistiche presso l'Università degli Studi di Udine, con uno studio sociolinguistico di una comunità immigrata locale. I suoi principali interessi di ricerca sono l'acquisizione delle lingue seconde, gli studi sulle migrazioni, la didattica della lingua italiana come lingua seconda e le nuove tecnologie. Al momento è un collaboratore esterno dell'Università degli Studi di Udine, insegna in corsi di italiano L2 e seminari.

Gianluca Baldo is a teacher of Italian as L2 with experience in public schools, universities and private institutes, both in Italy and abroad (Russian Federation and Canada). In 2012 he completed a PhD in Language Sciences at the University of Udine, with a sociolinguistic study on a local immigrant community. His main research interests are second language acquisition, migration studies, didactics of Italian as a second language and new technologies. At the moment he is an external Lecturer at the University of Udine, where he teaches courses of Italian as L2 and seminars.

Gerd Bräuer ist Konsulent für Unterrichtsfragen und Spezialist für Schreiben, er arbeitet stufenübergreifend für verschiedene Bildungsinstitutionen zur Verbesserung von Schreibförderprogrammen und entwickelt Materialien zum Schreiben und Lesen. In den letzten 20 Jahren war er weltweit an der Gründung von Schreibzentren und Schreibtutorenprogrammen unterstützend beteiligt. Er leitet zwei zertifizierte Fernstudienprogramme, eines für Schreibspezialist_innen, das andere für Entwickler_innen von Alphabetisierungsprogrammen und Aufgabenersteller_innen.

Gerd Bräuer is an educational consultant and writing specialist who works with institutions across the educational pyramid to optimize literacy programs and to develop support systems for writers and readers. In the past 20 years, he helped create many writing centers and writing tutor training programs across the world. He directs two certified distant-learning programs, one for writing specialists and the other for literacy program developers and task designers.

Ursula Doleschal ist Universitätsprofessorin für slawistische Sprachwissenschaft und Leiterin des SchreibCenters an der Alpen-Adria-Universität Klagenfurt. Ihr Forschungsinteresse gilt der mehrsprachigen Rede, der Genderlinguistik, der Grammatiktheorie, wissenschaftlichen Texten und der Didaktik des wissenschaftlichen Schreibens. Ihre Publikationen nehmen außer den slawischen Sprachen Deutsch und Italienisch in den Blick. Sie ist stellvertretende Präsidentin der *Gesellschaft für wissenschaftliches Schreiben* (GEWISSS) und des *Österreichischen Slawistenverbandes*.

Ursula Doleschal is Full Professor of Slavic Linguistics and head of the SchreibCenter at the University of Klagenfurt (Austria). Her research interests include bilingual speech, gender linguistics, theory of grammar, academic texts and the teaching of academic writing. Her publications are on German, Italian and Slavic languages. She is vice-president of the *Gesellschaft für wissenschaftliches Schreiben* (GEWISSS) and the Austrian Association of Slavists.

Zuzana Hajíčková je odbornou lektorkou češtiny jako cizího jazyka působící na Ústavu bohemistických studií Filozofické fakulty univerzity Karlovy. Na této fakultě také v roce 2009 vystudovala obory český jazyk a literatura, německý jazyk a učitelství pro střední školy. Je členkou Asociace učitelů češtiny jako cizího jazyka. Dlouhodobě se zabývá rozvojem dovednosti psaní a kreativním psaním v češtině jako cizím jazyku.

Zuzana Hajíčková is a Professional Lecturer of Czech as a foreign language at the Institute of Czech Studies at the Faculty of Arts, Charles University. She graduated in Czech language and literature, German language and Teaching for secondary schools at the same faculty in 2009. She is a member of the Association of Teachers of Czech as a foreign language. She focuses on the development of writing skills and creative writing in Czech for foreigners.

Damjana Kern je zaposlena na Centru za slovenščino kot drugi in tuji jezik pri Oddelku za slovenistiko Filozofske fakultete Univerze v Ljubljani. Dela kot strokovna sodelavka pri programu *Slovenščina za otroke in mladostnike*. Raziskovalno in strokovno se ukvarja s področjem jezikovnega načrtovanja ter učenja in poučevanja slovenščine v zamejstvu in izseljenstvu. Je soavtorica več učbenikov in priročnikov za poučevanje slovenščine kot drugega jezika.

Damjana Kern is employed at the Centre for Slovene as a Second and Foreign Language at the Faculty of Arts, University of Ljubljana. She works in the Slovene for Children and Teenagers' Programme. She is very interested in the field of language policy and teaching Slovene outside the borders of Slovenia. She is co-author of several teaching materials, textbooks and manuals regarding Slovene as a Second/Foreign language.

Mihaela Knez je zaposlena na Centru za slovenščino kot drugi in tuji jezik pri Oddelku za slovenistiko Filozofske fakultete Univerze v Ljubljani, kjer vodi program Slovenščina za otroke in mladostnike. Raziskovalno in strokovno se ukvarja s področjem usvajanja in učenja slovenščine kot drugega jezika. Je soavtorica *Sporazumevalnega praga za slovenščino* ter več učbenikov in priročnikov za poučevanje slovenščine kot drugega jezika za otroke, mladostnike in odrasle. Sodeluje tudi v različnih nacionalnih komisijah in pri pripravi nacionalnih dokumentov s področja načrtovanja jezikovnega izobraževanja.

Mihaela Knez is employed at the Centre for Slovene as a Second and Foreign Language at the Faculty of Arts, University of Ljubljana, where she is the head of the program *Slovene for children and youth.* Her research and professional field is language acquisition and language learning. She is co-author of *Threshold for Slovene* as well as several curricula, textbooks and manuals for teaching Slovene as a second language to children, adolescents and adults. She also participates in various national committees and in the development of national documents in the field of language education.

Sonja Kuri ist assoziierte Professorin für Germanistische Linguistik an der Universität Udine. Ihr Forschungsinteresse gilt Sprachvarietäten, Textlinguistik und didaktischen Fragestellungen zu Sprachenlehren und -lernen unter plurilingualen, multikulturellen, multimedialen Bedingungen und deren konkreter Anwendung. Neben ihrer Unterrichts- und Forschungstätigkeit begleitet sie als wissenschaftliche Konsulentin Bildungsprogramme und Bildungsinitiativen verschiedener Bildungsinstitutionen in Italien und Österreich.

Sonja Kuri is Associate Professor of German Linguistics at the University of Udine, Italy. Her primary research concentrates on language varieties, text linguistics and didactic topics on the teaching and learning of the German language in plurilingual, multicultural and multimedia conditions and their concrete application. Along with her teaching and research activities she participates in education programs and projects promoted by different institutions involved in education in Italy and Austria as a scientific consultant.

Anna-Maria Perissutti è Professore Associato di Lingua ceca all'Università di Udine. Si occupa di semantica e sintassi del ceco, acquisizione del ceco come lingua seconda, lessicografia e teoria e pratica della traduzione letteraria. Fa parte della redazione della rivista internazionale *Lingue antiche e moderne.* Ha partecipato a numerosi convegni di linguistica nazionali e internazionali; ha coordinato il progetto Wrilab2.

Anna-Maria Perissutti is Associate Professor of Czech Linguistics at the University of Udine. Her research interests include the semantics and syntax of the Czech language, second language acquisition, particularly Czech as a second language, lexicography and theory and the practice of literary translation. She is a member of the editorial board of the international review Lingue antiche e moderne. She has taken part in numerous national and international congresses. She has coordinated the project Wrilab2.

Ineke Vedder is Researcher and Senior Lecturer at the University of Amsterdam. Her research interests include instructed second language acquisition, particularly Italian as a second language, L2 writing, L2 pragmatics, language assessment and the development of complexity, accuracy and fluency in L2. Her publications have appeared in various edited books and journals. In 2014 she co-edited, together with F. Kuiken, a special issue of *Language Testing*, 'Raters' decisions, rating procedures and rating scales'.